MAY THE BEST
TEAM WIN

MAY THE BEST TEAM WIN

BASEBALL ECONOMICS AND PUBLIC POLICY

ANDREW ZIMBALIST

BROOKINGS INSTITUTION PRESS
Washington, D.C.

Copyright © 2003
Paperback edition copyright © 2004
THE BROOKINGS INSTITUTION
1775 Massachusetts Avenue, N.W., Washington, D.C. 20036
www.brookings.edu

The Library of Congress has cataloged the hardcover edition as follows:

Zimbalist, Andrew S.
    May the best team win : baseball economics and public policy /
Andrew Zimbalist.
        p.   cm.
Includes bibliographical references (p.   ) and index.
    ISBN 0-8157-9728-1 (cloth : alk. paper)
        1. Baseball—Economic aspects—United States. 2. Major League
Baseball (Organization). 3. Baseball—Law and legislation—United
States. 4. Antitrust law—United States. I. Title.
GV880.Z58 2003
796.357'0691—dc21   2002156494

        ISBN 0-8157-9729-x (pbk. : alk. paper)

Digital printing

The paper used in this publication meets minimum requirements of the American National Standard for Information Sciences—Permanence of Paper for Printed Library Materials: ANSI Z39.48-1992.

Typeset in Minion

Composition by Cynthia Stock
Silver Spring, Maryland

To my mother,

Dorothy Zimbalist,

with love and gratitude

Contents

Tables

Foreword

With the publication of *Baseball and Billions* in 1992, Andrew Zimbalist placed himself at the forefront of the ongoing discussion of baseball's economics.

In that highly respected work, and in subsequent books, articles, essays, and lectures, Zimbalist's carefully considered analysis brought welcome doses of logic and perspective to a subject fraught with partisan posturing and the emotions, resentments, and misperceptions of owners, players, media, and fans. From the start, it was clear that Zimbalist was himself a real baseball fan—after all, an academic's fascination with standard deviations and valuation analysis cannot alone account for the verve with which Zimbalist has pursued this topic through the years. And, after all these years, here is *part* of what Zimbalist finds:

Even now, when a compelling and coherent case for reform is available to them, baseball's owners continue to present misleading or exaggerated claims of financial distress, and to pursue questionable strategies (think "contraction"). This, of course, undermines their already shaky credibility and gives the Players Association and media critics plenty of inconsistencies, missteps, and absurdities to snipe at. It also diverts attention from what should be the central issue: economic inequities leading to significant competitive imbalance actually exist in baseball, and reasonable owners, players, and fans have cause to be concerned.

As coincidence would have it, the very season baseball's latest labor tussle came to a head also found the Twins winning the American League Central, the A's rolling on out West, and the Angels and the Giants, with payrolls outside the top ten, meeting in the World Series. This prompted the following assertion by many logic-impaired commentators: "What's all this stuff about competitive imbalance and small-market teams having no chance? Look at the Twins—now look at the Orioles and Dodgers—big payrolls and disappointing results. This *proves* that it's good management that matters, not payroll size." Yeesh. Where to begin?

We might note that the Angels and the Giants are hardly small-market teams and that their 2002 payrolls were still in the top half of MLB's thirty teams. With baseball's runaway economy in recent years, the *smaller* payrolls are well above what almost all the top payrolls were only a few years ago. Simply citing payroll rank ignores the huge growth in most payroll sizes in terms of raw dollars. But let's get back to the idea of what the success of a few small teams actually *proves*.

Let's suppose the issue is the life prospects of children raised in poverty as against those raised in affluence. As *evidence* that such differences don't really matter much and shouldn't concern us, I produce several Rhodes scholars from disadvantaged backgrounds. Have I made a good case? I don't think so. How is it, then, that the selective results of one season *prove* a point, but the overwhelming evidence of the preceding seven years is a mirage?

As Zimbalist explains, since the mid-1990s the relationship between payroll size and the *likelihood* of on-field success is direct, dramatic, and undeniable. Zimbalist never said, I never said, and no one with enough common sense to fill a thimble ever said that a low-payroll team couldn't *ever* succeed or that high-spending teams couldn't fail. What Zimbalist does say is that the *opportunities* for success are very significantly diminished by a smaller payroll, especially over the long term. As he wrote a couple of years ago: "The question is not whether there are exceptions. The question is whether there are patterns."

Despite these clear patterns, in their continuing effort to torture logic so as never to concede any points to ownership, we find some supporters of the players unwittingly arguing against the very reason to pay high salaries: to improve or maintain your team!

As I think about this new "It's not the money; it's the management" mantra, I can only conclude that George Steinbrenner has miscalculated. He has grossly overpaid for all his success. What he would be well advised to do is go to great lengths to get Billy Beane, architect of the low-payroll A's, to bolt the Bay for the Bronx—and upon securing him, tell him to cut the

Yankee payroll in half (it would still be more than Oakland's, after all). Good baseball and good business, right? Sure.

The Red Sox, in fact, very nearly succeeded in luring Beane to Beantown. Think they would have ordered him to operate with anything like Oakland's financial model? C'mon. If you can afford to spend big, you do. And if you also have competent management, you have a substantial competitive edge.

Many factors play into a team's prospects for playoff contention, but over time, payroll size is the most important. Baseball, like any professional sport, has a legitimate, indeed a compelling interest in creating a system that gives every team something closer to an equal *opportunity* to succeed, with good management and a little luck. As Zimbalist convincingly demonstrates, the question is not whether to promote greater playing strength parity, but how best to do it.

One of Zimbalist's arguments in *May the Best Team Win* is that many of baseball's problems would be effectively addressed by removing the industry's presumed antitrust exemption. He might be right, but Zimbalist recognizes that lifting baseball's exemption legislatively is a tall order. So he offers many insightful suggestions for improvement within the existing structure, along with other intriguing public policy proposals. As ever, Zimbalist provides plenty of food for thought, while clarifying our understanding of often complex issues.

And if you ask me, what else would we expect from the Robert A. Woods Professor of Economics at Smith College in Massachusetts? I've been there. Great school. Lots of tradition. Beautiful campus. A women's college by the way—although, I'm told Hootie Johnson's grandson is demanding admission next semester. Go figure.

Let me get out of your way now, as I turn it over to Professor Z.

BOB COSTAS
NBC and HBO Sports

Preface

Writing in the *New York Times* during the 2002 World Series, Hall of Famer Dave Winfield stated:

> As a kid, I played the big three sports: baseball, basketball and football. I was drafted in all of them, and as I said in my induction speech in Cooperstown, "Baseball is the best game of all."
>
> Players, owners and agents should act now to restore some of the luster and regain some of the respect, admiration and following that we have historically enjoyed and recently lost. It is time for America's pastime to look forward to the future.
>
> With the World Series starting last night, it is easy to forget there is trouble in paradise.[1]

Baseball's frequent missteps notwithstanding, the sport still holds a special place in American culture. The National Football League (NFL) may have won the television ratings war with Major League Baseball (MLB), but there are other indicators of baseball's transcendent popularity. During 2002, total attendance at major and minor league baseball games was 106.6 million. While not directly comparable, the NFL's total season attendance has never surpassed 17 million. Sales of baseball cards outnumber sales of football cards four to one. Almost twice as many tourists trek to Cooperstown, New York, as visit Canton, Ohio. And sportswriter Allen Barra asks, "Do hundreds of thousands flock to football's spring training, as they do for baseball?"[2]

Despite some pleasant surprises in the playoffs, baseball's 2002 season had mixed results: attendance fell by 6.2 percent, but television ratings rose modestly.[3] Surely the country's economic travails, along with ever-higher ticket prices and the looming work stoppage, contributed to problems at the ballpark. A breakdown reveals that an alarming twenty of MLB's thirty teams saw attendance declines during 2002.

Many argued that baseball's competitive imbalance problems had finally caught up with the sport. Fans in the cities with perennially poorly performing teams were simply losing interest. The simple slogan that for so long has governed notions of fairness and good sportsmanship—"May the best team win"—no longer seemed adequate. Fans today also care about how the best team got to be the best and whether other teams are also going to have their chance.

As Major League Baseball edged closer to the player-set strike deadline of August 30, 2002, Senator Arlen Specter of Pennsylvania played politicians' favorite baseball card. He threatened to sponsor legislation to remove MLB's presumed antitrust exemption if there was another work stoppage. As a baseball fan, his outrage was fully justified, but his strategy was tired and old. There must be a more enlightened public policy alternative than ineffectual saber rattling. This thought motivates the present book.

Since writing *Baseball and Billions* in the early 1990s, I have spent thousands of hours reading, consulting, talking, writing, and testifying about the baseball industry. The same issues keep coming up: teams demanding public subsidies for new stadiums and threatening to relocate (or, more recently, to self-destruct); viable host cities without a team reduced to practically begging for one from MLB; competitive dominance by high-revenue teams; migration of game telecasts to cable, along with ever higher cable prices; escalating ticket prices; and periodic work stoppages.

These recurrent problems have a common cause: monopoly. MLB is the only top-level professional baseball league in the country, and each of its teams is assigned an exclusive territory (save a few of the megacities, where the territory is shared between two teams). Monopolies have market power, which they use to derive higher returns, misallocate resources, and take advantage of consumers.

Sometimes it seems that baseball fans blame themselves for the game's problems. They continue to patronize the sport instead of boycotting it. Sports talk-radio hosts ask callers, if there is another work stoppage, whether they will pledge never to go to another game. But fans are a geographically dispersed, amorphous group for whom effective collective action is about as likely as the owners rehiring Fay Vincent as the next commissioner.

Instead of turning inward, fans should turn to their representatives in Congress and demand from them more than their roughly quinquennial ritual of admonishing MLB about its presumed exemption. Reasonable resolution of the abuses emanating from MLB's monopoly is within the grasp of public policy, as long as there is a will. To evaluate what Congress can do, however, it is first necessary to understand the industry and how it works. That's what this book sets out to do: describe and analyze the operation of the baseball industry, and then discuss what public policy measures make the most sense.

This book is written for a general audience, including fans, public policymakers, industry participants, and students. The material should be accessible to all these readers. I have made an effort to put virtually all the technical material in the endnotes. The reader will encounter a few statistical terms in chapter three and several tables, but I included them to make specific points and hope they will be tolerated for the clarity they add to my arguments.

I have many people to thank who over the years have shared their knowledge and experience with me. From the sports and entertainment industry I am particularly grateful to Clark Griffith, Don Fehr, Larry Baer, David Wolff, Gene Orza, David Sussman, Mike Weiner, Lauren Rich, John Moores, Jim Duquette, Gabe Paul, Ken Rosenthal, Jim Bouton, John Henry, Larry Lucchino, Marvin Miller, Mike Stone, David Feher, John Allen, Gene Budig, Dick Moss, Al Harazin, Robin Roberts, Curt Flood, Bob Costas, Jeffrey Kessler, Peter Gammons, Seth Grossman, Sandy Alderson, Dennis Lehman, Dick Jacobs, Fred Hanser, Chuck Armstrong, John Mansell, Rob Manfred, John Moag, George Nicolau, Tom Werner, John Genzale, Mark Lamping, Doug Pappas, Paul Alpers, Randy Levine, and Brian Cashman.

I also appreciate the assistance of many academic colleagues and friends who have helped me to clarify and sharpen my analysis of sports economics and sports law, including Steve Ross, Paul Weiler, Roger Noll, Gary Roberts, Brad Humphreys, Stefan Szymanski, John Siegfried, Allen Sanderson, Paul Sommers, Dan Marburger, Rob Baade, Jim Wetzler, and Roger Kaufman. Many of them read all or part of an earlier draft of this book and made useful comments.

I have benefited from the invaluable help of two excellent research assistants, Bhavani Harimohan and Zach Terwilleger, from the programming support of Lois Joy, and from the clerical assistance of Judy Fountain.

My editor at Brookings, Chris Kelaher, gets credit for pushing me to agree to write this book, expressing boundless enthusiasm, and offering good judgment along the way.

Mostly I thank my wonderful wife, Shelley, who raises Alex and Ella, loves Jeffrey and Michael, reads my drafts, encourages and supports me, and much, much more, always with a smile.

[NOTE TO THE READER: This expanded paperback edition includes a new postscript, beginning on page 161. —*The Publisher*]

MAY THE BEST
TEAM WIN

CHAPTER ONE

Introduction:
Cause for Concern

Many would say that the baseball industry had much to celebrate on November 6, 2001. The most scintillating World Series in recent memory, between the Arizona Diamondbacks and the New York Yankees, was decided in the bottom of the ninth of game seven. There had been no work stoppages for six-and-a-half years, the longest stretch in thirty years. Industry revenues in 2001 were 2.57 times greater than they were in 1995. Total attendance was at an all-time high. Major League Baseball (MLB) was in the midst of rich, long-term national television contracts, with Fox through 2006 for $2.5 billion and with ESPN through 2005 for $851 million. A new group of well-educated, business-proficient, and talented owners and executives were bringing intelligent and effective management strategies to many franchises. The industry could be proud of its patriotic sentiments, rituals, and contributions following the events of September 11, 2001.

Yet much was not right in the baseball world. Commissioner Allan "Bud" Selig went before Congress and once again pleaded poverty for his industry. MLB called for the contraction (elimination) of two teams, seeking to become the first major team sport league in the United States to reduce the number of its franchises. MLB's collective bargaining agreement with the players expired in early November 2001, and formal, substantive discussions for a new agreement did not commence until January 2002. After years of public good behavior, sniping between the commissioner's office and the Major League Baseball Players Association reemerged. (Public sniping among the owners was effectively curtailed when the commissioner imposed a gag order with a possible fine of $1 million for violating it.)

As 2002 proceeded, MLB was confronted with one new challenge after another. The Massachusetts attorney general accused the commissioner's office of rigging the sale of the Boston Red Sox and commenced an investigation. In the spring, the two co-owners of the New York Mets could not settle on a price for which one would sell the other his ownership share. Several court actions were filed, with Nelson Doubleday filing a counterclaim on August 5, alleging that his partner, Fred Wilpon, had conspired with the commissioner's office to generate an "outrageously low" assessed value for the team.[1] In July the former minority partners of the Montreal Expos (who had unwittingly become the minority partners of the Florida Marlins), representing several of the leading corporations in Canada, filed a RICO (racketeering) suit against the commissioner's office and Jeffrey Loria (owner of the Florida Marlins).

Left to its own devices, baseball again seemed to be mismanaging its affairs. Since 1922, MLB has benefited from a presumed exemption from the nation's antitrust laws. It is an unregulated, legal monopoly.[2]

Until 1992 the industry claimed that its "independent" commissioner would make sure that baseball did not abuse its market power and privilege. There is scant evidence that the commissioner ever consistently behaved independent of the owners' wishes, but whatever illusion of independence there may have been until Bud Selig, owner of the Milwaukee Brewers, was appointed acting commissioner in 1992 and then full commissioner in 1998 was now shattered.[3]

Capitalism draws its strength from the competitive process, a process that MLB has been largely insulated from at least since the 1922 *Federal Baseball* Supreme Court decision. Absent competitive pressures, arrogance, laxity, and inefficiency are bred.

In exploring the changing economics of our national pastime, this book examines the abuses and inefficiencies in the baseball industry and how these problems are connected to MLB's monopoly status, its presumed exemption, and public policy. Three issues from 2002 illuminate the relevance of monopoly analysis and public policy to the functioning of the baseball industry: MLB's contraction plan; the January 2002 sale of the Red Sox for approximately $720 million; and the standoff between Cablevision and the YES (Yankee Entertainment and Sports) network over the cablecasting of New York Yankees games.

Antitrust and MLB's Proposed Contraction

Baseball commissioner Bud Selig calls himself a history buff. Maybe, then, it was to confirm the Hegelian dialectic that on November 6, 2001, just one day after the Diamondbacks completed their exhilarating dethronement of the Yankees, Selig announced that Major League Baseball would contract by two teams for the 2002 season. Some had harbored the unrealistic hope that the commissioner instead would announce his readiness to commence substantive collective bargaining, something the Players Association had been waiting for since at least the previous spring. The existing agreement expired at the end of the 2001 World Series.

The last work stoppage in baseball had ended the 1994 season with less than one-third of the season remaining. No World Series was played in that year for the first time in ninety years. The first eighteen games of the 1995 season were also lost. The impact on the business of baseball was devastating. Average game attendance fell precipitously, from 31,612 during the first part of 1994 to 25,021 during 1995. Many fans swore they would never return to a game where spoiled millionaires and greedy billionaires couldn't decide how to divide their fortunes.

Fortunately for baseball, Cal Ripken was in the process of breaking Lou Gehrig's consecutive-games record. After Ripken surpassed Gehrig, along came Mark McGwire and Sammy Sosa to hit more home runs than Babe Ruth and Roger Maris. Then along came Barry Bonds to break McGwire's newly set home-run record. Baseball picked up a few other tricks and rode the country's 1990s economic expansion and stadium construction boom back into the hearts of American sports fans.

Yet in 2002 both the owners and players knew that the game could ill afford another work stoppage. They could not count on another Ripken or Bonds to come along every two years. Under the circumstances, wouldn't it have made sense for Selig to start labor negotiations as early as possible?

For a while it seemed that he might. Back in early 1999, Selig had established a blue-ribbon panel to study the game's economics. He got an early start, but took a false step. Selig's panel was one-sided, containing only individuals representing ownership. The Players Association was not invited to participate. Many believed that it would have made sense to seek a common and balanced view of the game's economic problems in preparation for collective bargaining.

Selig's panel included pundits Paul Volcker, a former chair of the Federal Reserve; Richard Levin, an economist and president of Yale University; George Will, a columnist and minority-interest baseball owner; and George Mitchell, a former U.S. senator and soon-to-be high-paid consultant to the Boston Red Sox. They worked with abundant resources and staff. The panel studied the economics of baseball for fifteen months and produced its report in July 2000. The report called for additional revenue sharing, a luxury tax on high payrolls, and the internationalization of the amateur draft, among other things. It did not recommend contraction. Indeed, the report explicitly stated that if the panel's recommendations were implemented contraction would not be necessary. (Interestingly, the panel's plan closely resembled one proposed earlier in 2000 by Bob Costas in his book *Fair Ball*.)

But the escrowed owner of the Milwaukee Brewers and present commissioner put aside the recommendations of his experts and called for the elimination of two teams. One of the targeted teams was the Minnesota Twins. Some said that Selig had a conflict of interest. If the Twins were eliminated, the Brewers' television market would extend many hundreds of additional miles to the west. Selig attempted to refute such claims by telling *Milwaukee Journal Sentinel* reporter Don Walker that they were nonsense because St. Louis was closer to Minneapolis than Milwaukee was.[4] The commissioner was off by over 275 miles.

Geographic gaffes aside, Selig wanted (or claimed he wanted) to reduce output in the baseball industry by two teams, or 6.7 percent. Since the 1994–95 work stoppage, baseball's revenues had grown at an average annual rate of 17 percent. Yet rather than first attempt to restructure the game to deal with its competitive imbalances—as recommended by Selig's hand-picked experts—the baseball monopoly proposed a reduction in industry output in the face of rapidly growing demand. In a normal monopoly, such behavior would run afoul of our nation's antitrust laws. Whether it does so in baseball seems to depend on which judge you ask and what judicial circuit you are in. More on this in chapter two.

Like all monopolies, MLB is wont to limit output in order to raise the price of its product. In the case of proposed contraction, baseball would reduce the number of franchises and hope to raise franchise value. Meanwhile, the consumers in Minnesota, Montreal, greater Washington, D.C., Portland, Oregon, and elsewhere potentially get shafted. It was as if GM bought up Ford, Chrysler, and Toyota and announced it would cease to sell cars in Oregon unless the state built the company a new assembly plant with public funds.

Some say baseball should be able to do what it wants. After all, if McDonald's has a franchise that is underperforming, it shuts it down. Sure, but McDonald's participates in a competitive industry. If it decides there will be no McDonald's in the nation's capital, then it cedes the market to Burger King and Wendy's and consumers are still served. Further, if McDonald's had a nationwide revenue growth rate of 17 percent annually, as MLB had from 1995 through 2001, then even if it closed down a franchise in one location it would open up new franchises in other locations. And, McDonald's does not require cities to subsidize the construction of its golden arches with public funds. Nor does it benefit from free, extensive, daily coverage of its business in the local media.

Thus it was appropriate for the U.S. Senate and House Judiciary Committees to call hearings during the 2001–02 offseason to inquire into the proper scope of MLB's antitrust exemption. At the House hearings in December, Commissioner Selig argued that contraction was necessary because baseball was losing money and it would improve the game's competitive balance. Selig promised that MLB would reveal all about the industry's finances to the House. Instead, he provided a few pages summarizing the teams' profits and losses. He claimed the industry lost $519 million in 2001. I consider the validity of this claim in detail in chapter four; for now, suffice it to note that more than a few members of the Judiciary Committee were unconvinced that the commissioner was leveling with them.

Selig's other proposition, that contracting two teams would improve competitive balance, is statistically incontrovertible. Consider a ladder. Lop off the bottom two rungs and there will be less distance from the top to the bottom rung. Of course, one could also lop off the top two rungs and achieve the same effect. One question, however, is whether addition by subtraction is the most efficient way to promote competitive balance, and another is whether the resulting distance from the top to the bottom would be acceptable.

Another question is how the contraction would play out in practice. Think about the lowly Detroit Tigers, for instance, who play in a two-year-old facility (completed in 2000 and built with the aid of over $160 million in public funds). With sixty-six wins and ninety-six losses in 2001, the team was able to draw only 1.9 million fans to the ballpark. Attendance in 2002 fell to 1.5 million. As long as the Tampa Bay Devil Rays are in the league and team owner Vincent Naimoli continues to keep his twenty-five-man payroll below $33.1 million, the Tigers would have a good chance of improving their record by beating the lowly Devil Rays.[5] In a postcontraction world without the Devil Rays, the Tigers will face, on average, tougher competition and, other things equal, have a still worse record. Their attendance and revenue likely will dwindle further.

Even if MLB were able to get away with it, it would make little business sense for baseball to contract. First, as the U.S. population and income grow and world transportation and communication systems bring us closer to our neighbors, the proper trajectory for the industry is growth, not stagnation or contraction.

Second, it is no secret that baseball remains considerably more popular in the over-fifty than in the under-twenty crowd. Yet MLB continues to follow policies that appear to disregard young fans, such as moving the World Series games to prime time; not opening the ballpark to fans until after the home team takes batting practice; reducing the number of discounted family days; and preventing fans from going on the field after the game. And MLB has failed to act affirmatively to redress other problems, such as the difficulty urban youth have finding space to play the game.

Little League participation is declining, even as the population grows. One good way to excite America's youth about baseball is to bring the game's stars to more of the nation's top cities. Let the ten-year-olds in Washington, D.C., Portland, Charlotte, Sacramento, and elsewhere see Barry Bonds, Pedro Martinez, and Randy Johnson play in person.

Third, expansion has made baseball more exciting by promoting record-breaking performances. Why, until 1998, were almost all of baseball's personal achievement records set between 1910 and 1930? Rogers Hornsby batted .424 in 1924, Hack Wilson knocked in 190 runs in 1930, Earl Webb whacked 67 doubles in 1931, Babe Ruth scored 177 runs in 1921, and Dutch Leonard had a 0.96 earned-run average (ERA) in 1914. Many believe that players in the good old days were better than today's players. Not so. Baseball stats are the product of competing forces and reveal little about the absolute quality of the players.

The reason has to do with relative degrees of talent compression. The distribution of baseball skills in the population follows a normal distribution (like a bell-shaped curve). For any given curve, the larger the number of people selected to play Major League Baseball, the greater will be the difference between the best and the worst players in the league. If the population grows and the number of baseball teams does not, then the proportion of the population playing will fall and the distribution of talent become more compressed. This is what happened in MLB between 1903 and 1960, when the population grew from 80 million to 181 million and the number of teams remained constant at sixteen.

Moreover, in the late 1940s baseball began to accept black players and to recruit Latin American players in greater numbers. This accentuated the compression, while better nurturance of baseball skills through the development of youth baseball leagues, and of physical abilities in general, offset the talent dispersion resulting from the growing appeal of football and basketball to American youth.[6]

With talent increasingly compressed, the difference in skills between the best and worst players grew more narrow, and it became more difficult for the best players to stand out. Hence, records ceased being broken, or even approached (save the asterisked performance by Roger Maris in 1961, the first year of MLB expansion).[7]

Thus it makes little sense to argue that Babe Ruth hit more home runs per season than Harmon Killebrew because he was stronger or had superior baseball skills. It makes more sense to conclude that Ruth played during a time when talent was more dispersed, so he faced many superb pitchers but also a much larger share of weak pitchers than did Killebrew. Similarly, Dutch Leonard and Walter Johnson (ERA of 1.09 in 1913) faced some spectacular hitters, but they also faced a much higher percentage of weak hitters than did Sandy Koufax, Ron Guidry, Roger Clemens, or Curt Schilling.

The ratio of the U.S. population to the number of major league players rose from 250,000 to 1 in 1903, to 307,500 to 1 in 1930, and 452,500 to 1 in 1960; thereafter it fell gradually to 385,000 to 1 in 1990, and 360,000 to 1 in 1998, after MLB's second expansion by two teams in the 1990s. Thus talent decompression gradually set in after 1960, and by 1998 the ratio had almost fallen back to the level in 1930.

So today the McGwires, Sosas, Rodriguezes, Martinezes, and Bondses can more easily excel. Some argue that the home-run heroics of Bonds and McGwire are the result of the use of androstenedione and steroids. This claim lacks evidence, at least for Barry Bonds, but it is also inconsistent with the outstanding pitching performances since baseball's 1992 expansion. The dominance of Greg Maddux, Tom Glavine, Randy Johnson, Roger Clemens, Pedro Martinez, John Smoltz, and Curt Schilling shows up clearly in statistics. For the eight years from 1985 through 1992, there were only two seasons where the top pitcher had more than 300 strikeouts and no seasons with more than 310 strikeouts. For the eight seasons between 1994 and 2001, there were four seasons when the leader threw more than 300 strikeouts and three in which he had more than 345 (despite 1994 and 1995 being strike shortened.) Similarly, 1985–1992 saw only two years in which the leading ERA was below 2.00, while 1994–2001 saw five such years. If baseball's outstanding performances since the mid-1990s were the product of artificial muscle-builders, it is improbable that the records of both pitchers and hitters would be so impressive. A more likely explanation lies in talent decompression.

Thus if baseball were to enter an era of contraction as the U.S. population and recruitment of players from outside the United States continued to grow, talent compression would reassert itself and we would expect fewer, if any, record-breaking performances. This would make the game less exciting and, with lower demand, more economically challenged.[8]

Finally, it is in baseball's interest to respect and honor its loyal host cities and fans. Teams' success and popularity inevitably go in cycles. To stop the clock at one moment in time, pick out the losers, and designate them for contraction is both irresponsible and counterproductive. The Twins, for instance, were rumored to be at the top of MLB's 2002 contraction list. This was not because the fans of Minneapolis–St. Paul (the nation's thirteenth largest media market) did not love their team. Indeed, back in 1988 the Twins became the first American League team to surpass the 3 million mark in annual attendance. It was because the citizens and politicians of Minnesota had just built the Metrodome with public money in 1982 and were reluctant to invest hundreds of millions of dollars in a new stadium—especially when the main beneficiary would be Carl Pohlad, one of the richest men in America, who had evinced little interest in building a championship club. Pohlad had made it clear that he had grown fed up with his failure to loosen the public purse strings for a new facility and was ready to sacrifice the team to contraction in return for a handsome buyout from MLB.

In 2002 divine justice seemed to intervene as the Twins—who would already have been defunct if Bud Selig had had his way—won first their division and then the American League Division Series (ALDS). Moreover, during the 2002 playoffs the Twins filled the Metrodome to capacity—something neither the Atlanta Braves nor the Oakland Athletics could manage. If the Twins were vulnerable to contraction in 2002, could any team deem itself safe from contraction in the future? This is not the message that MLB wanted to send out to its host cities or its fans.

There are, then, many good reasons why MLB should eschew, rather than embrace, contraction—enough good reasons to make one question whether the stated intention to contract was genuine.

Did the owners really believe on November 6 that they would be able to eliminate the Expos and Twins before the opening of training camps for the 2002 season in mid-February? They knew that the Twins had a specific performance clause in their signed stadium contract to play the 2002 season at the Metrodome.[9] They knew the Players Association has three levels of defense to impede contraction (calling for internal arbitration, charging unfair labor practices before the National Labor Relations Board [NLRB], and various actions before U.S. district courts). They knew that affected states and parties would also sue in state and district courts; and they knew that there would be very complicated operational matters regarding the dispersal of players on contracted teams and scheduling to be worked out.

A plausible alternative explanation for the contraction gambit is that the owners were seeking leverage in the stadium and players markets. Threaten to eliminate the Twins and maybe Minneapolis or St. Paul would finally put up the public funds to build the team a new facility. Threaten to eliminate the Expos and maybe the Washington, D.C., market would produce a solid ownership group and support stadium financing.

The contraction threat also meant that there was considerable uncertainty about player availability during the offseason. Would all of the Twins and Expos players (and their minor leaguers) become free agents, or would they be subject to a draft? Would the 2002 season be played with a normal schedule, or be played at all? This uncertainty, together with the weak economy, produced a weak players market. It surprised no one when "a high-ranking baseball official" told Buster Olney of the *New York Times*: "It's amazing. You could probably count the number of teams on one hand who are going to be aggressive financially in this market."[10] Opening-day player salaries in 2002 were up only 3.3 percent from 2001, after growing at a compound annual rate of 14.4 percent from 1996 through 2001.

Contraction also represents an explicit threat to the Players Association. Each team has a forty-man major league roster and forty union members. Not only would the union lose eighty members if two teams were eliminated, but the supply of players would remain the same as the demand for players fell by eighty, producing downward pressure on salaries.

The fact that Selig announced contraction plans before commencing substantive collective bargaining suggests that he hoped the announcement would give the owners additional leverage with the players. At the very least, it would give the owners an extra chip to put on the bargaining table. Jerry Colangelo, owner of the Arizona Diamondbacks, admitted as much in an interview on April 30, 2002, with the *Arizona Republic*. Colangelo asserted that the Players Association had been "totally, totally uncooperative" in adopting a system of salary restraints and added: "It's important to get someone's attention. Contraction might just do that."[11]

Of course, contraction did not happen for the 2002 season. But Selig soon threatened the game would eliminate two, and possibly more, teams before the 2003 season. Contraction in 2002 was thwarted principally by two actions: one, the successful suit of the Metropolitan Sports Facilities Commission in Minneapolis to force the Minnesota Twins to honor the specific performance clause in their stadium contract for the 2002 season; and, two, the grievance filed by the Players Association claiming that the owners failed to properly communicate and negotiate its contraction plan with the players. Contraction for 2003 through 2006 was postponed by the August 2002 collective bargaining agreement, but in return for the four-year moratorium on contraction the Players Association agreed not to challenge an owner effort to reduce the number of teams in 2007.[12]

Antitrust and the Sale of the Red Sox

As the 2002 contraction drama was reaching its apex, the protracted process to sell the Boston Red Sox was drawing to a close. Long-term Red Sox CEO and minority owner John Harrington had announced back in early October 2000 that he was putting the team up for sale.

According to Attorney General Tom Reilly of Massachusetts, MLB documents show that the commissioner's office was actively manipulating the composition of the bidding ownership groups and, ultimately, pressured the existing ownership of the Sox to accept a bid from the commissioner's favored group, despite the fact that it was $90 million lower than another bid. Under ordinary circumstances, such behavior would be vulnerable to an antitrust (restraint-of-trade) claim.

Harrington argued that he took the lower bid because he wanted new ownership to be in place by the start of the 2002 season. The group that made the lower bid, led by John Henry and including Larry Lucchino and Tom Werner, would gain immediate approval from Selig and the ownership committee. The groups making higher bids, led respectively by Charles Dolan of Cablevision and New York lawyer Miles Prentice (whose group included cable TV distributor and sports programmer Comcast), Harrington claimed, had various problems and would take the owners many months to consider, making it impossible to have the new owners in place for the beginning of the season. Haste, however, was a puzzling pretext for Harrington to assert, having procrastinated repeatedly since his announced plan to sell the team in 2000.

Henry, Lucchino, and Werner are all baseball men as well as friends and allies of Selig.[13] Selig, who, according to many accounts, spends many of his working hours on the phone cultivating allies, was entering treacherous terrain in late 2001.[14] Congress was questioning baseball's antitrust exemption. The commissioner was proposing previously unheard of contraction (which eventually would lead to the RICO charge against MLB), and he was about to start fighting a collective bargaining battle with the players. Selig was also attempting to increase revenue sharing among the owners.[15] The co-owners of the New York Mets were suing and denouncing each other in public. Bud Selig needed allies and ownership unity more than ever.

Henry, Lucchino, and Werner were all previously associated with small-market teams. As representatives of Boston, the sixth largest media market, it would be all the better if they continued to support more revenue sharing. Selig trusted Henry, Lucchino, and Werner; but he had never worked with Dolan or Prentice.[16]

Because 53.48 percent of the Red Sox was owned by the Yawkey Trust, which stipulates (a) that a large majority of its funds will go to Boston-area charities and (b) that the chair of the trust is obligated to maximize the value going to the charities, the state attorney general (AG) undertook an investigation of the sale. Unexpectedly, MLB's long-standing presumed antitrust exemption had come into conflict with the Massachusetts AG's duty to oversee the disposition of charitable trusts. Eventually, Attorney

General Reilly struck a deal with Harrington and Henry that obliged Henry to make extra contributions to Boston-area charities, but it still left the ultimate money transfer at least $60 million below the Dolan offer.[17]

As AG Reilly battled chief Yawkey trustee John Harrington and MLB, it came to light that Commissioner Selig had repeatedly violated an internal baseball rule that prevents owners from making loans to each other, either directly or indirectly, without first receiving the permission of the commissioner and all of the other owners. The stated purpose of this rule is to avoid the *mere appearance* of a conflict of interest. On one occasion, in 1995, while Selig was the acting commissioner and the owner of the Milwaukee Brewers, his team received a multimillion-dollar loan from a finance company controlled by Twins owner Carl Pohlad. Selig did not put the loan before baseball's other owners for approval.

The manipulated sale of the Red Sox and the interowner loan suggest once again that baseball was being run by a shrinking and self-selecting group, subject to no oversight and no competition. If baseball's leadership were guaranteed to be enlightened, perhaps there would be little cause for concern. But the point of representative, democratic government in politics and of competition in economics is that we cannot count on self-selecting leaders always to be enlightened and efficient.

Antitrust and the Cable Industry

When the 2002 baseball season began, 2.9 million of the 6.6 million television homes in the New York City media market did not have access to the 130 Yankees games scheduled to be telecasted on the new YES network. In previous summers, Yankees fans had grown accustomed to watching a good share of the team's games on the over-the-air free television channel WPIX.

Then, in the late 1980s Yankees owner George Steinbrenner got an offer he couldn't refuse from the then fledgling regional sports network MSG (Madison Square Garden). MSG signed a twelve-year television rights deal with the Yankees for $493 million. MSG then subcontracted with WPIX to carry approximately twenty-five games a year on free television, while it carried more than 100 games on cable. In some areas, MSG was carried on the expanded basic cable package; in others, it was carried as a premium service.[18]

The MSG deal ended in 2000 but was extended for one more year. Then the Yankees, with their YankeeNets partners, launched their own regional sports network (RSN), the YES network.[19] The 2002 plan was to carry all but thirty-two Yankees games on the YES network (twenty going to CBS-TV and twelve to exclusive national coverage as part of MLB's package deal with Fox and ESPN), and to insist that cable distributors in the New York market offer the YES network in their expanded basic package. YES would charge each cable distributor approximately $2 per subscriber per month to carry its programming. The subscriber fees alone under this plan would bring YES $163 million a year in the inner market (New York City and environs). There would also be tens of millions of dollars in the outer market (for example, upstate New York) and upwards of $50 million more in advertising revenue. That is, if the plan were fully implemented, the YES network could anticipate around $250 million in revenue in 2002. Most of it would be attributable to the Yankees.[20]

During the 2002 season the plan was not fully implemented. Cablevision would not go along. Cablevision is a vertically integrated company, owning cable distribution companies, two New York City RSNs (MSG and FSNY—Fox Sports New York), and two teams (the NBA's New York Knicks and the NHL's New York Rangers). Cablevision chairman Charles Dolan was less than pleased that his company, MSG, had lost telecasting rights to the Yankees and that his bid for the Red Sox was not accepted despite being some $90 million higher than the Henry group's bid.[21] But more important, Dolan was not pleased at the prospect that his two New York RSNs were going to face strong competition from the new upstart, YES.

Dolan's response was both clever and maddening. Dolan's Cablevision had exploited its immense market power over the years. Cablevision, the cable distributor, faced no meaningful competition in selling cable TV services to 2.9 million New York households. It had raised the monthly rate for its expanded basic package from $21.95 to $43.95 between 1993 and 2002.

The expanded basic package included sixty-five channels in early 2002.[22] Even if the consumer wanted only one or two of those channels, he or she had to purchase the whole package. Cablevision is a monopoly cable distributor, as are virtually all of the 9,924 cable distributors in the country, and is able to get away with bundling channels pretty much as it pleases. Bundling in many circumstances can be considered a restraint of trade. Imagine walking into a department store to buy a pair of slacks and being told by the salesman that in order to buy the pair you like you would also have to buy a particular shirt, a particular tie, and two pairs of socks.

Department stores do not attempt such bundling because consumers wouldn't stand for it. There are many places to buy slacks. Competition curtails abuse.

Some types of bundling are allowed. Certain restaurants, for instance, offer fixed-price menus. They bundle an appetizer, a salad, a main course, and a dessert (albeit often with choices within each category). The main reason why such bundling is legal is that consumers have a wide choice of restaurants to choose from—there is abundant competition. Secondarily, fixed-price menus also offer some efficiencies to the producer that can result in either lower prices or higher quality, or both.

Dolan's Cablevision also has enjoyed monopoly power by owning the only two RSNs in the NYC area until YES launched in early 2002 and by owning teams in two monopoly sports leagues. Yet when asked to make the YES network part of its expanded basic package at $2 per subscriber per month, something that the three other cable distributors in NYC and dozens more in the outer market agreed to, Chuck Dolan suddenly became a populist. He argued that it was unfair to bundle the YES network into the basic package and raise the rates of all subscribers, because not all subscribers were Yankees fans. True enough. On this argument Dolan should also cease to make ESPN, CNN, TBS, BET, and a host of other cable channels part of its basic package. Also on this argument, Dolan's Cablevision should not have put its own RSNs—MSG and FSNY—in the expanded basic package in roughly half of its New York markets.

These three cases—baseball's planned contraction, the sale of the Red Sox, and the Yankees/Cablevision dispute—share a common element: monopoly. As we shall see in subsequent chapters, other aspects of baseball's governance are also affected by the absence or weakness of competitive pressures on the industry. But before considering these other dimensions of MLB's monopoly, I turn to the history and meaning of the sport's presumed antitrust exemption.

CHAPTER TWO

Baseball's Presumed Antitrust Exemption

Major League Baseball was formed by the 1903 merger agreement between the National and American Leagues. Before this agreement was reached, the upstart American League (AL) had been challenging the National League's (NL) hegemony and its player reserve clause. The latter had been in effect since 1879 and allowed a team to have sole rights over a player. Because players under reserve could not solicit competitive bids for their services, their salaries were artificially depressed.

After the 1899 season, the American League's president, Ban Johnson, decided to make competitive offers to the NL's better players. He lured more than 100 players to the AL for the 1900 season. At the close of that season, Johnson declared the AL to be a major league. As the bidding war between the two leagues grew fiercer and player salaries continued to escalate, the AL grew in popularity. By 1902 the AL outdrew the NL, 2.2 million to 1.7 million attendees.

Both leagues decided it was in their economic interest to compromise and signed a truce in January 1903. Without competition for players, once again salaries languished. In 1911 the average player earned less than $2,500 (roughly equal to $45,000 in 2002 prices). But low salaries also provided an opportunity for a new rival league to challenge MLB. The Federal League (FL) was founded in 1913 as a minor league, but in August of that year it announced that it would seek major league stars and expand play in eastern cities. Significantly, the FL eschewed the reserve clause and offered players long-term contracts. While only eighteen players jumped to the FL in 1913, the doubling of their salaries led to massive defections in the following two years. As many as 221 major leaguers jumped to the FL in 1914–15.[1]

Not surprisingly, the advent of a rival league put strong upward pressure on player salaries, which on average doubled between 1914 and 1915. Yet the FL was still frustrated in its efforts to induce many of MLB's stars to sign with its clubs. MLB threatened to blacklist players who jumped to the FL, and it brought suit against many of the defectors.

In January 1915 the FL sued MLB for blocking access to the players' market. Considering the FL case in the Illinois U.S. District Court, Judge Kenesaw Mountain Landis declared: "As a result of thirty years of observation, I am shocked because you call playing baseball 'labor.'"[2] Landis then took the case under advisement to encourage settlement. Nearly a year had passed with no decision from Landis when the FL and MLB reached an accord in November 1915. The terms included an end to the FL and compensation to the FL team owners totaling some $600,000. Several FL owners became MLB owners, including Phil Wrigley, whose Wrigley Field was built originally for the Chicago FL franchise.

The FL's Baltimore Terrapins, however, were virtually excluded from the benefits of the settlement. MLB owners imprudently added insult to injury when White Sox owner Charles Comiskey derided the city by asserting, "Baltimore is a minor league city and not a hell of a good one at that." And Dodgers owner Charles Ebbets offered his own intellectually and syntactically challenged insight that Baltimore was one of the worst minor league cities because "you have too many colored population to start with."[3]

The Terrapins' owners rejected the insulting $50,000 settlement offer for their franchise from MLB and instead filed an antitrust suit in 1916. They won a $240,000 award in trial court in April 1919. This decision, however, was reversed in the District of Columbia Court of Appeals in April 1921. That court found, "The players . . . travel from place to place in interstate commerce, but they are not the game . . . [which] is local in its beginning and in its end. . . . The fact that the [owners] produce baseball games as a source of profit, large or small, cannot change the character of the games. They are still sport, not trade."[4]

The *Federal Baseball* Decision

This ruling was upheld on May 29, 1922, by the U.S. Supreme Court in a decision written by Justice Oliver Wendell Holmes, a former amateur baseball player, for a Court headed by former president William Howard Taft, himself an erstwhile third baseman at Yale University (and the first president to throw out a baseball to open the season).[5] Interestingly, Taft was also baseball's first pick to be commissioner after the 1919 Black Sox scandal. Taft waited to respond to the offer to see if the Republican, Warren Harding, would be elected president in 1920. Harding was elected, and Taft got his first wish: appointment as Chief Justice of the Supreme Court.

In the *Federal Baseball* decision, Holmes, echoing the court of appeals, reasoned that baseball exhibitions are "purely state affairs" and thus did not constitute interstate commerce. Traveling across state lines to stage these exhibitions is "a mere incident, not the essential thing." Further, he said, baseball was not even commerce because "personal effort, not related to production, is not a subject of commerce."[6]

It should be noted that the prevailing notion of what constituted interstate commerce at the time was much narrower than it is today, excluding, for example, basic manufacturing and service production. The idea was that if a good was produced within a state it was intrastate commerce and the production activities of the company were not subject to the Sherman and Clayton Acts. The concept of interstate commerce was broadened in the late 1930s to include production activities that affected (or were affected by) interstate commerce. Yet the plaintiff in *Federal Baseball* made a strong argument that the nature of an interstate sports league required the transportation of players across state lines, and it is quite likely that had the plaintiff sought relief under state law the defendants would have claimed that baseball was interstate commerce! Moreover, the respected lower court judge, Learned Hand, had previously held that a monopoly of vaudeville performances across state lines was interstate commerce, although, as in baseball, the only real interstate commerce was the travel to the entertainment event.[7] In sum, although the Holmes decision in *Federal Baseball* is understandable given the prevailing jurisprudence, it would also have been understandable if the Court had reasoned that because the players (as well as radio signals) crossed state lines in order to produce the game, baseball was involved in interstate commerce.[8]

The *Federal Baseball* ruling went untested for twenty-five years. Then, following World War II, the new Mexican League was formed. In June 1946, baseball commissioner Happy Chandler announced a five-year ban on all U.S. players who jumped to the Mexican League. Danny Gardella, a twenty-seven-year-old outfielder who in 1946 was offered $5,000 to play for the

New York Giants, was offered $8,000 plus a signing bonus of $5,000 to play in the Mexican League. Gardella chose to play in Mexico, but like other U.S. ballplayers who made this choice, he found the playing conditions there intolerable and wanted to return to MLB. But Gardella found himself blacklisted. He sued MLB for $300,000. After losing his case in trial court, Gardella appealed. The Second Circuit Court of Appeals found in Gardella's favor, ruling that the advent of radio and television had clearly involved baseball in interstate commerce and that the sport was therefore covered by the Sherman Act. The written decision did not mince words, stating that the reserve clause was "shockingly repugnant to moral principles that . . . have been basic in America . . . [since] the Thirteenth Amendment . . . condemning 'involuntary servitude' . . . for the 'reserve clause' . . . results in something resembling peonage of the baseball player."[9] Gardella was awarded damages of $300,000, and the 1922 *Federal Baseball* decision was seemingly reversed.

Baseball appealed the appeals court decision and announced amnesty for all Mexican League jumpers. Before the Gardella case could be heard by the Supreme Court, MLB and Gardella's lawyer reached a settlement. By settling, MLB was able to preserve some ambiguity about whether the 1948 appeals court decision or the 1922 Supreme Court decision was good law. MLB proceeded to seek congressional affirmation of its presumed exemption, leading to protracted hearings before the House Subcommittee on the Study of Monopoly Power in 1951. When the hearings opened in July, no fewer than eight antitrust cases were pending against MLB. There were also three bills that would have granted a legislated antitrust exemption to baseball and other sports. At the hearings Ty Cobb and dozens of other ballplayers and sportswriters, innocently echoing the owners' repeated refrain, testified that the reserve clause was necessary to preserve competitive balance in the game. The only dissenting voice within the baseball establishment was that of long-time team executive and owner Bill Veeck.

Given the prevalence of player sales throughout the years, it is remarkable that the reserve clause/competitive-balance myth was so tenacious. Economist Simon Rottenberg in 1956 was the first to suggest that as long as player sales were allowed, baseball talent would be distributed in proportion to teams' ability and willingness to pay, with or without a reserve clause. The chief difference between a reserve clause and a free-agency regime is not in the allocation of players but in the distribution of team revenues between owners and players. For reasons that I discuss in chapter three, competitive balance was actually improved after the introduction of free agency for the 1977 season.

In any event, the House hearings on baseball's antitrust exemption concluded without the adoption of any legislation. Many believe that the House committee thought that the 1948 appeals court ruling in *Gardella* had superseded the 1922 Holmes ruling in *Federal Baseball*. Accordingly, by not adopting new legislation to grant MLB an exemption, the House committee thought that the sport would be subject to the nation's antitrust laws.

The *Toolson* Decision

Congressional inaction meant that judgments on baseball's status were left to the courts. In 1953 the case of George Toolson and the New York Yankees went before the U.S. Supreme Court. Toolson had been a minor leaguer in the Yankees system. When the team attempted to reassign him to another minor league club, Toolson refused to report. While MLB's lawyers had assumed that the Holmes decision was no longer good law, the Supreme Court fooled them, reaffirming the 1922 *Federal Baseball* decision in a 7-to-2 vote. The Court's one-paragraph decision read as follows:

> In *Federal Baseball* . . . this Court held that . . . professional baseball . . . was not within the scope of the federal antitrust laws. Congress had the ruling under consideration but has not seen fit to bring such business under these laws by legislation. . . . We think that if there are evils in this field which now warrant application to it of the antitrust laws it should be done by legislation. Without reexamination of the underlying issues, the judgments below are affirmed on the authority of *Federal Baseball*.[10]

A plausible interpretation is that the Supreme Court and Congress were playing a game of cat and mouse. The Congress did not pass a bill lifting baseball's exemption because it thought it had already been lifted by the 1948 *Gardella* decision. The Supreme Court affirmed the Holmes decision because it thought Congress had given its sanction to the exemption by not passing new legislation in 1951.

There is strong irony, to say the least, in the fact that the Supreme Court chose to hide behind congressional inaction to justify a judicially conferred exemption. It is particularly troubling because the conception of interstate commerce—which might have justified the Court's 1922 decision in *Federal Baseball*—had clearly changed by 1953.

Baseball's exemption became even more anomalous in 1957 when the Supreme Court in *Radovich* v. *NFL* declared football to be subject to antitrust statutes and asserted that baseball's exemption was "unreasonable, illogical and inconsistent."[11] Of course, the *Radovich* decision correctly reflected the broader conception of interstate commerce prevalent since the late 1930s.

Congress did affirmatively join the sports antitrust exemption issue in 1961 with the passage of the Sports Broadcasting Act. This act permits the sports of baseball, basketball, football, and hockey to sign leaguewide package deals for national broadcasting rights on over-the-air free television. That is, the teams in a league are allowed to join together as a cartel for purposes of forming a single network agreement, and then to divide the rights fees equally among all teams. This revenue-sharing, in turn, is meant to promote competitive balance and enhance fans' interest in the sport. Of course, the effect of the act is stronger in leagues such as the NFL, with its massive national television contracts, worth in excess of $79 million annually per team in 2002, than in the NHL, which has diminutive contracts, worth only $4 million annually per team.[12]

The *Flood* Decision

A 1968 cover of *Sports Illustrated* declared that Curt Flood was baseball's best centerfielder. He wasn't bad with the stick either, batting over .300 six times in his career. After the 1969 season he was notified that he had been traded from the Cardinals to the Phillies. Wanting to stay in St. Louis, Flood sent a letter to MLB commissioner Bowie Kuhn asking him to nullify the trade. Flood's letter pleaded: "After twelve years of being in the major leagues, I do not feel I am a piece of property to be bought and sold irrespective of my wishes."[13]

When Commissioner Kuhn denied Flood's request, Flood filed an antitrust suit—funded by the Players Association—against MLB for $3 million, triple damages, and free agency in January 1970. Flood lost in district and appeals courts. The Supreme Court agreed to hear the case and on June 18, 1972, voted 5 to 3 to uphold the 1922 Holmes decision and reject Flood's claim.

This time the Court did not attempt to pin the blame on Congress. Though the Court's majority opinion, written by Justice Blackmun, called baseball's exemption an "aberration" and an "anomaly," the majority of the Justices argued on the basis of *stare decisis* (let the old decision stand), maintaining that too many long-term commitments had been made relying on the 1922 decision for the courts to lift the exemption. Justice Blackmun also made clear that the Court's decision was not just a formal application of *stare decisis*, but was rooted in a "recognition of baseball's unique characteristics and needs."[14]

Notably, the Court in *Flood* specifically rejected the grounds upon which *Federal Baseball* stood: "Professional baseball is a business and is engaged in interstate commerce."[15] One of the dissenters, William O. Douglas, went on record as having erred in voting with the majority in the 1953 *Toolson* case. Douglas's dissenting opinion stated: "This is not a romantic history baseball enjoys as a business. It is a sordid history."[16]

After the Supreme Court's *Flood* decision, a June 23, 1972, *New York Times* editorial opined: "The only basis for the judge-made monopoly status of baseball is that the Supreme Court made a mistake the first time it considered the subject 50 years ago and now feels obliged to keep on making the same mistake because Congress does not act to repeal the exemption it never ordered."

Baseball's anomalous treatment was underscored in 1984 by the Supreme Court's decision in the *National Collegiate Athletic Association* v. *Board of Regents of the University of Oklahoma et al.* In this case, the Supreme Court held that the NCAA's network football contract violated the country's antitrust laws, thereby subjecting even the nonprofit amateur activity of college sports to antitrust statutes.

Continuing Ambiguity

The scope of MLB's exemption, however, became ambiguous again in 1993, following the decision of U.S. District Court Judge John Padova in *Piazza* v. *Major League Baseball.*[17] This case involved MLB's rejection of Vincent Piazza (father of Mets catcher Mike Piazza) and Vincent Tirendi as lead investors in a Florida investment group trying to buy the San Francisco Giants and move them to Tampa Bay. Judge Padova ruled against Major League Baseball, interpreting the decision of Justice Blackmun in *Flood* to limit baseball's exemption to its reserve clause.[18] Padova's decision was never tested by the Third Circuit Court of Appeals because the matter was settled out of court by MLB for approximately $10 million.

In 1994 Florida's attorney general, Robert Butterworth, brought a state antitrust claim against the National League for not approving the sale of the San Francisco Giants to a Tampa Bay ownership group (excluding Piazza and Tirendi) for $115 million. The National League petitioned the Florida courts to disallow AG Butterworth's demands for information from baseball concerning the case. The petition went before the Florida Supreme Court in October 1994. The court agreed with the Padova decision that MLB's exemption was to be narrowly construed as applying only to its reserve clause and denied the NL's petition. The dispute was ultimately resolved when MLB agreed to admit Tampa Bay as an expansion team, to begin play in 1998.

However, matters grew murkier. When the Twins' owner, Carl Pohlad, proposed to sell his team to a group of North Carolina owners and then acting commissioner Selig said that MLB would allow the move, Minnesota's AG, Michael Hatch, brought suit to prevent the sale. Hatch issued a demand for information, and MLB petitioned to have the demands quashed. The Minnesota district court refused the petition, and the appeals court declined to hear the case. The matter went before the state supreme court in April 1999, where it was held that MLB's exemption from antitrust laws applied broadly to the whole business of baseball. (Interestingly, in its opinion the Minnesota Supreme Court recognized that "the Flood opinion is not clear about the extent of the conduct that is exempt from antitrust laws." Nonetheless, the court did not follow standard practice of construing exemptions narrowly.)

Then, in December 2001, following MLB's stated intention to eliminate two teams, Florida AG Butterworth, concerned that his state might lose minor league teams, spring training teams, or one of its two major league teams, decided to investigate possible antitrust violations by MLB. Butterworth issued demands for information, and MLB sought injunctive relief. The matter went before a U.S. district court in Tallahassee, where Judge Hinkle ruled in favor of MLB, holding that the exemption covered MLB's right to eliminate teams.

Thus since 1990 the judicial rulings on the status of MLB's exemption have stacked up evenly: one state ruling and one federal ruling held that the exemption applies only to the reserve clause; and one state and one federal ruling held that it applies broadly to the business of baseball. Together the rulings cover only three of the eleven judicial circuits in the United States, leaving ample ambiguity in the status of the scope of MLB's exemption in the remaining circuits.

The Curt Flood Act of 1998

One true clarification of the exemption's scope came with the Curt Flood Act, passed by Congress and signed by President Bill Clinton in 1998. Baseball's collective bargaining agreement of 1996 stipulated that both ownership and labor would urge Congress to lift MLB's exemption for labor relations issues. (The language of the act makes it clear that, apart from the change regarding labor relations, Congress was not legislating any changes in the status of MLB's presumed exemption.) The manifest rationale for the bipartisan support for the Curt Flood Act was that it would reduce the likelihood that baseball's labor disputes would end in a work stoppage, and increase the likelihood that they would end up in court.

Unfortunately, the Curt Flood Act provides little hope of pacifying MLB's labor relations. Part of the reason for this is the Supreme Court's 1996 decision in *Brown* v. *Pro Football, Inc.* The NFL Players Association (NFLPA) hired attorney Kenneth Starr (now well known in another context) to argue its case. Starr and the NFLPA lost the decision even though many believed that they had a very strong case. In finding against Brown and the NFLPA, the Supreme Court ruled that a labor union could not be protected at the same time by both labor law (which grants unions an exemption from antitrust prosecution) and by antitrust law. Thus any sports union seeking to challenge an attempt by owners to unilaterally impose new restrictive conditions on its labor market must first decertify the union before it can bring an antitrust complaint against the owners. The *Brown* decision thereby makes it more difficult for the MLBPA to take advantage of the antitrust tool it is granted in the Curt Flood Act.[19] (This is discussed further in chapter five.)

In his opening statement at the February 13, 2002, antitrust hearings before the Senate Judiciary Committee, its chairman, Senator Patrick Leahy of Vermont, made a striking observation. He stated that when Congress passed the Curt Flood Act in 1998 the recent judicial findings in *Piazza* and in *Butterworth* suggested a narrow interpretation of baseball's exemption— that is, that it only applied to the reserve clause. Leahy remarked:

It was against this judicial backdrop that in 1998 Congress finally did act and eliminated the judicially-created exception preserved in limited form by Justice Blackmun in the *Flood* case. . . . Between the narrowness of the way the Supreme Court had perpetuated baseball's antitrust exemption—only as it applied to labor relations—and our work in Congress, in which we struck the last remaining remnant of the judicially-created exception to the applicability of the antitrust laws, it seems that there is no longer any basis to contend that a general, free-floating baseball antitrust exemption somehow continues to exist. . . . In my view, the heavy burden of justifying any exception from the rule of law is, and should be, squarely on the proponents of any antitrust exemption.

As I have pointed out, others differ in their interpretation. Thus there is no clarity on whether the nation's antitrust laws apply to the industry and, if they do apply, what aspects of the industry are covered. Such ambiguity makes long-term decisionmaking difficult and begs for resolution.

That said, the Supreme Court has held that precedents are "not sacrosanct" and should be reconsidered when "the intervening development of the law" has "removed or weakened the conceptual underpinnings from the prior decision," or when the precedent "becomes outdated and after being 'tested by experience, has been found to be inconsistent with the sense of justice or with the social welfare.'"[20] Thus reasons appear to abound for either a judicial or a legislative reconsideration and clarification of baseball's antitrust status.

The Practical Effect of Baseball's Presumed Exemption

Whether MLB should enjoy antitrust immunity should sensibly be resolved by considering the impact either removing or granting such immunity would have on the game and its consumers. Would removing baseball's presumed antitrust exemption do more good than harm? To answer this question, I now turn to the practical meaning of MLB's presumed exemption.

Reserve Clause

Historically, the principal effect of MLB's exemption was that the teams could continue to employ the reserve clause. This right was in force until it was reversed in a baseball arbitration hearing involving players Dave McNally and Andy Messersmith in late 1975 (see chapter five). After the owners attempted several unsuccessful appeals of this arbitration ruling in federal court and imposed a lockout, MLB and the Players Association reached a collective bargaining agreement in July 1976 that granted free-agency rights to players with six years of major league experience. The reserve clause was gone and no longer needed the protection of baseball's exemption.

Amateur Draft and Minor Leagues

A second effect of the presumed exemption is that it has allowed MLB to follow restrictive labor market practices relating to its minor leagues. Every June, MLB conducts a draft of amateur players from U.S., Canadian, and Puerto Rican high schools and universities. Teams choose players according to their finish in the previous year's standings: the teams with the worst records pick first. Once chosen, players can either sign with the selecting team with a fixed salary ($850 a month for entering players) plus a sizable signing bonus for the top prospects, or they can stay out of professional baseball until the next year's draft.[21] Chosen players who sign with a major league team then spend up to four years in that club's minor league system before another team has an opportunity to sign them and move them up to a higher minor league or to the major league level. If, however, the drafting club puts a minor leaguer on its forty-man major league roster, then that player cannot be signed by another team until he has completed seven years in the team's system.[22]

These restrictions on minor leaguers are all restraints of trade. The amateur cannot receive competitive bids for his services at the time of the draft; nor can he receive bids from other teams (for up to seven years) after he is drafted. While in the minors, his salary is determined according to an owner-set scale. Since with few exceptions amateurs do not go directly into the unionized major leagues, and since there is no labor union of minor league players, there has been no collective bargaining wherein a player's representative bargained away free labor market rights in exchange for other benefits. Thus this practice is not protected by what is known as the "non-statutory" labor exemption.[23] The only thing that legally allows MLB to treat minor leaguers as a form of indentured servants is MLB's presumed exemption from the nation's antitrust laws.

If the exemption were definitively lifted, then a minor league ballplayer could sue MLB. But it is not clear that a minor leaguer would do this. Minor leaguers are, after all, young and ambitious.[24] They want to ingratiate themselves with, not alienate themselves from, MLB. They want to concentrate on developing their baseball skills.

If the exemption were lifted and a minor league player did sue MLB, it is not a forgone conclusion that the player would win. MLB could defend itself by arguing that the restraint of trade as it applies to minor league baseball is reasonable. Only restraints deemed "unreasonable" violate antitrust law. MLB could argue that the minor league system as it is presently constituted is part and parcel of the organization of professional baseball, that it is an increasingly popular summer spectator sport, and that it helps promote competitive balance in the major leagues. These arguments may hold water with some judges but not with others.

The point here and elsewhere about lifting the exemption is that it would permit judicial review of baseball's policies and actions. When MLB claims that the minors are necessary, as long as MLB is presumed to have a blanket antitrust exemption there is no judicial review. That is, there is no permitted discovery of facts and there is no analytical challenge of baseball's assertion. If MLB has no exemption, the plaintiff's lawyer can conduct discovery of the relevant information and present an analysis to be heard by an independent judge and/or jury. Given that MLB faces no direct competition (it is the only top-level professional baseball league in the United States) and that it is not regulated, the opportunity for judicial review would provide the only chance to limit the potential abuse of its monopoly powers.

Would the minor leagues, in fact, disappear if MLB lost its presumed exemption? The answer is complicated, and it depends in part on whether a minor leaguer sued and on the outcome of the litigation. More generally, it is likely that the minor leagues would change but not disappear.

In the 1990s several independent (from MLB) minor leagues emerged and they have survived.[25] Without an exemption, affiliated minor league clubs might lose their ties to the major league team, but they would not necessarily disappear. To be sure, even if MLB retains its presumed exemption, it is possible that the number of minor league teams will be reduced as part of an owner cost-cutting strategy.

Further, if minor leaguers did not "belong" to a particular major league club, then it is likely that competitive balance among major league teams would improve. Major league clubs would draft players out of the minors, not out of college and high school. These players would be more developed and their potential talent level more knowable. The reverse-order draft would confer a larger advantage on the low-finishing teams than does the present amateur draft. Several related points on baseball's draft system are discussed in subsequent chapters.

Rival Leagues

Baseball has not been challenged by a rival league since 1914–15. It was almost successfully challenged in 1959–60 by the Continental League and again in 1995 by the United Baseball League (UBL). The Continental League challenge reveals another advantage to MLB of its presumed exemption that is related to the reserve clause and the minor leagues.

One of the major obstacles experienced by the Continental League was its inability to sign major or minor league players who were contractually under reserve at the time. Thus the best and second-best talent pools were not accessible to the Continental League because MLB controlled the relevant labor markets. In May 1960, Senator Estes Kefauver called hearings around the issue of the establishment of the Continental League and his related bill to limit the number of minor leaguers who could be controlled by the existing major league teams. MLB did extensive lobbying, and the bill was defeated by the close margin of four votes (45 to 41) in the Senate. The bill was sent back to committee for reconsideration, however, with the outcome depending on whether MLB followed through on its pledged cooperation with the fledgling league.

After a few additional months of haggling, the Continental League was finally co-opted on July 18, 1960, when the NL voted to expand to ten teams and to form a committee including representatives from the Continental League to study how expansion should proceed. Shortly thereafter, the AL decided to expand as well. At an August 2 meeting, MLB promised the four new franchises to ownership groups from the Continental League.

Since the advent of free agency in 1977, the reserve clause for major leaguers no longer protects MLB from encroachments by a potential rival league and the barrier of access to minor leaguers is attenuated. This is because there are now several independent minor leagues, in addition to a more developed system of intercollegiate baseball as well as greater access to talent from foreign leagues.

Nevertheless, other barriers to entry for a new league have become more formidable. Access to signing players matters only if a new league can offer competitive salaries. To do this, a new league would need hundreds of millions of dollars per team in public subsidies to build new stadiums, gargantuan television contracts from the networks, and healthy local cable contracts. An upstart league would have none of these.

In the mid-1990s the United Baseball League contemplated an intermediate course, wherein each team would sign a top-tier player, several midlevel players, and a majority of low-salary players at its outset. As its following grew, the league would upgrade the talent level over time. Among its management group, the UBL included Curt Flood, Al Harazin (former general manager of the New York Mets), Dick Moss (former general counsel for the Players Association and a player agent), and Mike Stone (former general manager of the Texas Rangers). Initially, the UBL had eight cities with modest ballparks, a good share of its needed capital, and a long-term television contract with Liberty Media on a revenue sharing basis.

There is no telling whether the UBL strategy, which embraced profit-sharing with host cities and players, would ultimately have succeeded because its launch was aborted. A few weeks after the UBL signed and publicly announced its long-term television deal with Liberty Media, Liberty Media merged with Fox Sports. And within a few more weeks, Fox had signed a long-term contract for network broadcasting rights with MLB. Liberty Media reneged on its contract with the UBL. The UBL was dead.[26]

Broadcasting

The 1961 Sports Broadcasting Act (SBA) allows leagues to package national television rights for over-the-air broadcasting. The act does not permit packaging rights for pay television. More precisely, the act extends antitrust immunity to a league's sale of pooled rights for "sponsored telecasting of games." To clarify the meaning of "sponsored telecasting" courts have relied on the legislative history of the SBA. In testifying before Congress during hearings on the 1961 bill, the NFL commissioner and chief proponent of the SBA, Pete Rozelle, stated unequivocally: "This bill covers only the free telecasting of professional sports contests, and does not cover pay TV." Then, in 1982, the NFL counsel at the time and since 1989 commissioner, Paul Tagliabue, repeated to a Senate committee that "the words 'sponsored telecasting' were intended to exclude pay and cable. This is clear from the legislative history and from the committee reports. So, that statute does not authorize us to pool and sell to pay and cable."[27] This interpretation was affirmed in two subsequent court cases.[28]

Thus the NFL, NBA, and NHL national deals with cable stations and with special packages on DirecTV (such as *NFL Sunday Ticket*) are subject to antitrust review. In contrast, MLB's deals with ESPN and DirecTV (*Extra Innings*) are immunized from antitrust scrutiny if its presumed exemption is valid.[29] While this distinction is significant in theory, to date it has not been particularly significant in practice. The few challenges to pooled pay-TV deals in the NFL and NBA have all been resolved with little sacrifice by the leagues. Whether the distinction becomes more meaningful in the future remains to be seen.

Franchise Relocation and Contraction

Imagine owning a house and being told by a local politician that you will not be allowed to sell it to anyone whose last name begins with a J; or imagine owning a business in a state with high labor costs and even higher tax rates and being informed that you will not be allowed to move it to another state. It might occur to you that someone is interfering with your right to dispose of your assets as you please and that you are not enjoying the benefit of a free market. That same thought occurred to Al Davis, part-owner of the Oakland Raiders in 1980, when he tried to move his football team to Los Angeles and the NFL said that he could not do so.

Davis sued the league and won. The courts ruled that the NFL was engaging in an unreasonable restraint of trade. In particular, they said that the NFL was protecting the former L.A. Rams monopoly in the Los Angeles market and that the NFL's relocation voting rule was too stringent. The courts did not rule that a sporting league could not exercise some controls over a team's location; rather, they made it clear that such controls, when properly exercised, fall under a rule-of-reason defense. That is, there are good reasons why a league would want its teams to be both geographically stable and geographically dispersed. These reasons must be considered and offset against the negatives connected to prohibiting an owner from moving his or her team. The negatives include a reduction in an owner's rights of free trade and the possible retention of a team in a city with less interest in the sport than a prospective host city.

Each of these negatives is more complicated than may appear at first blush. From an antitrust perspective, the protection of a monopolist's rights would probably necessitate demonstrating that such protection is congruent with increasing efficiency or competition. In the case of two competing cities, one city's expression of stronger demand for a team may reflect the intensity of special interests or a temporarily stronger fiscal condition.

In the NFL, the NBA, and the NHL, which have no presumed blanket antitrust exemptions, the leagues have maintained some controls over team movement. In each league the relocation policy has evolved into one where most ownership proposals for relocation are negotiated. In the end, the owner generally is allowed to move but is compelled to pay the league a relocation fee on the order of tens of millions of dollars.

From the fans' perspective such a policy is less than optimal. Why, for instance, should the NBA be able to charge the owners of the Charlotte Hornets $30 million for permission to move from Charlotte to New Orleans? If the Hornets have to pay such a fee, the team will likely be able to exact a larger subsidy from New Orleans before agreeing to move. This is what happened to St. Louis when the NFL allowed the Rams to move there from Los Angeles. Whether such a fee can be charged and passed on to the city will be a function of the city's elasticity of demand for the team. The problem with monopoly leagues is that they create artificial franchise scarcity, which makes it more likely that such a fee will be passed on to the host city.

When he was still baseball commissioner, Fay Vincent referred to Washington, D.C., as an "asset" of baseball, even though no team was playing in the nation's capital. Why? Because Washington was and is a potential host of a team and could be used to leverage better deals from other cities. In a sense, baseball treated Washington as if it owned the town. This sense of ownership derives from the artificial scarcity of franchises that baseball enforces as a monopolist. Were there two competing major leagues, Washington, D.C., as the country's eighth largest media market and the nation's capital, would have one franchise, or perhaps two, in a heartbeat.

Thus MLB's presumed exemption may shield it from owner antitrust challenges and make it more difficult for teams to move. It should be noted, however, that where such moves are not in the public interest, team relocations could be prevented under a rule-of-reason defense even without an exemption.[30]

Sometimes team moves are in the public interest. The team moves to a city with a stronger demand for the game, and the abandoned city usually succeeds in attracting an expansion team.[31] This happened in the NFL with Baltimore, Cleveland, St. Louis, and Houston, and in the NBA with Charlotte, and seems likely in the NFL with Los Angeles. That is, relocation frequently leads to expansion and the servicing of additional cities. It is hard to argue that the public interest has been served by having a Major League Baseball team in Montreal instead of Washington, D.C., over the past ten years.[32]

It is also important to note that even though MLB has prevented certain teams from relocating, it has not hesitated to use its monopoly power to threaten team movement in order to extract larger public subsidies from existing host cities. MLB owners have threatened to move the Milwaukee Brewers to North Carolina and the San Francisco Giants to Florida, among others, before new stadium deals were put in place.

Threatened moves, however, have not always been sufficient to motivate a local community to support new publicly subsidized facilities. The voters in the San Francisco Bay Area rejected four different referendums seeking public funding for a new Giants stadium in the 1980s despite ownership threats to move the team to Tampa Bay. The voters in Minneapolis–St. Paul did not agree to build a new stadium for the Twins when Mr. Pohlad threatened to sell his team, first to an ownership group in Tampa Bay, and then to another group in North Carolina. Bud Selig even publicly stated that MLB would allow the move to North Carolina. Angered by Wayne Huizenga's barn sale of talent from the 1997 World Champion Florida Marlins, the people of South Florida were unwilling to put up hundreds of millions of dollars in public funds to build a new facility in Miami.

So MLB developed a new lever: contraction. As the Florida state legislature prepared to vote on public funding for a new Marlins stadium, on April 25, 2001, Commissioner Selig sent a threatening letter to State Senator J. Alex Villalobos. The letter read in part: "Unless [public stadium] funding was secured, the Marlins would be a prime candidate for contraction or relocation. Bluntly, the Marlins cannot and will not survive in South Florida without a new stadium."[33] For MLB, an advantage of threatening contraction rather than relocation is that it might not put the onus for the change on the local team owner. If baseball had eliminated the Marlins in the fall of 2001, this could not have been blamed on John Henry (then owner of the

Marlins). If John Henry, however, had threatened to move the team to Portland, Oregon, then he would have been the public culprit. Public culprits are less likely to loosen the purse strings of legislators or inspire sympathy among the voters.

The same threat loomed over the twin cities of Minneapolis–St. Paul during the 2001–02 offseason. The Metropolitan Sports Facility Commission (MSFC), which owns the Metrodome, sued the Twins and MLB because the Twins had signed a lease extension in September 2001 to play the 2002 season at the Metrodome. The MSFC won decisions in state trial and appeals courts and the state supreme court refused to review the case. These courts all rejected the Twins' attempt to liken their situation to that of a standard property lease, where the tenant only has to keep paying rent but is not obligated to continue living in the rental unit. The trial judge stated that sports leases are *sui generis* because the "welfare, recreation, prestige, prosperity, trade, and commerce of the people of the community are at stake."[34] Legally blocked from eliminating the Twins in 2002, MLB announced that it would delay contraction until 2003.

The MSFC then brought another lawsuit against MLB to prevent it from eliminating the Twins in 2003. This time the MSFC's lawyers deployed a different set of legal arguments. First, because a lease extension had been contemplated for 2003 in the 1998 lease agreement, the lawyers argued that this constituted "prospective contractual relations," which are recognized in Minnesota law as a form of property relations. Second, since MLB calls itself a custodian of a public asset, they maintained that under the good-cause standard a team should be able to move only if it is economically necessary to do so. In order to develop its case, the lawyers subpoenaed a variety of MLB financial documents. The court ruled that MLB had to release the documents; rather than do so, MLB agreed not to eliminate the Twins in 2003.

The MSFC cases did not rely on baseball's antitrust status. Attorneys general and other entities in other states, however, may bring antitrust cases against MLB in the future to prevent the elimination of major or minor league teams or spring training sites in their areas. As a monopolist, baseball should not be able to reduce output in order to increase the profits of cartel members, especially when the cartel's revenues have been growing at 17 percent annually since 1994. If MLB's presumed exemption were determined (either judicially or legislatively) to apply to all aspects of its business, then MLB would be insulated from such antitrust challenges to any proposed contraction.

Restrictions on Municipal Ownership

One straightforward and sensible way to right the relationship between baseball franchises and cities would be through municipal ownership. Given the large investment of community resources in a team, it would be proper for a city to hold an asset stake. If, for instance, a franchise's value increased by $150 million because the city invested $200 million in a new facility, then the city would reap part or all of the increased value, depending on what share of the team it owned. Of course, the capital gain would be unrealized unless the team were sold. But this is the point: the city itself could decide if it wanted to keep its baseball team.

MLB, however, does not allow municipal ownership of teams at the major league level. Indeed, back in the 1980s, Joan Kroc attempted to give her San Diego Padres to the city but was not allowed to do so. This prohibition on municipal ownership constitutes a restriction of trade in the market to buy and sell franchises. It is protected by MLB's presumed exemption. Without the exemption, MLB could argue that the restriction should stand a rule-of-reason test. But the NFL tried such a defense in *Sullivan* v. *NFL*, regarding its ban on public (corporate) ownership, and was unsuccessful.[35] Baseball would have the burden of demonstrating how municipal ownership would affect its ability to promote the game effectively.

Thus the status and scope of MLB's antitrust exemption are still vitally important, potentially affecting the industry's operation in a number of areas. After considering the issues of baseball's competitive balance, its profitability, its labor relations, and the economic impact of new stadiums, I shall return to the issue of MLB's antitrust status and a proper public policy toward the industry.

CHAPTER THREE

Competitive Balance: Leveling the Playing Field

Conventional wisdom has it that a successful team sports league must have a healthy dose of competitive balance or parity across its teams. Without such balance, there will not be the necessary uncertainty of outcome in individual games and in seasons to maintain fan interest. In its July 2000 report to Commissioner Selig, the blue-ribbon panel defined competitive balance like this: "In the context of baseball, proper competitive balance should be understood to exist when there are no clubs chronically weak because of MLB's financial structural features. Proper competitive balance will not exist until every well-run club has a regularly recurring hope of reaching postseason play."[1]

That is, the blue-ribbon panel wants to see team revenues redistributed sufficiently so that every *well-run* club has a regularly recurring chance to make the playoffs. Notice that the panel does not expect all clubs to have a chance to reach the postseason every year. First, the clubs must be well run. It is always possible for an owner to squander money by signing mediocre players to fat contracts, to assemble a team of players who don't complement each other, to hire a manager who sows anxiety and discord, and so on. High revenue does not guarantee success. Second, the panel calls for a "regularly recurring hope" of postseason play, not for a hope every year. Third, the panel does not call for a hope to make it to or win the World Series, just to make it to the postseason. In other words, the panel does not think that proper competitive balance entails equality of team strength.

Indeed, a league that seeks to maximize its revenue will not want each of its teams to have an equal chance to win the championship. Leagues want high television ratings. These are best achieved, generally, when teams from the largest media markets are playing in the championship series. Other things being the same, MLB would like to see the New York Yankees, the New York Mets, the Los Angeles Dodgers, the Anaheim Angels, the Chicago Cubs, and the Chicago White Sox appear in the World Series more frequently than the Milwaukee Brewers, the Cincinnati Reds, the Kansas City Royals, or the San Diego Padres. By the same token, MLB does not want to see the Yankees win or the Padres lose every year because that too would engender apathy in many cities.

In other words, identifying optimal competitive balance in a sports league is a complex matter. Baseball's blue-ribbon panel and the commissioner's office believe that MLB has crossed over the threshold of too much inequality and that it is hurting the game. To assess whether this view is correct and what, if anything, should be done about it, I shall begin by considering how best to measure competitive balance. Before prescribing a remedy, one must know whether the patient is sick, and if so, how sick.

Measuring Competitive Balance

There are almost as many ways to measure competitive balance as there are to score a run. Among the more frequently used metrics are the standard deviation of win percentages (in a given year for a league or over time for a team);[2] the ratio of the actual to the idealized standard deviation of win percentages;[3] the ratio of the top to bottom win percentages; the range of win percentages; the gini coefficient of win percentages[4] or of the concentration of championships;[5] and, excess tail frequencies.[6]

Which is the right index or the right combination of indices? The notion that competitive balance is important to sports leagues derives from an assumption that fans have a strong preference for uncertainty of outcomes, or, as Commissioner Selig has put it, fans want to begin each season with hope and expectation. It follows that the most relevant measures of competitive balance are the ones to which the consumers show greatest sensitivity.[7]

Competitive Balance in Comparative Perspective

I argue here that fans respond not only to the competitive outcome in a particular season, but also to the variability in outcomes over time and the process by which these outcomes are attained.[8] This is best perceived by

Table 3-1. *National Hockey League: Link between Payroll and Performance, 1995–2001*

	Correlation coefficient	
Year	Opening-day payroll	Trade deadline payroll
1995	.465	.583
1996	.341	.489
1997	.338	.431
1998	.237	.238
1999	.499	.593
2000	.471	.632
2001	.595	.646

Source: National Hockey League Players' Association data.

considering the experience with competitive balance in other major sports leagues.

Ice Hockey (NHL)

In terms of both the standard deviation of win percentages and the ratio of actual to idealized standard deviations, the NHL stands in the middle of the four major team sports leagues in the United States. Another perspective on competitive balance, and one that is likely to affect fan perceptions of the fairness of competition, is provided by the relationship between team payroll and team performance. If payroll and performance (such as win percentage) are highly correlated, then fans may conclude that the deck is stacked in favor of high-revenue teams. For the 1990s, the team payroll-performance link in the NHL was significant at the 5 percent level,[9] but the link was weaker (correlation coefficient, $r = .363$) than in the English Premier League, MLB, or the NBA.[10] The payroll-performance link is weakest in the NFL by a significant margin.[11] (The 5 percent level of significance is generally the lowest one used to denote a significant statistical relationship between two variables. The 1 percent level is generally the highest one used, denoting a highly significant relationship.)

An interesting pattern emerges in hockey's pay-performance relationship. Using data for opening-day and trade deadline payroll (about two-thirds of the way through the season) for each team from 1995 through 2001, the correlation coefficients between team win percentage and team payroll are shown in table 3-1.[12]

The pattern is clear: midseason payrolls are consistently more closely correlated with win percentages than are beginning payrolls. This result suggests that causality runs in both directions between pay and performance. Higher pay creates better teams, but better teams create higher pay. That is, teams performing well in midseason make an effort (by acquiring new players) to bolster their rosters in order to increase their chances for regular and postseason success. Of course, the causality from performance to pay may also appear between seasons, as winning teams have to spend more to retain their successful players.

Stated differently, owners exhibit a certain caution about payroll spending until they are convinced that their team will succeed. This suggests that owners believe the relationship between win percentage and revenue is nonlinear. Fans care little whether their team's win percentage is .400 or .430. Yet they care a great deal whether their team makes it to the playoffs (perhaps the difference between a .530 and a .560 win percentage), wins a division, or wins a championship. That is, fans are more responsive to improved performance at the top end.

Another interesting pattern has emerged in the NHL since 1990: the dynasties that dominated the sport for decades have not returned. Consider the following record of dynasties, according to who won the Stanley Cup: Montreal 1956–60; Toronto 1962–64; Montreal 1976–79; New York Islanders 1980–83; Edmonton 1984–85, 1987–88, and 1990. In contrast, since 1990, no team has won the cup more than two years in a row, and eight different teams have won the cup.

By the measure of concentration of championships, then, hockey appears to have become more balanced after 1990. The traditional policies related to competitive balance—revenue sharing or salary cap/luxury tax—however, have not been implemented in hockey. What might account for this post-1990 shift toward greater balance?

Since the arrival of Bob Goodenow as executive director of the National Hockey League Players' Association in 1991, players have followed a policy of salary disclosure. Together with the salary arbitration system, which allows players' salaries and productivity to be compared, this disclosure policy has helped boost player salaries appreciably. Further, the new collective bargaining agreement in 1995 brought the NHL its first system of unrestricted free agency for players over thirty-one years of age. This lifted the compensation of veteran star players still more. It seems plausible to hypothesize that the resulting rapid growth in hockey players' salaries in the 1990s, in the context of veteran free agency and arbitration, has made it more and more expensive to hold together winning teams—and easier to resurrect poorly performing teams.

Basketball

The NBA has been on the high end of most statistical measures of imbalance. The league practices no revenue sharing, other than income from the national television contract and NBA Properties, and it has had a salary cap since 1983, albeit a porous one until 1999. Indeed, the standard deviation of win percentages rose in the league by 14.5 percent during the 1980s, the decade when the cap was introduced, and has continued to increase since 1990.[13]

The NBA has an intermediate link between payroll and performance. In a simple regression of win percentage on team payroll from 1986 through 2000, the coefficient on payroll is significant at the 1 percent level ($r = .40$), and in yearly regressions the closeness of fit displays no particular trend (with correlation coefficients varying between .264 and .632).

The concentration of championships is high, especially since 1990.[14] The Chicago Bulls were crowned champions from 1991 through 1993; then when Michael Jordan tried his hand at baseball, the Houston Rockets won in 1994 and 1995, and with Jordan back, the Bulls won from 1996 through 1998, followed by the San Antonio Spurs in 1999 and the L.A. Lakers in 2000, 2001, and 2002.

Given the strong statistical evidence of imbalance, one might expect to see some impact in the form of diminished fan support. Some might argue that such a diminution has, in fact, happened. The difficulty, of course, is attributing the slightly reduced attendance and television ratings of recent years to competitive imbalance, rather than to the impact of the 1998–99 lockout, the temporary retirement of Michael Jordan, team and league pricing policies, or general macroeconomic conditions.

It might also be argued that, despite the concentration of championships, strong consumer support over the years has been maintained because fans perceive fairness in the way basketball's competition is structured. In particular, few would contest the proposition that the major reason for the Bulls' dominance during the 1990s had to do with their good fortune in drafting Michael Jordan. Because of the so-called (Larry) Bird exception (which allows a team to resign one of its own players without regard to the salary cap), teams tend to be able to keep their top players. In 1997–98, for instance, seven of the eleven top-paid players in the NBA still played for their original teams. Thus if Michael Jordan had originally signed with Milwaukee or Utah instead of Chicago, he probably would have played in one of those cities throughout his career. The Bulls' success in the 1990s had no discernible link to the fact that Chicago is the country's third largest media market.[15]

Another factor behind the NBA's success with its fans may be the successful promotion of the league by the commissioner's office. Commissioner David Stern constantly talks up his league and its players. As the Los Angeles Lakers prepared to sweep the New Jersey Nets in the 2002 championship, Stern remarked that it was wonderful to see the Lakers reassert their dominance—putting a positive spin on what many would see as an unfortunate circumstance. He added that the Lakers' success was achieved despite the leveling of team payrolls resulting from the 1999 collective bargaining agreement.

Football

The NFL has consistently had the highest actual standard deviation of win percentages; yet within U.S. sports leagues, it has also had the lowest ratio of actual to idealized standard deviations. Further, it has had a remarkably low concentration of championships: no team has ever won three consecutive Super Bowls.

The NFL employs several policies to promote competitive balance: extensive revenue sharing (approximately 70 percent of all league revenues are divided equally among the teams); a relatively hard salary cap; a reverse-order draft;[16] and an unbalanced schedule. The consequence of these policies is that the ratio of top to bottom team revenue and top to bottom team payrolls does not exceed 2 to 1, and often is considerably lower. In recent years, the average of the seven highest payrolls has not exceeded 1.5 times the average of the seven lowest payrolls in the NFL; the similar ratios in the NBA and MLB are 1.8 and 3.6 respectively.[17]

Revenue sharing in the NFL goes back to the league's inception in 1920 and the reinforcing policies of Commissioner Pete Rozelle in the early 1960s. It is ingrained in the NFL's contracts and its culture; hence, however desirable it might seem to some, it cannot be readily adopted by other leagues.

Many believe that the NFL has gone too far with its revenue sharing. Econometric work has made it clear that there is only a weak statistical link between team payroll and performance and that there is little, if any, profit incentive to win in the NFL. It remains to be seen whether this feature will eventually strain the fans' perception of the legitimacy of the league's competition.

English Soccer

The English Premier League, like soccer leagues throughout Europe and elsewhere, is based on a promotion/relegation system in which successful teams are promoted to higher leagues within a hierarchy and unsuccessful teams are relegated to lower leagues. From this, many tendencies ensue: stronger consumer demand, higher player salaries, better players, more competitive balance, and lower public subsidies, among others.

The greater expected degree of competitive balance in promotion/relegation leagues emerges from several factors. Perhaps most intriguing among them is that, because league membership is not fixed, teams do not have monopoly control over their territories. Any individual with sufficient capital and drive can create a lower-division team, invest in top players and coaches, and potentially rise up the divisional ladder to the top level. As a result of this characteristic, promotion/relegation leagues tend not to have monopolies or even duopolies in large cities. London has had nine different teams playing in the top-level English Premier League (PL) since 1990.[18] If a city has too few teams relative to its economic potential to support teams, then entrepreneurs are free to increase supply without paying the existing league for the permission to become an expansion team. Thus London PL teams do not enjoy the rent from the large market that is bestowed, for instance, upon baseball's Yankees.[19]

The team that has dominated the English PL since 1992–93 is Manchester United (Man U). Man U won the league championship seven out of the ensuing nine years. Between 1974 and 1999 the pay-performance link in the PL was stronger than it was for any U.S. sports league ($r = .583$).[20]

One might expect a negative fan reaction to this concentration at the top along with the apparent ability of a team to buy success. In fact, the era of Man U's dominance has coincided with a growth spurt in soccer's popularity in England. After four decades when average attendance per game fell by over 50 percent in English soccer, attendance at PL games shot up 41 percent between 1990 and 1998 despite rapidly rising ticket prices.

England's improved economy, new crowd-control policies at stadiums, John Major's love of the game replacing Margaret Thatcher's disdain, and more televised games, among other factors, all contributed to soccer's ascendancy in the 1990s, but it appears that the growing mystique of Man U played a role as well. A dominant team is not necessarily bad for a sport if fans perceive the team's success to be legitimately gained. In the case of Man U, the team did not benefit from the rent of being the only team in England's largest media market. On the contrary, there are approximately fifty professional league soccer teams within 100 miles of the Man U stadium. Rather, Man U's success seems to have its roots in an aggressive, well-executed management strategy.[21] The knowledge that poorly run teams can face demotion irrespective of their home city must also contribute to the sense of fairness of outcome.

Of course, another part of the legitimacy formula is the fans' confidence that the league is producing the highest possible quality of product. In the long run, the best guarantor of this is competitive labor markets. Promotion/relegation systems provide strong incentives for quality; purported single-entity structures, such as Major League Soccer in the United States, do not. Ultimately, successful leagues must strive for both relative and absolute quality.

Competitive Balance in Baseball

By the most commonly used measure of competitive balance, standard deviation of win percentage, MLB experienced a modest, gradual improvement in competitive balance between 1903 and the 1950s. With the introduction of the reverse-order draft in 1965, competitive balance improved further, and with the advent of free agency in 1977, competitive balance continued to improve in the 1980s.[22] Over the long haul, talent compression (primarily from the smaller share of the population playing Major League Baseball) also provided a balancing force. This gradual, long-term trend toward greater competitive balance in MLB, however, seems to have been interrupted and reversed in the mid-1990s. This reversal is clearly reflected in various statistical measures, such as standard deviation, championship concentration indexes, or Humphreys's ratio of competitive balance.[23]

Perhaps more troubling than the increase in the statistical measures of unequal performance is the clear evidence that the relationship between team performance and team payroll has grown stronger. The commissioner's office has issued two reports detailing the lack of balance since 1995. At first glance, the numbers are compelling. Consider, for instance, this one: during the seven years from 1995 through 2001 only four teams from the bottom half of payrolls reached the postseason, in which, altogether, they won a total of 5 out of 224 games (the top payroll teams had a win percentage of .978!).[24] None of these four bottom payroll teams went beyond the first round of the playoffs.

From 1980 through 1986, twenty of baseball's twenty-six teams made it to a League Championship Series (LCS). From 1995 through 2001, only eleven of baseball's thirty made it to an LCS. No team outside the top quartile in payrolls won a single World Series game during the period 1995–2001.[25] The only such team during this period to reach the World Series was the San Diego Padres in 1998. They were in the second payroll quartile at the time and were swept by the Yankees in that series.[26] The top-quartile dominance of the World Series was interrupted in 2002 when the Giants (with the ninth highest payroll) and the Angels (with the fourteenth highest payroll) met in the best-of-seven championship. Both teams were in the top half, but not in the top quarter, of payrolls. It was the first time that two wild card teams had met in the World Series.[27]

The apparent relationship between payroll and performance is reaffirmed by simple regression analysis. Table 3-2 shows the results from estimating the following equation for each year between 1980 and 2001: Win $Pct_i = \alpha + \beta\, Payroll_i + e_i$.

Table 3-2 shows that in eight seasons from 1985 through 1992, the relationship between payroll spending and win percentage was significant at the 5 percent level only three times, and never at the 1 percent level. In the nine seasons from 1993 through 2001, however, payroll was always significant at the 5 percent level and significant at 1 percent in all but the first two seasons. According to forty-man roster data, the relationship remained significant at the 1 percent level in 2002. Once again, it seems evident that the link between payroll and performance became significantly tighter in the mid-1990s.[28]

The relationship between a team's expenditures on its players and performance may well be closer than these tests suggest. This is because the

Table 3-2. *Major League Baseball: Yearly Relationship between Team Payroll and Performance, 1980–2001*

Year	α [t statistic]	β [t statistic]	r^2	n
1980	.484 [11.1]	3.24 E-09 [0.38]	.006	26
1981	.464 [9.06]	5.66 E-09 [0.73]	.002	26
1982	.489 [13.31]	1.46 E-09 [0.34]	.005	26
1983	.491 [12.82]	9.87 E-10 [0.26]	.003	26
1984	.418 [10.77]	7.48 E-09* [2.18]	.166	26
1985	.362 [5.26]	1.30 E-08 [2.05]	.149	26
1986	.460 [9.29]	3.41 E-09 [0.84]	.290	26
1987	.466 [9.65]	3.02 E-09 [0.74]	.220	26
1988	.393 [8.12]	9.37 E-09* [2.31]	.181	26
1989	.389 [9.10]	7.89 E-09* 2.69	.232	26
1990	.460 [9.46]	2.30 E-09 [0.84]	.028	26
1991	.420 [10.44]	3.14 E-09 [2.07]	.151	26
1992	.470 [10.72]	9.45 E-10 [0.70]	.020	26
1993	.398 [9.29]	3.17 E-09* [2.51]	.195	28
1994	.386 [8.39]	3.53 E-09* [2.57]	.203	28
1995	.382 [10.71]	9.45 E-09** [3.49]	.319	28
1996	.397 [14.93]	3.07 E-09** [4.13]	.396	28
1997	.392 [15.65]	2.72 E-09** [4.61]	.450	28
1998	.355 [13.42]	3.43 E-09** [5.89]	.554	30
1999	.389 [15.93]	2.26 E-09** [5.03]	.475	30
2000	.426 [17.67]	1.36 E-09** [3.33]	.284	30
2001	.408 [11.52]	1.37 E-09** [2.74]	.211	30

* Two-tailed test, significant at 5 percent.
** Two-tailed test, significant at 1 percent.

payroll figures employed do not include spending on player development (scouting, training, and minor leaguers' compensation). Some teams perform well with modest payrolls. This is often because they spend above the average on player development and are able to stock their major league rosters with young players not yet eligible for salary arbitration or free agency. Unfortunately, team-by-team data on player development expenditures is not publicly available and hence cannot be included in the statistical analysis.

The close statistical relationship between payroll and win percentage does not denote that payroll alone determines team performance. Even during the year of tightest correlation, 1998, only 55.4 percent of the variation in win percentage was determined by the variation in payroll. Other factors (for example, yearly variation in player performance, team cohesion, managerial choices, efficacy of the player development program, and luck) clearly affect a team's success. As Rangers owner Tom Hicks, Orioles owner Peter Angelos, and Mets owner Fred Wilpon, among others, will readily attest, the concern is not that high payrolls guarantee success or that low payrolls guarantee failure; rather, it is that high payrolls greatly increase the probability of strong team performance, while low payrolls greatly lower this probability.

Moreover, statistical correlation does not denote causality. A high correlation only means that the two variables move together; it does not tell us which variable affects the other, or indeed if both variables are affected by a third variable. As suggested in the case of the NHL, it is possible that team success in the short run causes payrolls to rise, rather than vice versa, or that causality runs in both directions. For instance, baseball teams with a strong chance of making it to and being competitive in the postseason may make midseason trades to acquire top players. The acquisition of these players, usually in exchange for minor league prospects, will lead to increases in team payroll. In this way, short-run performance can drive payroll. Further, if a team nearly reaches the World Series, owners may have an incentive to add another key player to the roster for the next season. Or, if a team wins the World Series and the owner wants to keep the team together, the players whose contracts have ended or are about to end can usually command higher salaries in their next contract.

There is a statistical model to test for causality that was developed by Clive Granger.[29] Applying this test to MLB during 1980–94 shows no evidence of Granger causality from payroll to performance. Since 1995, however, there is evidence that causality runs in both directions.

Sources of the Mid-1990s Shift

Aided by the introduction of the reverse-order draft and free agency, competitive balance in baseball steadily improved from 1965 through the 1980s.[30] Before free agency, when players were stuck with a team for their whole careers unless they were traded or released, big-city owners bought good players from small-city owners. The money (from the extra revenue produced by the player) went to the owner, not the player, and high-revenue teams disproportionately accumulated player talent. Once a championship team was assembled, the absence of competitive pressure on player salaries made it unlikely that this team would be broken up.

With free agency, however, it became more expensive to hold a winning team together, and weak teams became more able to improve themselves rapidly in the free-agent market. The era of team dynasties seemed to be gone forever and MLB's 1990 economic study committee found only a slight correlation between city size and team performance.

Then came the 1990s. At first, the news was good. Baseball signed a new national television contract with CBS and ESPN for 1990–93, which together with growing central licensing, superstation, and Copyright Royalty Tribunal revenues meant that each and every team received some $19 million a year from baseball's central coffers. In 1990 this was almost 40 percent of the average team revenue.

But in 1994 the value of baseball's new national television contract fell by over 60 percent. Exacerbating matters, certain big market teams, like the Yankees, were earning over $40 million a year in unshared local media revenue, and the era of the new big-revenue-generating stadiums was ushered in by Baltimore's Camden Yards in 1992. With centrally distributed monies below $8 million per club, teams with a big market or a new stadium found themselves with a rapidly growing revenue advantage.

The revenue disparity between the richest and poorest teams was around $30 million in 1989, but by 1999 it was $163 million. The disparity grew further, to $187 million in 2000 and $208 million in 2001. Local revenues (including all stadium-related and local media income) in 2001 ranged from a high of $217.8 million for the Yankees to a low of $9.8 million for the Montreal Expos.[31] The comparison is skewed somewhat by the special

Table 3-3. *Average Local Revenue by Revenue Quartile, 1995–2001*

Millions of dollars

Quartile	1995	1997	1999	2001
1	69.1	99.5	121.3	154.0
2	46.1	55.2	83.9	106.0
3	31.4	40.0	52.0	73.1
4	21.4	26.6	28.0	38.4

Source: Based on data from Major League Baseball.

circumstances of the Yankees and Expos, but the wide and growing disparity holds up clearly when the top and bottom quartiles of teams are considered.

The absolute difference in average local revenues between the top and bottom quartiles grew from $47.7 million in 1995 to $115.6 million in 2001 (see table 3-3). With the growing revenue disparity came sharpening payroll inequality. The top payroll (for a twenty-five-man roster) in 1995 was $58.2 million, and the lowest payroll was $13.1 million, a difference of $45.1 million. By 2001 the top payroll was $120.9 million, and the bottom was $17.1 million, a difference of $103.8 million.

Once again, the disparity remains sharp and growing when the top and bottom payroll quartiles are compared. In 1995 the average payroll of teams in the top quartile was $28.6 million higher than that of the bottom quartile, but by 2001 the top quartile spent on average $64.4 million more on payroll than the bottom quartile. Among other things, this widening differential meant that the top-payroll teams had more margin for error in their quest for competitive dominance.

To this volatile mixture add the emergence of new franchise owners who also own international communications networks or are attempting to build regional sports channels. The rapidly escalating franchise values limit ownership to extraordinarily wealthy individuals or corporations who, in addition to owning media entities, frequently own other businesses that have ties to the baseball team. These businesses include concessionaires, stadium management companies, real estate firms, consulting groups, financial entities, and transportation companies. These new owners value their ballplayers not only for what they produce on the field but also for what they produce for their media networks and other investments. When Rupert

Murdoch signed thirty-three-year-old Kevin Brown to the Los Angeles Dodgers for a seven-year deal worth an average of $15 million annually, he was thinking about the NewsCorp's emerging influence via satellite television in the huge Asian market. He was also trying to keep the Disney Corporation from successfully launching a competing regional sports network based on the Anaheim Angels in the greater Los Angeles market.

When George Steinbrenner opened up his wallet for David Cone ($12 million in 2000), Roger Clemens ($30 million for 2001–02, and 2003 at Clemens's option),[32] or Jason Giambi ($18 million per year average for 2002–09), he had in mind creating a new New York sports channel built around the Yankees. When Tom Hicks, owner of the Texas Rangers, signed Alex Rodriguez to a ten-year deal worth a minimum of $252 million, he was thinking about increasing the value of the 270 acres of land around the Ballpark at Arlington that he is developing, lifting the price for naming rights at the stadium, and promoting his investment company.

In 2001 the Angels, Braves, Blue Jays, Cubs, Dodgers, Indians, and Rangers were owned by media companies or media moguls. Several other teams, including the Yankees, Red Sox, and Phillies, either owned media companies outright or had joint ventures with them. In these and other instances, the owners of baseball teams do not treat their teams as stand-alone profit centers; rather, each team is a cog in the larger corporate machine or investment portfolio, used to maximize the long-term profits of the larger entity. As we shall see, MLB's post-1996 revenue sharing system provided a powerful incentive for all teams to develop ownership ties with the local media. The 2002 agreement seems to strengthen this incentive.

Players, then, produce value for these owners both on and off the ball field. In consequence, their differential productivity and value soars, creating still wider payroll gaps among the teams. Further, as argued in chapter one, baseball's expansion by four teams in the 1990s, while adding excitement to the game, makes the star players stand out more and thus makes it easier to buy a winning team. It is one thing for the Yankees to generate $217.8 million in local revenue while the Expos generate $9.8 million. But if Steinbrenner and General Manager Brian Cashman spend their budget on underperforming, overpaid players, then the Yankees are likely to squander their revenue advantage. Yet the more individual players consistently stand out, the more difficult it is for inept management to squander a revenue advantage.[33]

A recent study found the greater the talent compression (as measured inversely by the percentage of the population playing in the majors), the greater the competitive balance (as measured by a lower standard deviation of win percentage).[34] Another factor engendering greater imbalance since 1990 is the inversion of the amateur draft's leveling role. As team revenue disparities exploded, these inequalities were reflected in vastly different player development budgets across the teams. In 1999, for instance, the Yankees spent over $20 million on their player development system, while the Oakland Athletics invested less than $6 million.

One outcome of higher spending on player development is that the Yankees, by offering far more handsome signing bonuses, have greater success in signing foreign players who come to the United States as free agents. Only U.S. residents, Canadians, and Puerto Ricans (and foreigners enrolled at U.S. universities) are subject to the reverse-order amateur draft. All other foreign ballplayers come to the United States as free agents. In 2002, foreign-born players represented 26 percent of all major leaguers.

After the collapse of the former Soviet trade bloc and the ensuing meltdown of the Cuban economy, the supply of ball-playing Cuban defectors began to expand. Agents such as Joe Cubas exploited the opportunities and inspired still more defections.[35] More or less simultaneously, free-agency rules in Japanese baseball and government conscription regulations in Korea were liberalized, and many Asian ballplayers tested their market value in this country.[36]

As the foreign free-agent market developed, agents sought out players throughout the Caribbean and elsewhere and staged foreign-player workouts for prospectively interested teams. At first these workouts were attended by scouts from most teams, but as the signing bonuses grew, the number of represented teams diminished. Low-revenue teams realized that they wouldn't be able to compete for the best players.[37]

Complicating matters, as the signing bonuses for foreign free agents increased, U.S. amateurs, comparing their potential to the foreign players, demanded and often received higher bonuses. Occasionally, when a player didn't get the bonus he sought, he would refuse to sign and the drafting team in effect would lose a draft pick. The median signing bonus for amateurs signed in the first round of the draft increased from $225,000 in 1990 to $1.78 million in 2000—a compound annual growth rate of 23 percent! In 2000, White Sox owner Jerry Reinsdorf signed the team's first pick (but number twelve overall), Joe Borchard of Stanford University, for a record $5.3 million bonus.

Rather than lose draft picks, low-revenue teams began to skip over the top prospects, anticipating they wouldn't be able to sign them. The high-revenue teams, though lower in the drafting order, started to get better domestic, as well as foreign, talent. Thus the process of signing new talent, which had promoted competitive balance since 1965, today seems to be exacerbating the imbalance in baseball.

Ironically, the final factor contributing to baseball's imbalance is MLB's post-1996 revenue sharing system, a system that was introduced in the name of reducing imbalance. As it was applied in 2001, the so-called split-pool system involved taxing each team at 20 percent of its reported net local revenue (from local sources such as local television, cable, radio, gate, concessions, premium seating, and sponsorships, minus stadium-operating, debt-service, and rental costs). Of the monies collected from this tax, 75 percent was then divided equally among all thirty teams. The balance, or 25 percent, was distributed to the teams with net local revenue below the mean in proportion to how far below the mean each team was. Under this plan, in 2001 the Yankees, Mariners, Red Sox, and Mets were top net contributors at approximately $27.4 million, $17.2 million, $16.8 million, and $15.7 million respectively; the Expos, Twins, Marlins, and Royals were the top net recipients at approximately $27.7 million, $18.4 million, $18.3 million, and $16.0 million respectively.

Thus low-revenue teams had a powerful incentive to lowball team payrolls and perform poorly. The lower the payroll generally, the poorer the performance and the lower the team revenue. The lower the team revenue, the more revenue sharing from MLB's central fund. Under the 20 percent tax on the net local-revenue, split-pool system that applied in 2001, the marginal tax rate for above-average-revenue teams was 19.5 percent, and the rate for below-average-revenue teams was between 41 and 43 percent (see elaboration of this point in chapter five).[38] This perverse incentive structure produced ever-widening payroll disparities: the ratio of the top to bottom team payroll went from 4.85 in 1995–96 to 7.72 during 1997 through 2001.

These five factors—increased revenue inequality, more synergies from cross-ownership, the inversion of the draft's leveling role, talent decompression with the addition of four teams, and the post-1996 revenue sharing system—combined in the 1990s to exacerbate baseball's competitive imbalance.

The Meaning of Baseball's Post-1995 Competitive Imbalance

Many observers, while acknowledging that competition in baseball has been unbalanced since 1995, do not see a problem. They argue that baseball has had imbalance and dynasties in the past yet has continued to thrive. The present Yankee dynasty, for instance, is compared to the one between 1949 and 1965.

Yet the last period of Yankee dominance, in the 1950s and early 1960s, despite conjuring up romantic notions of the good old days, was not a time that baseball should seek to emulate. Between 1950 and 1965 average attendance at games grew by a total of less than 3 percent, even though real ticket prices remained virtually flat and real disposable incomes in the United States grew by 74 percent. Tellingly, only 10,454 people were in attendance at Fenway Park to watch the great Ted Williams play in his last game (and hit his last home run on his last at bat) on September 28, 1960.

Moreover, four and five decades ago baseball stood alone on the pedestal of popular team sports. Today it is challenged by professional basketball and football, as well as by a growing list of new professional sports and entertainment options, ranging from stock-car racing to professional wrestling to the Internet.

That is, even though baseball was able to stabilize its attendance during the previous Yankee dynasty, it is not clear that the sport can afford another protracted dynasty today. According to results from an econometric test, during the period 1950–65 one additional win increased the average team's yearly attendance by 14,819.[39] Between 1985 and 2000 one additional win increased the average team's yearly attendance by 31,325.[40] Alternatively, using the average ticket prices, one additional win was worth an average of $28,452 to team revenue during the period 1950–65, while it was worth an average of $315,443 during the period 1985–2000 (both figures in current dollars). These results support the view that attendance (and revenue) today is more sensitive to team performance than it was forty and fifty years ago.

Where does this review of baseball's competitive balance leave us? How serious are baseball's problems and how radical a reform is needed?

It merits repeating that a free-market solution to the competitive-balance problem has strong appeal. If monopoly sports leagues did not artificially regulate the number and location of franchises, then markets would be filled according to demand. A media market with 7 million households, such as New York, would host a third or a fourth team before a market with 830,000 households, such as Milwaukee, would host its first franchise. If New York had three or four MLB teams instead of two, then the revenue advantage of the Yankees and Mets would be greatly attenuated. However desirable and worthy a goal it may be, there is no indication that Congress is ready to force divestiture on MLB to create a competitive industry.

Competitive balance could also be rectified by introducing a promotion/relegation system like the one used in professional soccer leagues throughout Europe.[41] Baseball owners, however, are unlikely in the extreme to vote to abolish their monopoly power in favor of a more competitive system. Similarly, Congress cannot be expected to impose a European system of sports league organization on MLB.

Assuming that MLB's monopoly control will persist, there are alternative policies that would ameliorate baseball's imbalance. First, baseball's present problem is relatively new: it started in the mid-1990s. As additional teams get new facilities, as baseball's central Internet and national television revenues grow, as national sponsorship revenues increase by leaps and bounds, and as some teams relocate to stronger markets, revenue inequalities among franchises are likely to diminish even without more internal revenue sharing. Second, as we have shown, some of baseball's imbalance problem can be fixed by simply adjusting the incentive system in its present revenue sharing system. This could be accomplished without raising the underlying tax rates.

Third, the introduction of an international and competitive-balance draft would also go a long way toward equalizing the distribution of player talent across teams, particularly if it were accompanied by a scale for signing bonuses given to amateurs.[42] New rules allowing the trading of draft picks, granting additional first-round picks to low-revenue teams, and further limitations on the acquisition of player talent in midseason, among others, would also promote greater balance.[43] That is, much could be accomplished even without increasing revenue sharing tax rates and without introducing a luxury tax on high payrolls. Further, it is not known what level of competitive imbalance is optimal for baseball in the long run. Nor is it known how responsive the various measures of imbalance will be to changes in the revenue sharing or luxury tax rates. Given all this, there was little reason during the 2002 negotiations for either side to insist upon sharp adjustments in the underlying tax rates.

While owners have claimed that they want more revenue sharing and a luxury tax on high payrolls in order to level the playing field, it is apparent that they are also seeking to control the growth in player salaries. Higher revenue sharing taxes lower the net marginal revenue product of players, and, other things equal, lower their salaries. Luxury taxes on high payrolls have a similar effect. The owners also called for additional measures to reduce salaries.

Hence it is naive to believe that the solution to baseball's competitive-balance problem will be resolved in isolation from the issues of the sport's finances and its collective bargaining. For this reason, in the next chapter I turn to a discussion of the evidence of MLB's profitability. In chapter five, I take a closer look at collective bargaining.

CHAPTER FOUR

Profitability

The gospel according to Commissioner Selig has it that Chicken Little was right. After the July 2002 All-Star Game, the commissioner proclaimed that one team might not meet payroll the next week and "likely would be forced out of business," and "a second team is so deep in red ink it may not be able to finish the season."[1]

Selig's musings sent reporters scurrying to identify the woebegone franchises. First they contacted the two most obvious candidates, the Devil Rays and the Tigers. Devil Rays owner Vince Naimoli did not mince his words: "It's not true, not true, not true. It's the same old crap. We don't have a problem. We're fine cash flow wise." Tigers GM Dave Dombrowski was also unequivocal: "[There's] no danger of missing payroll and [the team] faces no bankruptcy threats. . . . I don't know where they got that report. There's no truth to that."[2]

Then the reporters went down the list of the usual suspects, and again there was one firm denial after another. Selig's right-hand man and MLB's chief operating officer, Bob Dupuy, tried to bail out the commissioner the next day when he told the press: "I believe that the immediate crisis has been solved regarding the team that could have missed payroll." But Selig insisted, saying that "nothing had been resolved" and that DuPuy's assessment "isn't quite accurate." The commissioner went on to state that, unlike in the 2001 season, when he had "arranged loans that kept two or three teams afloat," this year he had "no choice but to allow the two clubs in question to fail. . . . I'm done [with bail-outs]."[3] Exactly how baseball would proceed with its 2002 schedule without one or two of its clubs, or how the disappearance of two teams would affect the availability and cost of future financing for MLB, was left unexplored. Felicitously, MLB never had to confront these eventualities; all thirty teams finished the 2002 season and none declared bankruptcy.

No More Secrets

Eight months earlier Selig had testified before the U.S. Congress that the game's economic system was broken and that in 2001 baseball's thirty teams lost a total of $519 million. Before testifying, the commissioner had pledged that MLB would open up its books to Congress and that there would be no more secrets; and during his testimony, Selig assured the members that MLB was withholding no relevant information. This surprising assurance prompted California representative Maxine Waters to warn Selig on three separate occasions: "Sir, let me remind you that you are under oath."

Many prominent journalists joined the fray. Leonard Koppett expressed his incredulity in the *New York Times*: "What shocks me is [the baseball owners'] utter lack of patriotism. How? By refusing to share, with the rest of the American business community, the secret of their greatest discovery: how to lose millions year after year, stay in business and even double their revenue."[4]

Tom Boswell, the *Washington Post*'s preeminent baseball writer opined: "What never changes is that baseball says whatever it wants to say, then changes what it has said, then pretends that everything it has ever said is exactly what suits it at that particular moment. Fans say baseball will never see another .400 average. When it comes to telling a straight story, that's what Selig bats every year."[5]

It is reasonable to ask what is going on here. Is MLB perpetrating another Enron or Worldcom accounting scandal on the U.S. public? Is it benignly massaging its books, or is it leveling with Congress and the American people when it claims the sky is falling?

Interest, Depreciation, and Amortization

The next edition of *Bartlett's Familiar Quotations* will do its readers a disservice if it does not include former MLB chief operating officer (COO) Paul Beeston's warning about baseball teams' financial statements: "Under generally accepted accounting principles, I can turn a $4 million profit into a $2 million loss and I can get every national accounting firm to agree with me."

Using Paul Beeston's admonition as inspiration, let us take a closer look at the numbers Bud Selig provided to Congress. During his initial testimony at the December 6, 2001, hearing before the House Judiciary Committee, Selig stated: "Although this year's audits are not yet final, the consolidated loss for all 30 clubs in 2001 will be approximately $519 million. Twenty-five clubs lost money, and five made money this year. . . . The total industry debt is currently over $3 billion. . . . If you add deferred compensation and future guaranteed obligations to players, that number approaches $8 billion. Needless to say, these numbers are the highest in baseball history, and incredibly they are still growing rapidly."[6] If these numbers accurately told the whole story and if 2001 had been a typical year, there would indeed be cause for alarm about baseball's economic future. The numbers, however, are misleading, and 2001 was a year of recession, low advertising expenditures, and the devastating September 11 terrorist attack.

The first adjustment that needs to be made is that the $519 million represents book, not operating, losses. It includes amortization, depreciation, and interest expense. These items are almost always excluded when analyzing a business' ongoing economic viability. This is because depreciation and amortization do not represent cash expenditures to operate a business, but are accounting conventions to prorate previous investments over their useful life. Interest expense is excluded because it generally relates to how a company is capitalized, not how it is run. Consider two companies, each worth $1 billion. One owner uses his own savings to purchase his company. The second owner uses his savings for half the purchase price and borrows the other half at 10 percent. The first owner will pay no interest. The second owner will pay interest of $50 million a year. If each company earns $40 million in profit yearly before interest they are equally viable, even though one will show a $40 million book profit (assuming no depreciation charge) and the other will show a $10 million book loss.

There is perhaps even less reason to pay attention to amortization, depreciation, and interest in the case of baseball franchises. Partly as a result of a successful tax case involving Bud Selig and his Milwaukee Brewers in 1984, baseball owners generally may attribute 50 percent of the price they pay for a franchise to the value of player contracts and then amortize that value over five or fewer years.[7] Thus if a team is purchased for $400 million,

$200 million of that may be amortized at $40 million annually for each of the first five years of ownership. If this team had operating profits (before amortization, depreciation, and interest) of $30 million, it could then show a book loss of $10 million.

The problem with amortizing the presumed value of player contracts is threefold. First, there is little reason to assume that players' contracts have any asset value. If a player produces $10 million of value annually to a team (that is, he generates $10 million in net incremental revenue) and gets paid $10 million, then he produces no asset value. Some players, of course, produce a value above what they are paid and some produce a value below what they are paid. Because their salaries are governed by market forces, it is reasonable to assume that, on balance, free agents and arbitration-eligible players produce a value similar to their salaries.[8] The only group of players who systematically tend to produce a value above what they are paid are those who have not yet become eligible for salary arbitration. These are players with less than roughly 2.2 years of major league experience, and they are few in number on typical major league active rosters. It is difficult to imagine that the net asset value of such players would even approach 10 percent of a team's purchase price. In addition, these pre-arbitration players are regularly replaced by minor leaguers. The asset class of pre-arbitration players, therefore, is perpetual and does not depreciate.[9]

Second, unlike buildings and mechanical equipment, major league players on average do not depreciate. Most players improve during the first half or more of their careers; only those in their waning playing years decline in productivity. During any given year, more than half of the players are appreciating in value.

Third, players' salaries are already expensed (deducted as an expense from revenue). It makes no sense to both expense and depreciate the same item.

Now suppose that our hypothetical team valued at $400 million was purchased by a partnership and that the general partner loaned the partnership $100 million at 10 percent in order to raise sufficient capital for the purchase. The general partner could instead have put up that $100 million as equity capital, but chose not to do so. Because it is debt capital, each year the general partner receives $10 million in interest payments from the partnership that owns the team. The team's book profit is now its operating profit of $30 million minus $40 million player contract amortization, minus $10 million interest, or a reported $20 million book loss.

If we make the same adjustment to Selig's $519 million book loss in 2001 by deducting depreciation, amortization, and interest charges, the result is an operating loss of $232 million—less than half of the book loss.[10] Herein emerges another curiosity. MLB's COO, Bob Dupuy, gave an interview in July 2002 wherein he asserted: "Put aside interest, put aside depreciation. Just in operations alone, the clubs last year lost over $300 million." One wonders where the additional $70 million came from. Dupuy ended his thought with arrogance and defensiveness: "The numbers are flat accurate. Period. End of story. All right?"[11] He didn't tell us, however, whether his numbers or Selig's were "flat accurate." Going with the commissioner's numbers, if there were no other massaging of the accounts, MLB's operating loss in 2001 would be $232 million. There is cause to believe, however, that some massaging took place.

Selig's claim that there were no secrets and that Congress had all the relevant information on the clubs' finances was implausible. The commissioner provided only four pages of summary revenue and cost data to Congress for baseball's thirty teams. His office also threatened to sue the Players Association if it shared additional information on the clubs' finances with Congress. Yet as anyone at all familiar with the business of baseball knows, any serious examination of the game's economics has to *begin* with the financial statements of the individual franchises, each around fifteen pages in length. After that, one would want to look at payroll forms and financial ledgers detailing individual transactions. Next one would need to examine the books of related businesses operated by the owner. What Selig provided scarcely scratches the surface.

Nonetheless, scrutinizing the Selig data raises some serious questions, particularly when it is compared with other information that has been provided by individual teams.

Baseball's Central Office

In 2001 MLB's central fund revenues (from national TV, radio, Internet, sponsorship, and licensing) averaged $24 million per team, yet distributions per team were only $17.9 million. The difference was retained by the central office, which therefore had a budget of at least $184 million.

In the early 1990s this budget was less than $25 million. Why did the budget balloon? In addition to growing salaries, perquisites, and staff in the commissioner's office, tens of millions of dollars were spent developing MLB's new Internet site, and a similar sum reportedly was stashed away to build a war chest in the event of a new work stoppage.[12]

Indeed, *USA Today's* Hal Bodley reported that the owners' war chest was as large as $210 million. If we assume that the operating cost of MLB's central office is $40 million, then MLB would have set aside at least $144 million for investment and work stoppage security purposes in 2001. Under ordinary circumstances that same sum would have been distributed to the teams.[13] If the $144 million had been distributed, the operating loss of the teams in 2001 would have fallen from $232 million to $88 million.

Team Revenues

I proceed here by first observing some discrepancies between the revenue figures reported by Selig and those reported by the teams, and then trying to explain the source of these and other discrepancies.

During 1997 the Padres, attempting to obtain public financing for a new stadium, released a financial statement. According to this statement, the Padres' revenues in that year were $79.81 million. According to the figures Selig gave to Congress, the Padres' revenues in 1997 were $76.22 million, or $3.6 million below those in the club's statement.

In February 2000, the new YankeeNets holding company issued an offering prospectus to sell $250 million in seven-year senior notes in a private placement. The prospectus reported the Yankees' revenues in 1997 as $157.72 million. Selig reported them to be $135.12 million, net of revenue sharing.[14] If we net revenue sharing out of the Yankees' figure, the adjusted team revenues in 1997 become $147.09 million, or $12 million more than Selig's number.[15]

Using the offering prospectus numbers again for 1998 yields a reduced, but still sizable, discrepancy with the commissioner's numbers. The prospectus reports revenue of $179.67 million in 1998, which net of revenue sharing becomes $164.89 million. Selig reports this figure to be $157.87 million, a discrepancy of $7 million.

There appears to be a pattern of underreporting of revenue in the data Selig supplied to Congress. This pattern is confirmed by team data from the Indians, the Red Sox, and the Diamondbacks. The Indians' former owner, Dick Jacobs, took approximately 30 percent of his team public in 1998. In addition to an offering prospectus, Jacobs was obliged to provide quarterly and yearly financial statements to stockholders. These statements put team revenue, already adjusted for revenue sharing, at $140.03 million in 1997 and $144.55 million in 1998. The commissioner's numbers were lower, $113.75 million in 1997 and $125.74 million in 1998, $26.3 million and $18.8 million less than the owner's own figures.

The Boston Red Sox were sold to John Henry and partners in January 2002 for approximately $720 million. Before the private auction, the team issued a prospectus that reported revenue of $100 million in 1997 (or $96 million net of revenue sharing) and $114 million in 1998 ($107.3 million net). Selig's numbers were $85 million and $105 million, $11 million and $2 million less than the team's.

Finally, the Arizona Diamondbacks released their 1998 financial statement to the press showing revenue of $105.2 million ($102.5 million after revenue sharing). The commissioner reported the team's revenue at $101.5 million, a modest discrepancy of only $1 million.

Related-Party Transactions

The most common cause of revenue discrepancies is related-party transactions. Many team owners today own entities that do business with the team (such as TV, cable, and radio stations; facility management companies; concessions; and catering companies). When the owner does business with himself he can charge whatever prices he likes—it is money in one pocket or the other. This practice, known as a related-party transaction or transfer pricing, can reduce franchise revenues substantially. Let's look at how it affects the finances of several different teams.

Chicago Cubs

According to Selig's figures, in 2001 the Chicago White Sox's income from local TV, radio, and cable was $30.1 million, and that of the Chicago Cubs was $23.6 million. These numbers are a curiosity, to say the least. Everyone knows that the Cubs are the far more popular team in the Windy City, and TV ratings bear this out: in 2001 the Cubs' average ratings were 6.8 on over-the-air broadcasting and 3.8 on cable; the White Sox's were 3.6 and 1.9 respectively. And this doesn't take account of the fact that the Cubs games are shown on superstation WGN, which reaches 55-million-plus homes nationally.

So, what's going on? The Cubs are owned by the Tribune Corporation, which happens also to own WGN. The Tribune Corporation transfers revenue away from the Cubs and correspondingly lowers the costs of WGN. According to *Broadcasting and Cable*, the industry's authoritative source, the Cubs' local media earnings were $59 million. If the Cubs had reported this figure instead of $23.6 million, then their reported $1.8 million loss would have become a $33.6 million profit in 2001![16]

Why would the Cubs (and several other teams) want to reduce their reported revenues? Let me count the ways. First, since 1996 MLB has had a revenue sharing system that levies a tax on a team's net local revenue. In 2001 this tax was 20 percent. Thus for every dollar in local revenue not reported, the team saves just under 20 cents.[17] Since WGN pays no such tax to the broadcasting industry, it is preferable for the parent corporation, Tribune, to have the profits appear on WGN's books.

Second, baseball teams (and even the Cubs, who were pleading for public permission to erect higher left-field stands in 2002) seek various kinds of public support for their facilities. They believe that the more impecunious they appear, the more likely such support will be forthcoming.

Third, every few years the owners negotiate with the players over a new collective bargaining contract. The owners always seek new restrictions in the labor market to lower salaries. Invariably, one of the justifications for these restrictions is that the teams are losing money. Whether or not the Players Association is persuaded by such arguments, it appears to be permanently fixed as part of the owners' foreplay.

Fourth, MLB is the only professional sport in the United States that has a presumed antitrust exemption. Periodically MLB is called before Congress to justify this special treatment. One of the arguments that MLB has repeatedly trotted out—most recently by Selig before the U.S. Congress in December 2001—is that the industry can't possibly be abusing its market power because it is not profitable.

Atlanta Braves

Another striking example of a broadcasting related-party transaction that lowers team revenue is that of the Atlanta Braves and national cable channel (formerly superstation) WTBS. WTBS in 2001 carried ninety Braves games. Turner South carried thirty-four games. Both WTBS and Turner South are owned by AOL/Time Warner, which owns the Braves.

Doug Pappas, the chair of the business of baseball comm[...]
ety for American Baseball Research, suggests that the [...]
WTBS's rights for its ninety Braves games is to com[...]
According to Pappas, each airs about ninety games per year an[...]
ried on virtually every cable system in the country.[19] During 2000, br[...]
games on TBS had an average rating of 1.6, while ESPN games averaged 1.0.
ESPN also has higher production costs because it airs more regional games,
involving more travel, more announcers, and more crew. ESPN pays MLB
an average of $135.8 million per year for its rights.

Now, TBS's rights are not worth that much, in part because TBS has no
postseason broadcasting rights, and in part because TBS does not promote
itself as a national sports channel. But if we assumed that TBS's rights were
worth only 40 percent of ESPN's, then TBS's rights fee payments to the
Braves in an open market would be $54.3 million. Selig's numbers put the
total revenue received by the Braves for local media rights at $20 million.
According to *Broadcasting and Cable*, in 2001 the Braves received $5 million
for local radio from WSB, $4 million from the regional Fox Sports Net, and
$12.5 million from Turner South. Putting the *Broadcasting and Cable* and
Selig numbers together suggests that the Braves received minus $1.5 million
from TBS to telecast ninety games nationally!

More realistically, if the TBS rights are worth $54.3 million and the
Braves make $20 million in "superstation" payments to MLB, then the
Braves should receive net revenue of $34.3 million from TBS. Selig's num-
bers imply that they receive minus $1.5 million. If the difference of $35.8
million were added to the Braves' bottom line, the team's $25 million loss
would become a $10.8 million profit.

New York Yankees

In July 1999 the Yankees formed a holding company, YankeeNets, with
the NBA New Jersey Nets. In August 2000 the holding company bought
the NHL New Jersey Devils for $175 million. Neither the NBA nor the
NHL has local revenue sharing. In September 2001, Goldman Sachs paid
$340 million to buy a 40 percent stake in YES, the new regional sports
network that began broadcasting in 2002. At $340 million for a noncon-
trolling interest of 40 percent, the implied market value of the YES network was in excess of $850 million. YES has the exclusive right to air 130
Yankees games.

For 2002, YES reached a deal with Time Warner Cable and Comcast, two of the three big cable distributors in the metropolitan market, to carry its 130 Yankees games for approximately $2 per subscriber per month. This would yield approximately $88 million in subscriber fees in greater New York City. There is also an "outer" market of more than 2 million households, served by other cable distributors, where the charge would be an estimated $1.70 per month, yielding roughly another $40 million in fees. On top of this, YES sells advertising during the games, from which it should be able to clear another $30 million. Together these sources would provide YES with over $150 million in revenues, even without an agreement with Charles Dolan's Cablevision and its 2.9 million subscribers. If and when a deal with Cablevision is reached, it could add an additional $100 million in subscriber fees and advertising revenues annually. YES will also derive revenue from its deal with DirecTV and its sale of the rights for twenty games to CBS-TV in New York for $10 million.

Thus YES's annual revenues should have been in excess of $160 million in 2002 and could have surpassed $260 million if a deal with Cablevision were in place. YES will carry New Jersey Nets games next year (and eventually Devils games as well), and some share of the revenue properly belongs to them. If we generously attribute $20 million to the Nets and subtract another $20 million in production and front office costs, YES should have netted at least $120 million in revenue in 2002 that is attributable to the Yankees. Yet according to reports in the New York press, YES was scheduled to pay the Yankees only between $52 and $54 million in 2002.[20]

Obviously, it is advantageous to the YankeeNets partnership to attribute a larger share of YES revenue to the Nets because this revenue does not have to be shared with other NBA teams. In contrast, Yankees local revenue in 2002 was subject to a 20 percent sharing tax, and this rate will rise in 2003. The upshot is that the Yankees appear to be sheltering upwards of $60 million from baseball's internal tax system.

It is also likely that the Yankees, as well as other teams, are sheltering income from the revenue sharing tax by inflating stadium expenses. The tax is on "net local revenue" or local revenue minus stadium expenses. When this tax was phased in beginning in 1996, the Yankees stadium operating expenses mysteriously began to balloon. According to the YankeeNets offering prospectus, the Yankees reported stadium expenses of $9.5 million in 1995, $14.2 million in 1996, $16.2 million in 1997, and $20.1 million in 1998. Based on the data Commissioner Selig provided to Congress, I estimate that the Yankees stadium expenses continued to rise gradually to more than $21 million in 2001.

A modest part of the increase in the Yankees' stadium costs is attributable to a small increase in rental payments (which are proportional to gate receipts), which rose from $4.90 million in 1996 to $7.86 million in 1998. The Yankees' lease with the city of New York stipulates that the team may subtract any maintenance and improvement expenses from their rent. Thus the team can get double credit for any improvements it makes in Yankee Stadium, first by deducting the expenditures from its rental obligation, and second by deducting them from its taxable revenue to MLB. If the improvements also generate additional revenue, and the net cost of the related investment is negative (100 percent reimbursement from New York City and 20 percent reimbursement from MLB), the rate of return is infinite.[21] This enviable and strange circumstance is topped off by Rudy Giuliani's parting mayoral gift to the team of $5 million annually in city funds to defray design and location study costs for a new stadium.[22]

Boston Red Sox

In 2001 the Red Sox, through the team's partnership, New England Associates (NEA), owned 80 percent of the New England Sports Network (NESN). During the 2001 season, NESN went from being a premium channel in most of New England to an expanded basic channel, and revenue rose sharply from roughly $39 million in 2000 to an estimated more than $50 million. With some $15 million in costs, NESN probably cleared $35 million before paying rights fees to the Bruins and Red Sox.

In the Selig data, the Red Sox report $33 million in local media revenue for 2001. Approximately $10 million of this came from the local Fox channel, WFXT, for the rights to broadcast sixty-seven Sox games on over-the-air television and another $5 million from WEEI for radio rights, suggesting that the Sox received only $18 million from NESN.

Based on NESN cost data from 2000, after paying rights fees to the Sox and Bruins, NESN would have produced a net income of about $14 million in 2001, and 80 percent of this, or $11.2 million, would have gone to the New England Associates partnership that owned the Red Sox and 80 percent of NESN.[23] This $11.2 million, however, would have been recorded as NEA, not Red Sox, revenue and thus would have skirted MLB's revenue sharing system.[24]

Table 4-1. *Reported Marlins Income Statement, 1997*
Millions of dollars

Revenues		Costs	
Ticket sales	23.9	Payroll	53.5
Broadcasting	23.2	G&A and player development[a]	5.1
Team operations	18.9	Scouting	5.1
Concessions	1.8	Latin American operations	0.6
Other	10.0	Stadium operations	5.0
Total	58.9	Total	88.2

a. G&A refers to the general and administrative expenses of the front office.

Florida Marlins

Although the machinations of former Marlins owner Wayne Huizenga do not affect the numbers produced by Selig in 2001, it is instructive to review his use of related-party transactions to hide team profits back in 1997. The Marlins won the 1997 World Series in seven games. Huizenga, trying to persuade south Florida to build his team a new stadium, claimed the Marlins lost $33 million that year.

When no stadium was forthcoming, Huizenga attempted to arrange a cozy sale of the Marlins to his long-standing associate and team president, Don Smiley, for $169 million. Putatively to stop the team's financial bleeding, Huizenga also conducted the most radical fire sale of players in baseball history, lowering the Marlins' payroll from $53 million in 1997 to $13 million in mid-July 1998. Though Huizenga refused to provide any details about the team's 1997 finances, Don Smiley issued a confidential report on the team to prospective partners in his effort to buy the team. Smiley's "Private Placement Memorandum" reports a variety of financial information for 1997 (see table 4-1), as well as projections for 1998. The operating loss suggested by these numbers is $29.3 million ($3.7 million below Huizenga's claim). Quibbling over a few million dollars aside, what's the problem? Did Huizenga's Marlins really lose close to $30 million? Of course not.

Huizenga happened to own Pro Player Stadium and the team's cablecaster at the time, SportsChannel (now Fox Sports Florida). Pro Player was built in 1987 and is amply stocked with all the revenue-generating accoutrements of a modern sports facility. A quick look at the team's reported revenues reveals that there is no income from luxury boxes, despite the fact that Pro Player

Stadium has 195 suites that rented for between $55,000 and $150,000 a year, and no income from club seats, notwithstanding the existence of 10,209 club seats at Pro Player that sold for between $900 and $3,500 a year. Bob Kramm, president of the stadium corporation, estimated that in 1997 an average of sixty-five luxury suites and 5,000 club seats per game were sold.[25] If we assume that the average suite rented for $100,000 and the average club seat sold for $2,000, then the gross revenue from these two sources would have been $16.5 million. Huizenga attributed none of this revenue to the Marlins and all of it to his separate business entity, Pro Player Stadium.

Similarly, Huizenga sold naming rights to the stadium for $2 million a year. Since the stadium is shared with the NFL Dolphins (also owned by Huizenga), we can assume that roughly half of this value emanated from the Marlins. Parking for approximately 788,000 cars during the baseball season at $5 a car in 1997 would have brought in an estimated $3.9 million. Sales of signage, advertising, and merchandise at the park and in the team program should have produced $6 million or more. But that additional ballpark revenue of approximately $10.9 million was attributed to the stadium company, not to the Marlins.

Further, the revenue from concessions appears to have been substantially understated. With total Marlins attendance in 1997 of 2.364 million and an average expenditure of roughly $10 per attendee, net concessions income should have been around $9.4 million (using a standard 40 percent of gross spending.) Yet only $1.8 million is attributed to the Marlins, a deficit of $7.6 million. The total additional sources of stadium revenue that are not reported as Marlins income come to $35.0 million ($16.5 million from luxury and club seating; $7.6 million from additional concessions; $6.0 million from signage, advertising, and merchandise sales; $3.9 million from parking; and $1.0 million from the Marlins' share of naming rights).

Huizenga played the same game with SportsChannel. According to Smiley's prospectus, an independent appraiser estimated that the Marlins' contract with the cable station was undervalued by more than $2.1 million a year. Herein lies a powerful reason why Huizenga wanted to sell his team to Don Smiley rather than to the other suitors. Huizenga's deal with Smiley included an extension of the SportsChannel contract through 2024, which, because of the below-market rights fee it was paying the Marlins, increased the station's value from an estimated $85 million to $125 million. After the extension was signed, Huizenga sold the station.[26]

Together, in the related-party transactions between the team, on the one hand, and the stadium and cable station on the other, there was a transfer of $37.1 million ($35.0 million from the stadium and $2.1 million from SportsChannel) in revenue away from the team in 1997. Finally, in the "Private Placement Memorandum" Smiley reports that he intended to lower general and administrative expenses by $3 million a year, suggesting there was that much padding in the team budget.

In short, if the Marlins' financial statement was adjusted for related-party transactions and bloated costs, what appeared to be a $29.3 million operating loss in 1997 would become instead an operating profit of $10.8 million (−$29.3 million + $37.1 million additional revenues + $3 million in bloated costs). Why else would Don Smiley, who as team president knew its financial predicament as well as anyone, have wanted to buy the team?

Texas Rangers

Tom Hicks bought the team in January 1998 from a partnership that included George W. Bush (who had invested $600,000 of borrowed money and took home some $15 million after persuading the state legislature and the city of Arlington to finance 84 percent of the new stadium). Hicks owns many other businesses with potential connections to the team, including Southwest Sports Group (SSG). SSG joined together with Fox Sports Net Southwest to form Lone Star Mobile Television. Lone Star produces audio and video feeds from sporting events and counts the Rangers among its clients. Fox Sports Net owns the television rights (ten years for $200 million) and the cable rights (fifteen years for $300 million) to carry the Rangers' games. Fox Sports Net also has a fifteen-year deal to carry the NHL Dallas Stars' games. The Stars are also owned by Hicks. These linkages, and others, give Hicks the opportunity to shift around substantial revenues and costs.

Los Angeles Dodgers

Fox Entertainment Group, which is controlled by Rupert Murdoch, owns the Dodgers. It also owns twenty-two off-air stations with 176 affiliates, the Fox Sports Channels, and the Regional Fox Sports Networks, among other cable and news entities.

Until 2002 the Dodgers' broadcasting partner was KTLA-TV, which is not owned by Fox. Its cable partner, Fox Sports Net 2, carried eighty Dodgers games in both 2001 and 2002. According to *Broadcasting and*

Cable, the Dodgers received rights fees of $15.5 million from KTLA in 2001 for fifty games, but in 2002 received only $8 million from Fox station KCOP for the same fifty games.[27] That is, Fox paid the Dodgers (whom Fox owns) $7.5 million less for the same product than an independent station paid the Dodgers the previous year.

Beyond that, if the Dodgers received $15.5 million from KTLA for broadcasting rights to fifty games in 2001, then Selig's figure for the Dodgers' local media revenue of $27.3 million leaves only $11.8 million to be generated by eighty games on cable and by the contract with the KXTA-AM radio network, which includes twenty-six stations. Given that Los Angeles is the nation's second largest media market and that cable revenue involves both rights fees and advertising, $11.8 million would seem to be a significant understatement of market value.

Toronto Blue Jays

The principal owner of the Blue Jays is Rogers Communications, a major telecommunications company in Canada. Among other firms, Rogers owns Rogers Sportsnet, which carries more than ninety Blue Jays games. The Blue Jays also have a cable contract with TSN and a radio contract with CJCL-AM, which Rogers is slated to buy. According to Selig, the Blue Jays' local media income in 2001 was $14.46 million (in U.S. dollars). This sum is $4.5 million below the reported MLB average, despite the facts that Toronto is a major metropolitan area with a population of 2.5 million and 7.7 million people live within a 100-mile radius of the city.

Other Teams

The Philadelphia Phillies contract with Comcast to cablecast 109 of their games, and the Phillies are part owners of Comcast SportsNet. Minority owners of the San Francisco Giants also own the team's broadcaster (KTVU) and the team's radio station (KNBR). Other teams with media and entertainment companies as minority investors include the Arizona Diamondbacks (Gannett and Pulitzer), the Cincinnati Reds (Gannett), the Colorado Rockies (E. W. Scripps and Clear Channel Communications), and the Pittsburgh Pirates (CBS and Blade Communications).[28]

Several other teams have the opportunity to hide media revenue because they retain and market their own television or radio rights. Other franchises are planning to establish regional sports networks based on the teams.

But related-party transactions extend well beyond media operations, as the example of the Florida Marlins under Huizenga illustrates. The owners of the Diamondbacks, for instance, own a company, REM, that manages the luxury suites at Bank One Ballpark and generates $4 million income annually. An owner of another team also owns an aircraft company and spends $2.5 million a year, charged to the team, renting a jet for personal and non-team business use.

The San Francisco Giants have a wholly owned subsidiary, Giants Enterprises, that is responsible for all nonbaseball events at PacBell Park, such as bowl games, the circus, concerts, and dinner receptions in the clubhouse. During its first year and a half, Giants Enterprises reportedly recorded over $10 million in revenue. While owing its success to the team, Giants Enterprises records its revenue separately.

The list goes on. In the aggregate, it is reasonable to assume over $100 million is sheltered from MLB revenue (or added to MLB costs) that is attributable to related-party transactions each year—more than enough to wipe out the adjusted aggregate MLB operating loss of $88 million in 2001 estimated above. Last, in assessing baseball's 2001 results, one would do well to remember the impact of September 11 and the recessionary economic conditions.

Accounting Gimmickry and Waste

But necessary adjustments to MLB's figures do not end here. It appears to be a common practice for teams to expense signing bonuses, especially for amateurs. The proper treatment would be to prorate these bonuses over the expected useful life of a player's contract. Expensing these bonuses artificially adds to present costs and lowers profits. To be sure, some teams even expense signing bonuses in the first year when the bonus itself is paid out over a series of years.

Many owners take a high, six- or seven-figure salary or consulting income for themselves from the team. It is also common to find family members employed in front office executive positions. Owners also benefit by having their own first-class travel, lodging, meal, and entertainment expenses charged to the team.

Baseball's alleged financial difficulty also does not adjust for the presence of significant waste in baseball's management. On November 14, 2000, Jerry Colangelo, managing general partner of the Arizona Diamondbacks, told

Table 4-2. *Major League Baseball Economic Data, 1996 and 2001*
Millions of dollars

	1996	2001
Total revenue	1,775	3,548
Player payroll	939	1,972
Difference	836	1,576

Source: Based on data from Major League Baseball.

the *Arizona Republic* that he would cut front office expenses by $10 million without affecting the team's operation or the product. If the quality of the team could be maintained with $10 million less, then why was this money being spent in the first place? The possibility of excess is highlighted by the numbers shown in table 4-2, derived from Selig's presentation to Congress.

Between 1996 and 2001, MLB's revenues doubled. With players' salaries increasing 2.1 times, the players' share of total revenue edged up from 52.9 percent to 55.6 percent. However, before attributing any economic problems in the industry to the players, it should be noted that, *after paying the players*, the owners' revenues increased from $836 million in 1996 to $ 1.576 billion in 2001. That is, revenues after salaries grew at an annual rate of 13.5 percent. Over the same period, the Consumer Price Index in the United States grew at 2.45 percent per year. Even adjusting for higher stadium costs, including debt service, and higher insurance premiums for players and facilities,[29] it seems that with sound management baseball should have been able to turn a financial profit in 2001.

It should also be noted that the players' higher share in 2001 may well prove to be an aberration. Eliminating 1994 and 1995 because of the strike, the players' share between 1992 (53.7 percent) and 2000 (52.4 percent) was between 52 percent and 54 percent, save in 1998, when it was 51.3 percent.[30]

Beyond the Bottom Line

Even if an unadulterated bottom line is red, the owner may still be getting a satisfactory return on his or her investment. A loss in one year often becomes a profit in the next. There is no guarantee in capitalism that a business will be profitable every year—particularly a poorly managed one.

David Glass, owner of the small-market, old-stadium Kansas City Royals, one of the reputed hawks among the ownership ranks, put it this way in a June 21, 2002, interview with the *Kansas City Star*: "What I've said all along is we're going to have years when we lose money and years when we make a little money. What I'd like to do, overall, is come close to breaking even as we go forward."[31] If Mr. Glass would truly be content to break even financially over time, then he must be contemplating indirect or nonfinancial returns on his investment. Most owners do.

What are these indirect or nonfinancial returns? Increasingly, as discussed in chapter three, owners treat sports teams as part of their entire investment portfolio. Often, the team itself is not managed as a profit center, but as a vehicle for promoting the owner's other investments. Owners can take their investment returns in a number of ways. For instance, George Steinbrenner used his New York Yankees to create the YES regional sports network in the nation's largest media market. YES has a market value upward of $850 million. Rupert Murdoch recently admitted that his purchase of the Dodgers had already paid off because it enabled him to prevent Disney from creating a regional sports network in southern California.[32] Tom Hicks hopes to use his ownership of the Rangers to develop some 270 acres of commercial and residential real estate around the ballpark in Arlington and to grow his Southwest Sports Group, among other things. Dick Jacobs exploited his ownership of the Indians to promote the value of his downtown real estate. And so on.

Other owners seek return in gaining access to politicians and corporate executives. Such access can enhance their business opportunities. Still others experience ownership as a consumption good and seek fulfillment, notoriety, ego gratification, power, and fun.

Listen, for instance, to John Henry describe his experience in owning the Boston Red Sox: "I am a very fortunate man allowed to work with bright, committed people and be a part of an institution that I hope to play a positive part in—passing it on eventually to the next stewards. One can generally only dream of being in the position I find myself today."[33]

Lastly, most owners enjoy tax benefits and eventual capital gains when they sell the team. Herein lies a perennial paradox of sports team ownership. How do teams with reported yearly losses go up in value? The evidence of appreciation in franchise values is clear (see table 4-3). Sports investment banker John Moag estimates that the annual rate of return to baseball

Table 4-3. *Major League Baseball Franchise Sale Prices*

Millions of dollars

Team	Most recent sale price[a]	Year	Previous sale price	Year
Angels	146.7	2000	120	1996
Diamondbacks	130[b]	1998	...	
Braves	12[c]	1976	6.2	1962
Orioles	173	1993	70	1988
Red Sox	700+	2002	100	1994
Cubs	20.5[c]	1981	.5	1975
White Sox	20[c]	1981	10.7	1975
Reds	67	1999	n.a.	
Indians	323	2000	35	1986
Rockies	95[b]	1993	148	2001
Tigers	82	1992	53	1983
Marlins	150	1999	95	1993
Astros	115	1992	19	1979
Royals	96	2000	22	1983
Dodgers	350	1998	4.1	1950
Brewers	10.8[c]	1970	...	
Twins	36[c]	1984	.36	1919
Expos	120	2002	75	1999
Mets	400+	2002	80.8	1986
Yankees	600	1999	8.8	1973
Athletics	85	1995	12.7	1980
Phillies	30.2[c]	1981	.23	1943
Pirates	90	1996	22	1985
Padres	100	1994	75	1990
Giants	100	1992	8.5	1976
Mariners	106	1992	80	1989
Cardinals	150	1995	3.75	1953
Devil Rays	130[b]	1998	...	
Rangers	250	1998	80	1989
Blue Jays	140	2000	7	1976

Sources: Levin and others, *The Report of the Independent Members of the Commissioner's Blue Ribbon Panel*; Team Marketing Report, *Inside the ownership of Professional Sports Teams*, various years; James Quirk and Rodney Fort, *Pay Dirt* (Princeton University Press, 1992).

n.a. = not available

a. Values are approximations in current prices. Only transactions when a majority share or a minority share of 20 percent or more is sold are recorded; the implied value for the whole is estimated without using a minority discount.

b. Expansion price paid to Major League Baseball. This price rose from $7 million in 1977 to $95 million in 1993, and to $130 in 1998.

c. If we use a typical revenue multiple for baseball teams of 2.5, the estimated franchise values for these clubs in 2002 were Braves, $400 million; Cubs, $410 million; White Sox $270 million; Brewers, $290 million; Twins, $188 million; Phillies, $235 million.

franchise ownership was 12.4 percent between 1960 and 2002—well above the rate of return to common stock ownership for the same period (6.9 percent annually for the S&P 500 through June 30, 2002).[34]

Consider the case of the Boston Red Sox. According to Selig's numbers, the Red Sox had operating losses of $13.7 million in 2001 and $21.93 million from 1995 through 2001. Yet four former baseball team owners (Tom Werner, John Henry, Larry Lucchino, and John McMullen) wanted to buy the team and its assets for over $700 million. Why would a team losing so much money be appreciating in value? The answer must be either that it is not, in fact, losing money, or that there are substantial nonfinancial returns to ownership, or both.

Bud Selig says that the Red Sox are the exception that proves the rule. They are an aberration as a storied team in the nation's sixth largest media market. But what kind of an exception are they if Selig's numbers—showing operating losses for the franchise during the period 1995–2001—are to be believed? And if the Sox are healthy at present but the industry as a whole is in serious economic distress, why doesn't that distress affect the value of the team, especially if both the owners and the players agree that one way to diminish the distress is by increasing revenue sharing from the rich to the poor teams?

All things considered, it is difficult to accept the sky-is-falling analysis. Rejecting the catastrophic prognosis, however, does not mean that the game does not have economic problems. It does. There is too much imbalance, and there may be eight to ten teams with perennial financial problems that are not due to poor management. At this writing in 2002, the game needs economic reform, not revolution, and economists can rest assured that the theory connecting monopoly and profitability is firmly intact.

CHAPTER FIVE

Collective Bargaining

History provided little solace to baseball fans as the 2002 season proceeded. Since MLB's first collective bargaining agreement in 1968, every basic agreement has been marked by either a strike or a lockout.[1] The baseball Players Association is often characterized as the most militant and successful union in the United States today. With average salaries in 2002 at $2.4 million and the absence of a salary cap as exists in the NBA and NFL, many baseball owners feel as if they have been on the short end of collective bargaining agreements since 1977.

Former Yankee pitcher and author Jim Bouton describes the relationship between baseball players and owners this way: the owners exploited the players from the advent of the reserve clause in 1879 until the advent of free agency in 1977, nearly a hundred years, and the players have exploited the owners for the past twenty-five years; the players have seventy-five years to go before they get even.

Many owners, of course, have no intention of letting that happen. Bud Selig, who has been an owner since 1970 and has experienced one frustration after another at the bargaining table, is such an owner. Perhaps the most frustrating confrontation for Selig and the other owners was the 1994–95 strike, when the World Series was interrupted and the owners lost hundreds of millions of dollars. After the owners started the 1995 preseason with strikebreakers, the players prevailed in an unfair labor practices suit. The union remained intact and the real players went back to work under the terms of the old contract. The subsequent 1996–2001 collective bargaining agreement did little to deter the growth of players' salaries. Thus, to understand the expectations, the attitudes, and the behavior of each side in the 2002 (and subsequent) negotiations, it is important to retrace how collective bargaining in baseball got where it is today. After outlining this history, I turn to an evaluation of the 2002 labor agreement.

The Background

In the spring of 1954, unhappy over the progress in discussions for an improved pension plan, the players formed the Major League Baseball Players Association (MLBPA), with Bob Feller elected as the first president. Although not a bargaining unit at the time, the MLBPA did articulate a series of demands that were represented to the owners through its executive committee. The resulting agreement stipulated that 60 percent of TV revenues from the All-Star Game and the World Series would finance the players' pension fund. At the time, the owners set the minimum salary at $6,000.

The Players Association was not an active force until after 1966. Indeed, its legal counsel and de facto director was Judge Robert Cannon, a man who aspired to be baseball's next commissioner; he supported the reserve clause and praised the players' pension plan as the finest in the world.[2] On the players' economic status, Cannon told Congress in 1964, "We have it so good we don't know what to ask for next."[3] Historian James Edward Miller reports that when Cannon was selected to serve as the MLBPA's first executive director at $50,000 a year in 1966, the owners were so pleased that they voted to put aside 35 percent of the profits from the All-Star Game to pay for a New York office for Cannon.[4] But Cannon turned down the offer and Marvin Miller, a longtime negotiator for the United States Steel Workers, was chosen in his stead.

Before Marvin Miller had a chance to work his magic, Don Drysdale and Sandy Koufax double-handedly set out to make baseball economic history. Dissatisfied with their 1965 salaries, before the 1966 season they formed a two-person negotiating team and hired a lawyer to represent their salary interest. They asked for a combined $1 million over three years. Dodger president O'Malley was outraged, vowing that he would never bargain with an agent. After a short joint holdout, the players received substantial increases: Koufax's salary nearly doubled, to $125,000, and Drysdale got $115,000.[5] Later that year, the MLBPA and the owners signed their first agreement altering the pension financing system. They scrapped the old formula that took a percentage of All-Star Game and World Series proceeds in favor of a flat $4.2 million annual contribution from the owners, which virtually doubled all the players' benefits.

The first comprehensive collective bargaining agreement between the MLBPA and the owners was signed in February 1968. The agreement established a formal grievance procedure with the limitation that the owner-appointed commissioner was designated as the final arbiter. It raised the minimum salary from $6,000 to $10,000 and set up a joint study group on the reserve clause.

The Dismantling of the Reserve Clause

Notwithstanding dissent from a few players, most notably Carl Yastrzemski, the MLBPA financed Curt Flood's challenge to baseball's reserve clause (see chapter two for the full story).[6] In January 1970, Flood filed suit against MLB for $3 million, triple damages, and free agency. Flood lost round one in federal district court. He appealed in January 1971, but lost again in the Second Circuit Court of Appeals. Flood appealed to the Supreme Court, which heard the case and on June 18, 1972, voted 5 to 3, with one abstention, to uphold Holmes's 1922 *Federal Baseball* decision.

Flood's personal setback, however, shook the foundations of the reserve system. The Players Association's sights were now clearly fixed on winning in collective bargaining what they could not win in the courts. A first step was taken with the agreement signed in 1970. Not only did the players succeed in raising the minimum salary to $15,000 by 1972 and reducing the maximum salary cut to 20 percent, but more important, they gained the right to impartial arbitration of grievances outside the commissioner's office.

The first industrywide players' strike occurred during early April 1972 over funding for the players' pension plan. The players struck for fourteen days (nine during the regular season) (see table 5-1). The players wanted to be able to use the surplus that had accumulated in the pension fund to augment their pensions. The owners, apparently unaware of the surplus, refused to increase their contributions. Leonard Koppett wrote a summary of the 1972 strike in the *New York Times*:

Players: We want higher pensions.
Owners: We won't give you one damn cent for that.
Players: You don't have to—the money is already there. Just let us use it.

Table 5-1. *Industrywide Work Stoppages, 1972–95*

Year	Nature	Length[a]	Regular season games lost
1972	Strike	14 days	86
1973	Lockout	12 days	0
1976	Lockout	17 days	0
1980	Strike	8 days	0
1981	Strike	50 days	712
1985	Strike	2 days	0
1990	Lockout	32 days	0
1994–95	Strike	232 days	938

a. Counts both preseason and offseason dates.

Owners: It would be imprudent.

Players: We did it before, and anyhow, we won't play unless we can have some of it.

Owners: Okay.[7]

It was a modest victory for the players, but it was a victory nonetheless. The 1972 strike established the union as a contending force. It also seemed to adumbrate the conflicts that lay ahead and to have more to do with each side staking out some turf than with the issues at hand.

Negotiations over the third basic agreement commenced in November 1972. The Flood case had put free agency at the top of the players' agenda. The owners offered to end the reserve clause for players with five years of major league service if their team offered them less than a $30,000 salary, and for players with eight years of service if their team offered less than $40,000.[8] This was the kind of bargaining that usually made for long work stoppages. Yet the so-called lockout of 1973 affected only the early, voluntary reporting of players to spring training in mid-February. A settlement was reached on February 25, and the camps were opened several days before the exhibition games were to begin. The Players Association and owners agreed to introduce player salary arbitration and to postpone the reserve clause issue to the next round of bargaining. Salary arbitration was to take effect following the 1973 season. It enabled all players with two years plus one day of major league service to go before an impartial arbitrator to resolve salary disputes with an owner. Today, all observers recognize salary arbitration as a powerful weapon in the players' arsenal, and the owners have been trying to vitiate the arbitration system ever since.[9] The players also exacted another concession from the owners, the so-called 10-and-5 Rule (a.k.a. the Flood Rule). The rule stated that any player with ten years of service, the last five with same team (as Curt Flood had), had the right to veto any trade. The rule signified the first time since 1879 that players were granted any control over where they played.

In 1974, Catfish Hunter signed a two-year contract with Charlie Finley of the Oakland A's. One provision in the contract called for half of Hunter's salary to be paid into an insurance company fund during the season, for the purchase of an annuity. During the 1974 season Finley made no payments into the fund, and Hunter filed a grievance against Finley after the season. The three-person arbitration panel, headed by Peter Seitz, ruled in December 1974 that Finley had violated the contract and that Hunter was no longer bound by it; that is, he was a free agent. Hunter went on to sign a lucrative multiyear contract with the Yankees, making him the only player in MLB to be playing with a multiyear contract in 1975.[10]

Both Dave McNally of the Montreal Expos and Andy Messersmith of the Los Angeles Dodgers were dissatisfied with the 1975 contracts offered by their clubs, and each refused to sign a new contract. The clubs exercised their rights under the renewal clause of the standard contract, which permitted a club to renew any contract for one additional option year without the player's signature. When the 1975 season ended, McNally and Messersmith claimed they had played out their option year and were no longer bound to their clubs. They were assaying an unprecedented challenge to the reserve clause in baseball based on a literal interpretation of the renewal provision.[11] Again the case went before a grievance panel headed by Seitz. This time the ramifications of the ruling were infinite and the implications profound. Seitz urged the owners and the players to resolve the matter outside of arbitration at the bargaining table. Four weeks went by before Seitz issued his decision on December 21, 1975. In a sixty-one-page decision Seitz ruled that players were free to bargain with other clubs once their contracts expired. He again urged that a suitable procedure be established in the new basic agreement. The owners immediately fired Seitz and then appealed the decision in federal district court and the Federal Circuit Court of Appeals. Each court rejected the appeals, the last in March 1976.

The owners then took out their frustration on the players and the fans by locking the players out of spring training. Urged to do so by Walter O'Malley, Commissioner Kuhn persuaded the owners to reopen the camps on March 17. The baseball season proceeded without a new basic agreement. Negotiations continued and an accord was reached in July. The players won the right to free agency for all players with six years of major league experience as well as those players in the Messersmith category of having played out their contracts.[12] For the 1977 season, 281 players signed multiyear contracts.[13] The average salary almost tripled between 1976 and 1980.

By 1979 the owners had regrouped and were ready to do battle. Three preparatory steps were taken. First, in 1979, each team contributed 2 percent of its home gate receipts to a strike war chest.[14] Eventually, the owners took out a $50 million strike insurance policy with Lloyds of London and accumulated a $15 million strike fund.[15] Second, at their November 1979 meeting, the owners decided military discipline was imperative and imposed a gag rule, prohibiting owners from discussing labor relations issues with the media. Violators were to be fined $50,000. The rule was more than hortatory for owners who did not toe the party line. The Brewers' co-owner at the time, Harry Dalton, was hit with the full fine during the negotiations when he commented that he thought the players were trying to reach a compromise and he hoped the owners would do the same. Third, the owners hired a new chief negotiator, Ray Grebey, to head their Player Relations Committee (PRC). Grebey previously had earned a reputation as a tough negotiator working for the General Electric Company. His appointment was a clear signal that the baseball owners were going to take a hard-line position. Indeed, one leading baseball labor historian writes that Grebey was hellbent on breaking the union.[16]

The 1976 basic agreement expired on December 31, 1979, but serious negotiations did not begin until February 1980. The players wanted to reduce the free-agency eligibility from six to four years of service and to eliminate the five-year waiting period before a player could become a free agent for a second time. The owners were determined to stop the rapid salary growth that had started in 1976 and were not about to make further concessions that would strengthen free agency. On the contrary, their strategy was to weaken it through the introduction of a plan to compensate teams who lost free agents by penalizing teams who signed them.

Under the 1976 basic agreement the only compensation for loss of a player to free agency was an amateur draft choice, which, due primarily to the lesser development of college baseball compared to college football or basketball, was much less significant in baseball than in the other sports. The owners wanted to add a major league player to the compensation package. With the negotiations stalled, the players voted to authorize a strike beginning on May 29. A strike was averted in May when the two sides agreed on a deal that included everything but free-agent compensation and followed Marvin Miller's suggestion to set up a joint study committee to look into the compensation issue. The committee was to report its plan by January 1, 1981. If this did not lead to a compromise, the owners would be able to impose their compensation scheme. But in this case, of course, the players would be able to strike. This is precisely what happened.

Baseball fans remember 1981 as the split season, with division winners in each half and a one-game playoff at the end. The strike began on June 12, 1981, and lasted until August 1, seven days before the owners' insurance policy was to run out of money.[17] Fifty days and 712 games were lost. Owners' losses from the strike were estimated to be over $72 million, and the players' losses in forgone salary totaled around $34 million.[18]

The final compromise did little to alter the cost of signing a free agent. Indeed, Miller claims the compensation formula they agreed upon was basically the one he had proposed before spring training.[19] The new plan maintained the amateur draft pick and added compensation from a major league player pool. Each team signing a Type A free agent (a player ranked in the top 20 percent according to various performance criteria at his position) would have to put all but twenty-four protected players into this pool. Teams losing a Type A free agent could select any player from this pool, not necessarily one from the team who signed the free agent. Clubs that did not sign a Type A free agent could protect twenty-six players, and up to five clubs could become exempt from the compensation pool by agreeing not to sign Type A free agents for three years.

The 1980–81 basic agreement expired on December 31, 1984. Negotiations began in mid-November 1984, with hopes of reaching an accord before spring training. Peter Ueberroth had replaced Bowie Kuhn as commissioner on October 1, 1984, and he made his influence felt immediately. Three issues stood out. First, baseball's new national television package with

NBC and ABC quadrupled the annual value of its previous contract, and the MLBPA, now directed by Donald Fehr, sought a commensurate increase in the owners' pension contributions, from $15.5 million to $62 million. Second, the MLBPA wanted to eliminate the free-agent compensation pool. Third, the owners wanted to weaken salary arbitration.

In February a snag arose in the discussions when the owners requested a recess in order to review a "serious financial situation."[20] The owners pleaded financial distress. In the past, when the MLBPA had requested it, the owners had refused to open their books. Since they were now invoking economic hardship as a relevant factor in the negotiations, by National Labor Relations Board (NLRB) precedent the owners were required to show the MLBPA their books. Ueberroth successfully prevailed upon the reluctant owners to do so.

The "opened" books showed a $42 million combined loss in 1984, with twenty-two of twenty-six teams losing money. Moreover, MLB's accounting firm of Ernst & Whinney was projecting losses of $58 million in 1985, $94 million in 1986, $113 million in 1987, and $155 million in 1988.[21] (Of course, reality evolved quite differently as media contracts continued to grow handsomely and the licensing of major league products became a $100-million-plus annual business.) The MLBPA hired Stanford University economist Roger Noll to decode the books. Noll concluded that the industry really had an operating profit of $9 million for 1984.

With matters once again approaching a stalemate, Ueberroth indicated that in order to head off a work stoppage he might invoke Rule 12A, which allowed the commissioner to make any decision deemed to be in the best interest of the game. Of course, Ueberroth's Rule 12A powers in this regard only extended to his control over the owners' ability to declare a lockout. It did not trump the players' right to strike under national labor law. And strike they did. This time the strike had lasted only two days when the two sides reached a five-year agreement. The players got a $32.7 million annual contribution for their pension fund,[22] and the owners got the service requirement for arbitration eligibility lifted from two to three years beginning in 1987. Minimum salaries were raised from $40,000 to $60,000, with cost-of-living increases for future years.

The owners agreed to open up the free-agent market by eliminating both the free-agent reentry draft and the professional player compensation for type A free agents.[23] Amateur draft pick compensation was all that remained. Type A free-agent losses would be compensated by a first-round draft pick from the signing club.[24] Type B free agents (players who ranked between the twentieth and thirtieth percentile in performance by position) would be compensated by a "sandwich" pick between the first and second rounds.

Thus Ueberroth's heavy hand contributed to an efficient negotiating process and a quick compromise. Yet what Ueberroth's heavy hand accomplished over the bargaining table it took away under the table. Ueberroth was preparing the owners not to bid on free agents.

Ueberroth began sowing the seeds of collusion as soon as he took office. At an owners' meeting in October 1985 during the World Series in St. Louis, he reportedly scolded them for overspending on mediocre free agents. Lee MacPhail, director of the owners' Player Relations Committee, delivered a speech arguing that players with contracts of three years and more spent nearly 50 percent more time on the disabled list than those with one-year contracts and that the average player with a three-year contract or more experienced a nearly twenty-point decline in his batting average after signing the contract.[25] At owners' meetings later in October and in mid-November came more reprimand and admonition from Ueberroth, as he called long-term contracts "dumb" and said "he would want to know the economics of clubs that signed free agents."[26] Soon, Ueberroth would turn the owners' meetings into criticism/self-criticism sessions, with owners volunteering mea culpas.

Teams began announcing a policy to sign no contracts longer than three years for hitters and two years for pitchers. Star players such as Kirk Gibson found that teams were not bidding for their services. Of the thirty-three free agents between the 1985 and 1986 seasons, twenty-nine went back to their former teams without receiving bids from any others. The four who did move were marginal players whose teams announced they did not want them anymore. Free-agents' salaries grew by only 5 percent in 1986, and two-thirds of them received just one-year contracts. In February 1986 the MLBPA filed its first grievance (Collusion I).

Following the 1986 season, free agents again encountered a barren market. Star players, such as Jack Morris, Andre Dawson, Bob Horner, Bob Boone, Tim Raines, and Lance Parrish, were attracting little or no interest from the owners. Something had to be amiss. Every year between 1984 and 1987 new attendance records were set. According to their own figures, in

1986 MLB had its first pretax operating profit in eight years, and in 1987, with average salaries down 2 percent and revenues up 15 percent, operating profits grew to $103 million.

Andre Dawson's agent, Dick Moss, decided to test the owners' resolve. He left a blank contract in the Cubs' general offices with the message to fill it out as they saw fit. Then he told the press what he had done. After screaming expletives at Moss, the Cubs' management filled it out, lowering Dawson's base salary by 60 percent from his 1986 salary. The average salary of free agents in 1986–87 declined 16 percent, and approximately three-quarters of them got only one-year contracts. On February 18, 1987, the MLBPA filed its second grievance (Collusion II).

In September 1987, arbitrator Thomas Roberts ruled in Collusion I that the owners were guilty as charged. This led the clubs to soften their approach to the 1988 crop of free agents. Their new plan was to create an information bank where clubs reported their bids on players to each other. On January 19, 1988, the MLBPA filed its third grievance (Collusion III).

In July 1988, arbitrator George Nicolau found the owners guilty in Collusion II. And in July 1990, Nicolau found the owners guilty in Collusion III as well, reasoning : "[The Information Bank] converted the free-agency process into a secret buyers' auction, to which the sellers of services—the players—had not agreed and the existence of which they were not even aware" and "it is evident that many clubs used the Bank to report offers to free agents and to track just how far they would have to go with particular players."[27]

Monetary damages from collusion were fixed in stages. First, Roberts, using the average of three statistical methodologies, found the salary shortfall in 1986 due to collusion to be $10.5 million. Then, Nicolau, in September of 1990, also on the basis of statistical studies, found the salary shortfall to be $38 million in 1987 and $64.5 million in 1988. To these salary shortfalls were added lingering salary effects from multiyear contracts, losses due to shorter contracts, fewer guaranteed contracts, fewer option buyouts, fewer and smaller performance and award bonuses, fewer and smaller signing bonuses, and fewer no-trade clauses.[28]

A settlement for total collusion damages of $280 million was reached by the MLBPA and MLB on December 21, 1990. Owners paid the MLBPA $120 million on January 2, 1991, and were scheduled to pay the balance in four equal installments of $40 million each on July 15, 1991, September 15, 1991, November 15, 1991, and April 15, 1992.

Psychic damages from collusion still have not been settled. The owners' behavior during this period engendered a deep-seated distrust in the union. In his 2002 book, former MLB commissioner Fay Vincent is emphatic on this point: "The effects of collusion so thoroughly polluted the whole relationship between the union and the owners that the impact is still being felt. . . . Selig and Reinsdorf, two ringleaders of collusion, were the ones who were the most adamant in saying, 'We've got to find some way to get around this union, we have to see if we can break them.'"[29]

The next basic agreement negotiations brought yet another work stoppage. This time, without the imposing leadership of Peter Ueberroth, it was a longer work stoppage—a thirty-two-day lockout by the owners during the 1990 spring training. The regular season was delayed, but with some scheduling contortions it was played in full. The most contentious issue was eligibility for salary arbitration: the players wanted to revert to the two-years-of-service eligibility requirement, the owners proposed to do away with salary arbitration altogether and replace it with a complex pay-for-performance formula for players with between two and five years of service. The owners also proposed to introduce a salary cap, as existed in professional basketball at the time, at 48 percent of defined gross revenue.[30] The rationale given was that such a cap would preserve competitive balance in the game. Eventually, the owners backed off from the salary cap and pay-for-performance plans, but insisted on not lowering the eligibility requirement for arbitration below three years of service. The ultimate settlement involved a small concession from the owners. Seventeen percent of the players with more than two but fewer than three years of service (amounting to thirteen players in 1991) would be eligible for salary arbitration.

Other parts of the new basic agreement included an increase in the minimum salary from $68,000 to $100,000 in 1990, with a cost-of-living increase in 1992; an increase in the yearly pension fund contribution from $34.2 million to $55 million; and triple damages for any future owner collusion around the signing of free agents. The agreement lasted until December 31, 1993.

While a thirty-two-day work stoppage was long by the standards of 1990, the next negotiations would set a new watermark. In December 1992 the owners exercised the option in the existing four-year basic agreement to reopen the agreement. This reopening made a lockout or a strike in the final year of the basic agreement a legal possibility. In early January 1993, Don

Fehr, head of the Players Association, received a letter from Dick Ravitch, the owners' chief negotiator, conveying a sense of great urgency that the two sides meet frequently during January and February to resolve matters before the start of spring training. Fehr took the communication as a threat that a lockout was coming, but Ravitch quickly backed off, explaining that the only reason the owners reopened the basic agreement was to begin negotiations early. As it turned out, the owners did not convene a single collective bargaining session with the players between January and late July.

Ravitch adopted a strategy of first persuading the owners to increase revenue sharing among the teams and then selling the idea of a salary cap to the players. In the past, the Players Association had often said that if it was true that some teams were in financial distress, then the owners should help each other out rather than pressing the players for givebacks. Ravitch apparently assumed that this meant the players would accept a salary cap if the owners shared more revenue.

On the contrary, although the Players Association had never categorically ruled out a cap, Fehr had made it clear that it would be difficult to convince the players to accept a compensation system that tells the owners they are not allowed to pay the players as much as they want to pay them. Fehr had also made it clear that if a salary cap were to be seriously negotiated certain conditions would have to be met. First, the owners would need to share more revenue. Second, the owners would have to open their books completely to the Players Association. This is logical, since under a cap salaries would be set as a percentage of revenues, and players would have every right to verify that revenues were not being hidden. Third, since players' salaries would vary with the game's revenues, the players would take a direct interest in major financial decisions that affected revenue flows, such as a new national television contract. Hence the players would want some input into or veto power over such decisions. Fourth, an appropriate cap level would have to be agreed upon by both sides.

Ravitch's strategy, then, seemed ill-advised if his goal was to reach a negotiated agreement—unless, of course, the cap idea was simply a tactical maneuver to extract other concessions from the players. It is dubious that even the latter (and lesser) goal was achieved. Ravitch postponed several dates for the owners to come forward with their revenue sharing plan. The problem was that it was not an easy matter to get the big-city owners to part with their income. They argued that they paid more for their franchise than the small-city owners and were entitled to the extra revenues (which were capitalized in the team's value at purchase time). If the smaller-market clubs tried to force too much revenue sharing on them, the issue would likely end up in court.

Ravitch, it seems, predicated his sales pitch to the big-market owners on the assumption that whatever funds they gave up to the small-market owners would be replenished by reduced player incomes from the salary cap and by a healthier game with higher franchise values. At *USA Today Baseball Weekly's* Town Meeting, held at the July 1993 All-Star Game, Fehr expressed concern that Ravitch's refusal to initiate bargaining until a revenue sharing plan was in place was a delaying tactic. Since the owners receive 80 to 90 percent of their network television money from the postseason, the players' greatest bargaining leverage comes at the end of the season. By postponing substantive talks until the end of the season or beyond, Ravitch may have been seeking the upper hand. If the talks didn't progress to the owners' liking after the completion of the season, the owners could have declared a bargaining impasse and imposed their last offer to the players as the contract plan for the next season. Of course, the players could then have struck in March or April, but the players' greatest leverage comes at the end, not the beginning, of the season. Still another option—often overlooked—is that the players could have played the next season through August or September and then gone on strike. Selecting this option could have meant playing one season under the owners' imposed system.

Equally ominous was that when Ravitch finally was ready to talk to the players he had invested at least eight months in preparing the owners' position—a position that was fashioned without meaningful input from the players. This likely led to a stronger commitment to a more rigid plan on the owners' part as well as to greater divergence between that plan and what the players deemed acceptable—hardly an auspicious way to begin a collective bargaining process.

The owners had taken one additional step that did not augur well for a negotiated settlement. Because Commissioner Fay Vincent had forced the owners to open their spring training camps after the thirty-two-day lockout in March 1990 in the name of the best interest of baseball, the owners did not want him around limiting their strategic options for the 1993–94 negotiations. In September 1992 they forced Vincent's resignation and replaced him "on a temporary basis" with the owner of the Milwaukee Brewers, Bud

Selig. For the first time an owner was acting as commissioner. It was reasonable to assume that the best interest of baseball would now be more perfectly equated with the best interest of the owners—not a very encouraging thought to Don Fehr and the Players Association.

It turned out that the small-market owners did have an ace in the hole. Under U.S. copyright law, the home team owns the rights to a "performance." Baseball teams had long-standing agreements among themselves that permitted visiting teams to televise games in the visiting team's home market. The existing agreement expired in 1993. The small-market teams threatened not to sign a new agreement unless the big-market teams agreed to additional revenue sharing among the owners. At the owners' meeting in January 1994, they agreed to both a new television agreement and a new revenue sharing regime, but the latter was contingent on the Ravitch plan for a salary cap.[31] (When the AL and NL merged administratively in 2000, the new constitution included an article that permanently grants rebroadcast rights to visiting teams. This provision can only be overturned by a three-quarters vote of the owners.)

As also happened in the 2002 negotiations, the owners did not begin substantive bargaining until after the previous agreement had expired. In both cases, by delaying the talks the owners appeared to be jockeying for position, but there is little evidence that they achieved any advantage. Instead, they squandered potentially valuable months of discussion and subverted any hope of establishing more open and trusting lines of communication.

The first negotiating session was in Tampa, Florida, in March 1994. Little, if anything, was accomplished at that meeting or in the sporadic meetings over the ensuing three months. It was not until June 14 that the owners made their formal proposal for a salary cap. It is noteworthy that the owners opted to reopen the previous agreement in December 1992, and it was not until nineteen months later that they put their key goal—a salary cap—on the table.

The June 1993 cap proposal was different from the one proffered by the owners in 1990. Players would receive 50 percent of the industry's revenues (approximately 3 percentage points below what they were getting at the time), and each team's payroll would have to be between 84 and 110 percent of the average team payroll. The owners also proposed to eliminate salary arbitration. In its place, the owners offered to introduce free agency after four years of major league service (instead of six), but a player's team would have a right of first refusal after the player's fourth and fifth years.

The players doggedly countered that eligibility for salary arbitration should be reduced to two years, certain restrictions on free agency should be eliminated, and the minimum salary should be raised to $175,000. Owners rejected these proposals. The sides were doing a typical collective bargaining dance: early posturing with extreme positions and finding no common ground. On July 28, 1994, with average game attendance records being broken, the Players Association set August 12 as a strike deadline.

The owners then stuck out their collective chest and refused to make payments to the players' pension fund in August. The players responded with an unfair labor practices suit, which they later won. On August 12 the players stopped work, and on September 14 Commissioner Selig announced that he was canceling the remainder of the season, including the World Series. It would be the first time since 1904 that there was no World Series.

Bargaining proceeded irregularly throughout the early offseason. President Clinton appointed a former secretary of labor and renowned miracle worker in labor disputes, William J. Usery, as mediator. Usery was able to extract new ideas with modest compromise from both sides, but the gap was too large to bridge. On December 23, 1994, the owners declared an impasse in the negotiations and unilaterally implemented their salary cap proposal. The union filed another unfair labor practices suit, claiming, among other things, that the negotiations were ongoing. In January the owners announced their plan to begin the season with strikebreakers if the players remained on strike.

On January 26, President Clinton ordered William Usery to bring both sides back to the negotiating table. When talks resumed on February 1, the owners removed their demand for a salary cap and instead proposed a luxury tax on high payrolls: a 75 percent tax on payrolls between $35 million and $42 million, and a 100 percent tax on payrolls over $42 million. With discussions proceeding, the owners unilaterally revoked the authority of clubs to sign player contracts, eliminated salary arbitration, and ended the anticollusion clause.

On February 7, President Clinton called both sides to the White House and asked them to submit to binding arbitration. The players agreed. The owners demurred. On February 8, the players filed another unfair labor practices suit in response to the owners' last unilateral action.

The 1995 preseason eventually began with strikebreakers, but without the Baltimore Orioles. The Orioles' owner, Peter Angelos, was also a labor lawyer who refused to use strikebreakers during spring training or the regular season. Before the regular season began, American League president Gene Budig canceled the Orioles' games; this would have preserved Cal Ripken's streak of consecutive games played had the season commenced with substitute players. As it turned out, the regular season did not begin with strikebreakers in early April, but with the real players on April 26.

The National Labor Relations Board agreed with the players' unfair practices claims and, seeking an injunction to prevent the owners from implementing a new labor system, referred the case to federal district court in New York. On March 31, Judge Sonia Sotomayor, appointed to the federal bench by President George H. W. Bush in 1992, ruled in the players' favor and issued an injunction that compelled the owners to restore all the terms and conditions of the previous collective bargaining agreement. The owners decided that it was too financially risky to lock out the players at this point and the players went back to work.[32]

Sotomayor also ordered the two sides back to the bargaining table.[33] Negotiations on a new agreement went on during the 1995 season. On October 24 the two sides reached a tentative agreement, but on November 6 the owners voted 18 to 12 to reject the settlement. However, shortly after this vote, White Sox owner Jerry Reinsdorf, who had reportedly been a hawk during the negotiations, signed Albert Belle to a then record five-year contract worth $55 million. Reinsdorf's capriciousness was too much for the other owners. On November 26, 1996, they voted to approve the October 24 agreement.

The new agreement contained some significant changes. Most prominent among them, MLB introduced its first revenue sharing system. The system was phased in between 1996 and 2001 (the last year of the agreement). By 2001 each team was taxed at 20 percent of its net local revenue (all local revenue minus stadium expenses). Three-quarters of the revenue thus collected was distributed equally to the thirty teams; one-quarter was distributed only to clubs with below-average team revenue, in proportion to how far they were below this mean. Approximately $168 million was redistributed via this system from the top- to the bottom-revenue teams in 2001 (see table 5-2 for team details). This new system replaced previous forms of local revenue sharing, primarily from gate revenue.[34]

Although this system was intended to level the playing field for high- and low-revenue teams, it instead seems to have exacerbated competitive imbalance. The problem was straightforward. If an owner did not anticipate his or her team's being able to make it to the postseason (and it is probable that half or more owners felt this way each year), then the owner's profit-maximizing strategy might have been to lowball payroll. Reducing payroll would likely mean that team performance would suffer and team revenue would be decreased, but this would lead to higher revenue sharing transfers from MLB's central office. More precisely, if the reduction in payroll plus the additional revenue sharing transfer exceeded the drop in team revenue, then lowballing payroll would be a maximizing strategy.

Many owners behaved rationally and simply pocketed the lion's share of the revenue sharing money they received instead of using it to improve their clubs. Thus owners were rewarded for doing poorly, and the 1996 revenue sharing system probably increased, rather than narrowed, the performance differential between high- and low-revenue teams.

The second innovation of the 1996 agreement was the introduction of baseball's first luxury tax on high team payrolls. The intent of the tax was obvious. It substituted, albeit weakly, for a salary cap and was intended to be a drag on high team payrolls. Beginning in 1997 the teams with the top five payrolls paid a tax of 35 percent on the amount by which their payroll was above the midpoint between the payroll of the fifth and sixth highest team payrolls (the "threshold"). The 1998 tax was 35 percent on the top five payrolls for the amount they were above 1.078 times the 1997 threshold. The 1999 payroll tax was reduced slightly, to 34 percent on the top five payrolls for the amount they were above 1.071 times the 1998 threshold. The luxury tax was phased out—as the revenue sharing system was phased in— and did not apply in 2000 or 2001. This baroque formula, which I have simplified here, is indicative of the bargaining contortions that often lead to a final accord.

A third noteworthy element of the agreement called for the establishment of an "Industry Growth Fund" (IGF) to promote the growth of the game in Canada, the United States, and throughout the world. The players contributed 2.5 percent of their 1997 and 1998 salaries to this fund, and the owners contributed a matching sum (largely out of the proceeds from the

Table 5-2. *Outcomes of Different Revenue Sharing Schemes*

Millions of dollars

Team	Split-pool simulations				Straight-pool simulations				
	20 percent	22.5 percent	25 percent	27.5 percent	20 percent	30 percent	34 percent	40 percent	50 percent
Anaheim	9.83	11.06	12.29	13.52	6.29	9.44	10.70	12.59	15.73
Arizona	−4.36	−4.91	−5.45	−6.00	−0.37	−0.56	−0.63	−0.74	−0.93
Atlanta	−9.32	−10.49	−11.65	−12.82	−5.33	−8.00	−9.06	−10.66	−13.33
Baltimore	−6.81	−7.66	−8.51	−9.36	−2.82	−4.23	−4.80	−5.64	−7.05
Boston	−16.75	−18.84	−20.93	−23.03	−12.76	−19.13	−21.69	−25.51	−31.89
Chicago Cubs	−7.50	−8.44	−9.38	−10.32	−3.51	−5.27	−5.97	−7.03	−8.79
Chicago White Sox	−3.32	−3.74	−4.15	−4.57	0.30	0.46	0.52	0.61	0.76
Cincinnati	12.40	13.95	15.50	17.05	7.46	11.20	12.69	14.93	18.66
Cleveland	−13.20	−14.85	−16.50	−18.15	−9.21	−13.81	−15.65	−18.42	−23.02
Colorado	−6.51	−7.33	−8.14	−8.95	−2.52	−3.78	−4.29	−5.05	−6.31
Detroit	8.49	9.55	10.61	11.67	5.68	8.52	9.66	11.36	14.20
Florida	18.26	20.54	22.82	25.11	10.13	15.19	17.22	20.26	25.32
Houston	−4.88	−5.49	−6.10	−6.71	−0.89	−1.33	−1.51	−1.77	−2.22
Kansas City	16.00	18.00	20.00	22.00	9.10	13.65	15.47	18.20	22.75
Los Angeles	−8.47	−9.53	−10.59	−11.65	−4.48	−6.72	−7.62	−8.97	−11.21
Milwaukee	1.21	1.37	1.52	1.67	2.37	3.55	4.03	4.74	5.92
Minnesota	18.38	20.68	22.98	25.27	10.19	15.28	17.32	20.37	25.46
Montreal	27.65	31.11	34.56	38.02	14.41	21.61	24.49	28.81	36.01
New York Mets	−15.68	−17.64	−19.60	−21.56	−11.69	−17.53	−19.87	−23.37	−29.22
New York Yankees	−27.39	−30.82	−34.24	−37.66	−23.40	−35.10	−39.78	−46.81	−58.51
Oakland	10.83	12.18	13.53	14.89	6.75	10.12	11.47	13.49	16.86
Philadelphia	10.81	12.16	13.51	14.86	6.74	10.11	11.45	13.47	16.84
Pittsburgh	1.93	2.18	2.42	2.66	2.70	4.05	4.59	5.39	6.74
San Diego	9.40	10.57	11.75	12.92	6.10	9.14	10.36	12.19	15.24
San Francisco	−6.81	−7.66	−8.51	−9.36	−2.82	−4.23	−4.79	−5.64	−7.05
Seattle	−17.24	−19.39	−21.55	−23.70	−13.25	−19.87	−22.52	−26.49	−33.12
St. Louis	−7.44	−8.37	−9.30	−10.23	−3.45	−5.18	−5.87	−6.91	−8.63
Tampa Bay	8.51	9.57	10.64	11.70	5.69	8.54	9.68	11.38	14.23
Texas	−7.53	−8.47	−9.42	−10.36	−3.54	−5.31	−6.02	−7.09	−8.86
Toronto	9.50	10.69	11.88	13.07	6.14	9.22	10.44	12.29	15.36
Total redistributed	163.21	183.62	204.02	224.42	100.04	150.06	170.1[a]	200.09	250.11

Source: Estimates generated by the author based on 2001 team revenues.

a. This sum is $5 million below the estimate of MLB because it is based on the pre-audited 2001 revenues that Selig provided to Congress. The MLB estimate is based on final audited 2001 team revenue figures, which are apparently some $40 million higher. Positive numbers denote that a team is a net recipient of funds; negative numbers, that it is a net payor.

luxury tax). Perhaps the most significant aspect of the IGF was that it was jointly administered and signaled the willingness of both sides to begin building a partnership between players and owners.

Finally, the agreement contained an unprecedented clause stating that both labor and management would go to Congress to seek a partial lifting of MLB's antitrust exemption as it applied to collective bargaining. Congress complied in the Curt Flood Act of 1998. As discussed in chapter two, this act gives the players a clear opportunity to sue MLB if the owners attempt unilaterally to impose new restrictive conditions on baseball's labor market. To pursue this avenue, the Players Association first has to be decertified as a union because the Supreme Court (curiously to some) ruled in 1996 that workers cannot be protected by both labor law and antitrust law at the same time.[35] The practical significance of the Curt Flood Act is discussed further in chapter seven.

MLB under the 1996 Agreement

Baseball took a powerful initial hit from the 1994–95 strike. Average game attendance fell from 31,612 in 1994 to 25,021 in 1995, a drop of 20.9 percent. Serendipitously for baseball, the magic of Cal Ripken's streak of consecutive games, the sustained economic and stock market expansion in the country, and the new stadium construction boom, followed by the home run heroics of Mark McGwire, Sammy Sosa, and Barry Bonds, led to a gradual recovery in attendance (which reached 30,050 in 2001) and to a rapid growth in industry revenues (which doubled between 1996 and 2001). But as chronicled in chapter three, baseball's competitive imbalance grew more acute, and there was growing evidence of financial problems for a number of teams.

Early in 1999, Commissioner Selig handpicked a panel of four experts and twelve owners to study baseball's economic system and make recommendations about how to improve it. Significantly, Selig's blue-ribbon panel made no pretense of representing the players' perspective. The Players Association was not invited to join the panel. This unilateralism seemed to contravene the spirit of partnership adumbrated in the 1996 agreement.

With abundant resources at its disposal, after fifteen months of study and deliberation the panel produced a report in July 2000. The report contained three basic elements. First, it recommended that MLB increase its revenue sharing system by raising the tax on net local revenue from the 20 percent level of 2001 (under the split-pool scheme) to between 40 and 50 percent (under the straight-pool scheme). To avoid free-riding by owners, the panel also recommended that teams have a minimum payroll of around $40 million before they qualified to receive revenue sharing transfers.[36]

Second, the panel called for the reintroduction of the luxury tax, recommending that the amount of team payrolls over $84 million (using the forty-man roster) be taxed at 50 percent. Third, the panel suggested several changes in baseball's draft system. In 1965, MLB introduced the reverse-order amateur draft, which gave the team finishing lowest in the previous year's standings the first pick among U.S. amateurs. Before this, amateurs were signed as free agents by whichever team offered them the largest signing bonus. For many years the reverse-order draft gave a modest advantage to baseball's weakest teams. However, over the past decade, amateur signing bonuses have escalated to the point where many low-revenue teams are unable (or unwilling) to sign their top draft picks. The unsigned players reenter the next year's draft and frequently are passed over by low-revenue teams.[37] The highest-rated players often end up signing with the high-revenue teams.

Further, amateurs who do not reside in the United States, Canada, or Puerto Rico are not subject to the draft. Forty percent of all players signed to first-year contracts today fall into this category. Some are amateurs from the Caribbean or elsewhere; others are professionals in Japan or South Korea who come via a transfer arrangement between their home league and MLB or free agency. The signing of this 40 percent is based on team resources (scouting, baseball camps, bonus money, and salary).

The blue-ribbon panel sought to restore the balancing effect of the amateur draft. Among other proposals, the panel recommended that all international players be included in the draft, that changes be made to make it more unattractive for amateurs to not sign and reenter the draft the following year, that playoff clubs not be allowed to draft in the first round, and that draft picks be allowed to be traded.[38]

These were the principal proposals of the owners' panel.[39] After Selig excluded the players from participating as regular panel members, one might have thought that he would seek to initiate discussions around these recommendations with the Players Association as soon as possible.[40] The 1996 agreement was to end after the 2000 season, although there was a provision allowing the Players Association to extend the contract for one year (which it did in late August 2000).

But Selig did not call for negotiations. It was not until the Spring of 2001 that the commissioner delegated MLB COO Paul Beeston to begin informal negotiations with the players. According to the Players Association, these negotiations went on productively for several weeks until suddenly Selig ended them without explanation in June. Eventually Beeston, who had an excellent rapport with the Players Association, was dismissed from his post. And on November 6, 2001, when the 1996 agreement expired, Selig still had not initiated formal, substantive negotiations with the players.[41] Instead, he launched a grenade at the Players Association by announcing that the owners had voted to contract (eliminate) two teams for the 2002 season. This plan would mean the reduction of union membership by eighty players; and lowering demand for players by eighty relative to supply would put downward pressure on salaries.

To some it seemed that Selig was not interested in negotiating anything, but that his real interest was in busting the union. To others Selig's delaying tactics were reminiscent of Dick Ravitch's strategy in 1994 (performing on behalf of then acting commissioner Selig). In 1994 and again in 2002, somehow Selig believed that postponing negotiations would deliver him bargaining leverage and would be more constructive than talking to the other side. And somehow a large share of the media was willing in 2002 to hold the Players Association responsible for the possible setting of a strike date when the time for negotiations was running out on the season.

The owners did not put their core demands on the bargaining table before December 2001, and Selig himself did not attend a bargaining session until January 2002. The owners' bargaining demands included not only the principal proposals (modestly tweaked) of the blue-ribbon panel, but also some hefty items not mentioned in the panel's report. In addition to his plan for contraction (which the blue-ribbon panel explicitly stated would not be necessary if its other ideas were implemented), Selig wanted the owners' 60/40 rule ratified in the collective bargaining agreement, the establishment of a fund of $100 million that the commissioner could use at his discretion, the right of owners to release players whose salary arbitration figures were deemed to be too high, and a new pension plan contribution system. Let us consider the meaning and weight of these bargaining demands.

Selig announced in late March 2002 that he was going to dust off the long-dormant 60/40 rule and begin implementing it during the 2002 season. This rule, first introduced by the owners in December 1982, stated that teams were required to maintain a ratio between assets and liabilities of at least 60 to 40. At the time, the players filed a grievance that the rule would affect salaries and thus was a mandatory subject for collective bargaining. In his errant ruling of January 1985, arbitrator Richard Bloch upheld the owners' right to unilaterally implement the rule, arguing that it was a matter of fiscal responsibility and management prerogative.

When Selig announced that the owners would have to comply with the 60/40 rule by June 2002, he stipulated new implementation guidelines. According to press reports and a legal complaint filed by former Mets co-owner Nelson Doubleday, among these guidelines were the franchise valuation rule that a team's value equaled only two times its (trailing) annual revenue and the liability instruction that long-term player contracts would count as liabilities.[42] Selig threatened that noncompliers would be subject to possible fine, loss of payments from the central fund, or being put into trusteeship. On the surface, once again, the implementation of 60/40 may have smacked of financial prudence, but the reality was otherwise.

Under Selig's franchise valuation rule the Boston Red Sox, which sold for approximately $720 million in January 2002, would be worth two times the team's reported 2001 revenue of $160.5 million, or $321 million. Yet based upon the 2002 sale price, and assuming that the Sox's 80 percent stake in NESN is worth $200 million and the 10.7 acres of real estate around Fenway Park is worth $75 million, the team's value is around $445 million.[43] Selig's revenue multiple of two is well below the implied ratio of 2.77 in the Sox sale as well as the market-generated revenue multiple for other baseball franchises. Indeed, MLB's financial and valuation consultant, Robert Starkey, employed a revenue multiple of roughly 2.4 in his very conservative valuation of the New York Mets in April 2002.[44] If franchises have lower value, then their asset values are reduced and they must, correspondingly, decrease their debt under the 60/40 rule.[45] For instance, if the Sox are valued at $321 million, then their allowed debt under the rule is $128.4 million. If they are valued at $445 million, their allowed debt is $178 million.

Under the liability accounting instruction, long-term player contracts count as debt. This makes no economic sense.[46] As of June 2002, when the Selig rule was to kick in, the Red Sox had a remaining obligation to outfielder Manny Ramirez of around $120 million. For the rest of the squad,

the Sox had approximately another $70 million in long-tern
the team's total in long-term contract obligations alone v
million; that is, it was already $60 million plus over the d
counting the $40 million of preexisting debt the new own...
the $200 million the new owners borrowed from Fleet Bank to buy ...
team. The Sox would have to do some massive payroll cutting not to be in
violation of Selig's 60/40 rule.

And the Red Sox are not an aberration. According to Selig, at the end of
2001, MLB teams had over $3 billion in debt, or over $100 million per team.
Using Selig's two-times-revenue multiple to value teams and his figure of
$112.1 million average team revenue in 2001, it follows that the average
franchise was worth $224.2 million. With an average debt of $100 million
plus (and this is before long-term player contracts), the average team, with
a 55.4/44.6 asset-to-debt ratio, was already in violation of the rule.[47]

In his counterclaim of August 5, 2002, Mets owner Nelson Doubleday
provides a similar analysis of the 60/40 rule:

> Using the Yankees as an example, this would mean excluding from the
> team's asset calculations television contracts that will produce over
> $50 million annually and treating the contracts of superstars such as
> Derek Jeter and Jason Giambi (the team's greatest assets) as liabilities.
> As such, the Yankees, almost certainly the most profitable and valuable
> team in baseball, would potentially be judged as non-compliant with
> Selig's 60/40 rule. In other words, although the Yankees are capable of
> adding additional star players to their payrolls, they are suddenly cal-
> culated as having too much debt and prevented from taking on any
> more "liabilities" (i.e., long-term player contracts).[48]

Doubleday goes on to critique the Selig rule that a team's value is arrived at
by multiplying its last year's revenues by a factor of only two.

> The 60/40 rule devalues every single franchise in baseball, regardless
> of the size of the team's home market or the amount of its revenues.
> The New York Yankees are valued at $484 million under the 60/40
> rule. No other published estimate of the team is below $600 million.
> At the other end of the spectrum, the Montreal Expos, baseball's low-
> est revenue team, had revenues of $34 million in 2001 (yielding a
> 60/40 valuation of $68 million), yet Major League Baseball itself pur-
> chased the Expos this year for $150 million.[49]

Whatever Richard Bloch may have believed back in 1985, it is clear that the 60/40 rule would function as a back-door salary cap in 2002. Selig was supposedly implementing the rule in 2002 under the authority of Bloch's ruling, but he must have recognized its vulnerability and hence put it on the bargaining table for labor ratification. The rule, however, was much too draconian in its potential effects to be acceptable to the Players Association.

Why, then, did Selig put it on the table? Is he so out of touch with what is in the realm of possibility? Not likely. More likely he put it on the table as a bargaining chip to loosen the players' position on other issues. This is part of the bargaining game played by both sides.

The demand for a commissioner's discretionary fund of $100 million (later reduced to $85 million) was only a little bit more benign. The discretionary fund could have been used by the commissioner to reward teams who followed the gospel as laid down by Selig. The Players Association believed that this would provide a further drag on salaries. If a substantial fund were needed to help financially distressed franchises, then the players surely wanted it to operate according to set rules or be coadministered, much like the Industry Growth Fund from the 1996 accord.

The right of owners to cut loose players who asked for high salary arbitration awards would undermine the value of the long-standing arbitration system to the players. Unless the owners were willing to substitute an equally effective mechanism, such as earlier free agency, it was not conceivable that the players would accept such a change.

The proposal for a new pension plan contribution system called for teams with higher payrolls to put more into the plan. However, players would still receive the same pension benefit. This proposal, in effect, would constitute an indirect tax on high payrolls, supplementing the impact of the luxury tax proposal.

Selig, then, loaded the bargaining table with what the players perceived to be harsh, unacceptable demands. None of these demands were incorporated into the final settlement, and there is no evidence that they yielded any incremental bargaining leverage for the owners.

The Final 2002 Settlement

After the usual bargaining dance, with each side posturing for advantage and resorting to brinksmanship to intimidate the other, on August 16 the players set a strike date of August 30. Negotiations intensified. Logic and sanity for once prevailed, when a last-minute agreement was reached just in time for the Cardinals to play the Cubs in an afternoon game at Wrigley Field on August 30.[50]

Although Selig's claim in announcing the agreement to the press that this was the first time in baseball's collective bargaining history that no games would be lost was false, it was the first time since 1972 that there was no strike or lockout declared (see table 5-1).[51] Each side was duly scared about the enormous costs another work stoppage would create. The short-term financial losses for the owners would reach around $1 billion for the 2002 season.

The long-term damage to the game would be practically incalculable. Unlike 1994–95, when the economy was in the middle of a ten-year expansion, the stock market was experiencing a burgeoning bubble, and the stadium-building boom was in full swing, the economy in 2002 was weak, the stock market bubble had burst, and the building cycle was drawing to a close. The stigma of being on strike on the first anniversary of September 11, 2001, would not have helped matters. Further, fans would certainly have had a stronger negative reaction if the World Series were canceled midseason for a second time and there were no Cal Ripken or Mark McGwire around to set new records. And it was unlikely that Barry Bonds would break his new record of seventy-three home runs because pitchers had taken to walking him with such frequency that if one didn't know better one might suspect he were a 5th Avenue poodle (he ended up with a record 198 walks in 2002).

As Don Fehr put it: "All streaks come to an end sometime and this one was long overdue." So there was no work stoppage in 2002, and this was clearly a victory for the owners, players, and most of all the fans. But will labor strife be avoided in the future, and will the elements of the new collective bargaining agreement be sufficient to resolve the game's economic problems or at least to put the game on the right course?

Other than the improvement in the players' benefit fund, the lifting of the minimum salary from $200,000 to $300,000, and the introduction of drug testing for steroids, the main items in the agreement came from the blue-ribbon panel's report.

Increased Revenue Sharing

The blue-ribbon panel called for the net local revenue tax to increase from 20 percent (using the split pool) to between 40 and 50 percent (using the straight pool). The owners' initial demand was for a 50 percent tax using a straight-pool system.

The players resisted such a substantial increase. Revenue sharing was being called for in the name of competitive balance, but the players were concerned that at such high tax levels it would also function as a strong deterrent to player salary increases. They reasoned something like this. Suppose that George Steinbrenner believes that Jason Giambi will add $20 million a year to the New York Yankees' local revenues. That being the case, Steinbrenner should be willing to offer Giambi a salary of up to $20 million. Now suppose that MLB informs Steinbrenner that it will tax away 50 percent of any local revenue generated by the Yankees. Suddenly, Giambi is no longer worth up to $20 million to Steinbrenner. He is now worth only $10 million, and Steinbrenner's pay offer would be scaled down accordingly.[52]

With this concern, the players countered that they would accept an increase in the net local revenue tax from 20 percent to 22.5 percent under the split-pool system (the system prevailing in 2001). It will be recalled that under the split-pool system, of the monies collected from the net local revenue tax, 75 percent is distributed equally to all teams and 25 percent is distributed only to teams with below mean revenues (in proportion to how far they are below the mean). Under the straight-pool system, 100 percent of the collected monies are distributed equally to all clubs.

The players favored the split- over the straight-pool system because the split pool, at any given level of total sharing, redistributes more money to the bottom teams and takes less money away from the top teams. The players wanted more money to go the bottom teams because the bottom teams need it the most, and the pressure for salary controls and additional revenue sharing comes most intensely from the bottom. They wanted proportionately less money taxed away from the high-revenue teams because they did not want strong penalties on building a successful club. Moreover, it is the high-revenue teams that generally drive the salary structure upward.

We can see the differential redistributive effects by comparing the results of a 25 percent tax under the split pool with a 40 percent tax under the straight pool. Each system generates approximately the same amount of total redistribution; the former shares $204 million, the latter $200 million. The four bottom-revenue teams in 2001 (Marlins, Royals, Expos, and Twins) would receive $12.6 million more under the split pool, and the four top-revenue teams (Yankees, Seattle, Red Sox, and Mets) would be taxed $26 million less under the split pool (see table 5-2).

The owners preferred the straight pool for many of the same reasons. They wanted ongoing pressure to increase revenue sharing and retard salary growth. They wanted to penalize the high-spending Yankees as stiffly as possible. Further, more teams experienced larger benefits under the straight-pool system, so it was easier to gather the necessary ownership votes to approve a straight-pool model.

The bargaining began with the sides seemingly far apart: the owners asking for a 50 percent tax under the straight-pool system and the players offering 22.5 percent under the split pool. The owners' proposed tax rate was more than twice as high as the players, but as table 5-2 shows, the actual amount redistributed under the owners' system was only 34 percent higher ($250 million in contrast to $184 million under the players' system). More important, as is always the case in collective bargaining, these proposals were only the initial negotiating gambits. If the players were moving in 2.5 percentage point increments and the owners in 10 percentage point increments, then at the very next set of proposals (25 percent under the split pool and 40 percent under the straight pool), the sides would find a meeting place. It was a forgone conclusion that the revenue sharing issue would be worked out.

The eventual agreement on revenue sharing provided for a 34 percent net local revenue tax rate on a straight-pool basis. Based on team revenues in 2001, this plan would redistribute $175.8 million from the top to bottom half of teams.[53] This sum would be supplemented by an additional $43.3 million in 2003 to come out of the MLB central fund, and an additional $10 million to come out of a $333,333 assessment on each team.[54] The $43.3 million from the central fund would increase to $57.7 million in 2004 and to $72.7 million in 2005 and 2006, while the $175.8 million would stay the same (again based on 2001 revenues), so the total amount redistributed would rise from $229 million in 2003 to $243 million in 2004, and to $258 million in 2005 and 2006.[55]

The redistribution of the $43.3 million (and subsequent higher amounts) coming from the central fund will be done on a split-pool basis. Thus, over the four years, on average just under 75 percent will be redistributed on a straight-pool and just over 25 percent on a split-pool basis. With this in mind, we can estimate the combined marginal tax rates for teams at different revenue levels. For 2003 the combined marginal rate faced by the top-revenue teams will rise to approximately 0.37 from 0.195 in 2001 (see table 5-3), while that for the bottom teams will stay at roughly 0.41. However, when the system is fully implemented in 2005, the marginal rate

Table 5-3. *Marginal Tax Rates under Revenue Sharing Plans*

Team	2001 total local revenue (millions of dollars)	Straight pool					Split pool			
		0.2	0.3	0.34	0.4	0.5	0.2	0.3	0.4	0.5
Anaheim	67.33	0.193	0.290	0.329	0.387	0.483	0.416	0.624	0.832	1.040
Arizona	106.65	0.193	0.290	0.329	0.387	0.483	0.195	0.293	0.390	0.488
Atlanta	122.45	0.193	0.290	0.329	0.387	0.483	0.195	0.293	0.390	0.488
Baltimore	103.9	0.193	0.290	0.329	0.387	0.483	0.195	0.293	0.390	0.488
Boston	152.58	0.193	0.290	0.329	0.387	0.483	0.195	0.293	0.390	0.488
Chicago Cubs	105.37	0.193	0.290	0.329	0.387	0.483	0.195	0.293	0.390	0.488
Chicago White Sox	87.28	0.193	0.290	0.329	0.387	0.483	0.426	0.639	0.852	1.065
Cincinnati	46.48	0.193	0.290	0.329	0.387	0.483	0.414	0.621	0.828	1.035
Cleveland	137.84	0.193	0.290	0.329	0.387	0.483	0.195	0.293	0.390	0.488
Colorado	107.41	0.193	0.290	0.329	0.387	0.483	0.195	0.293	0.390	0.488
Detroit	82.39	0.193	0.290	0.329	0.387	0.483	0.417	0.626	0.834	1.043
Florida	36.15	0.193	0.290	0.329	0.387	0.483	0.409	0.614	0.819	1.024
Houston	110.23	0.193	0.290	0.329	0.387	0.483	0.195	0.293	0.390	0.488
Kansas City	39.29	0.193	0.290	0.329	0.387	0.483	0.411	0.617	0.822	1.028
Los Angeles	119.21	0.193	0.290	0.329	0.387	0.483	0.195	0.293	0.390	0.488
Milwaukee	88.95	0.193	0.290	0.329	0.387	0.483	0.423	0.634	0.845	1.057
Minnesota	31.87	0.193	0.290	0.329	0.387	0.483	0.409	0.614	0.819	1.023
Montreal	9.77	0.193	0.290	0.329	0.387	0.483	0.402	0.603	0.804	1.006
New York Mets	158.23	0.193	0.290	0.329	0.387	0.483	0.195	0.293	0.390	0.488
New York Yankees	217.81	0.193	0.290	0.329	0.387	0.483	0.195	0.293	0.390	0.488
Oakland	51.07	0.193	0.290	0.329	0.387	0.483	0.415	0.623	0.830	1.038
Philadelphia	57.11	0.193	0.290	0.329	0.387	0.483	0.195	0.293	0.390	0.488
Pittsburgh	84.31	0.193	0.290	0.329	0.387	0.483	0.422	0.633	0.844	1.055
San Diego	55.32	0.193	0.290	0.329	0.387	0.483	0.416	0.624	0.833	1.041
San Francisco	145.89	0.193	0.290	0.329	0.387	0.483	0.195	0.293	0.390	0.488
Seattle	178.03	0.193	0.290	0.329	0.387	0.483	0.195	0.293	0.390	0.488
St. Louis	108.06	0.193	0.290	0.329	0.387	0.483	0.195	0.293	0.390	0.488
Tampa Bay	62.34	0.193	0.290	0.329	0.387	0.483	0.417	0.626	0.834	1.043
Texas	110.51	0.193	0.290	0.329	0.387	0.483	0.195	0.293	0.390	0.488
Toronto	54.08	0.193	0.290	0.329	0.387	0.483	0.416	0.624	0.832	1.041
Total	2,827.91									

Source: Estimates generated by the author based on 2001 team revenues.

for the top teams will rise to 0.39, and for the bottom teams it will climb to around 0.47.[56]

The implied marginal tax rates for the Yankees under this combined system would be approximately 39 percent in 2005; that is, for every additional dollar of net local revenue, 39 cents would be taxed away.[57] This rate is approximately double the marginal rate faced by the Yankees in 2001. It should provide some deterrent to Yankee payroll expenditures.

While the marginal tax rates on the top teams become significant, those on the bottom teams rise even higher, to around 47 percent. This is a matter of concern. Under the former system, the bottom teams faced a marginal rate of just over 41 percent; the new rate starts at this level in 2003 but rises to around 47 percent in 2005 and 2006. This means that if the Kansas City Royals were to lift their payroll by $10 million in 2005, and the club were to improve and generate an additional, say, $12 million in local revenues, almost half of this would be lost in lower revenue sharing transfers. The net effect on the Royals from raising their payrolls in this illustration would be negative $3.64 million.

Conversely, if the Royals lowered their payroll and performed more poorly (aggravating competitive imbalance), they would be rewarded with an increase in transfers from the revenue sharing system. For every decrease in revenues of $1, the Royals would see their transfers increase by 47 cents. So, if the decrease in payroll plus the increase in transfers exceeded the decrease in revenues, the Royals' profit-maximizing strategy would be to lower payroll. With such incentives, it is questionable whether baseball's new revenue sharing system will motivate the low-revenue clubs to improve the talent on their teams.

Recall that high-revenue teams naturally tend to outperform the low-revenue teams in the effort to sign marquee free agents. This is because the expected incremental revenue contribution of the star is greater in larger markets and in markets with new stadiums. Sometimes this imbalance is aggravated by the ability of an owner to use the baseball team to drive revenue for other, related businesses, such as a regional sports channel. The differential marginal tax rates confer yet an additional advantage on the top-revenue teams, who face a lower rate (though the differential is smaller than it was under the 1996–2002 system).

From a slightly different perspective, consider the situation faced by a low-revenue team owner before and after the revenue sharing system. The owner will offer a player a salary up to the player's expected incremental contribution to team revenue. The fact that the owner receives a revenue sharing transfer from MLB does not increase the value of a player's incremental contribution. It does the opposite. If the player increases (pretransfer) team revenue, then the team's transfer will decrease and the net revenue contribution of the player will be smaller. Thus it is not surprising that the Tampa Bay Devil Rays' owner, Vince Naimoli, when asked whether all of the increase in transfers under the new system would go into payroll, "stopped short of committing to spend the additional money on [player] payroll," saying that he "might instead use some to pay down the team's revolving line of credit."[58]

Largely for this reason, the commissioner's blue-ribbon panel and the owners themselves in their initial proposal to the Players Association called for a minimum team payroll. Teams whose payrolls fell below this minimum would not be eligible to receive revenue sharing transfers. This mechanism was intended to ensure that owners would put their transfers into improving the talent on their teams rather than into their pockets. The owners' initial proposal put the minimum at $45 million for the forty-man roster, including benefits. In 2001 only three teams fell below this threshold (San Diego, Montreal, and Minnesota), and none of the three teams was more than $3 million below it. By 2002 only two teams (Tampa Bay and Montreal) fell below this level, and neither team was more than $1.5 million below it.[59]

The Players Association alternately said that this minimum payroll threshold was too low and that they were against payroll minimums because they violated the spirit of a free labor market and were likely to lead to a maximum payroll (salary cap). The claim that this threshold was set too low is understandable if it would have affected one or two teams at most. The latter claim is puzzling. Baseball's labor market already contains a variety of restrictions, one of which is a minimum individual salary that has been in place for several decades and has never led to a maximum individual salary.

There are also possible practical problems with the operation of a minimum payroll if it is set at an effective level. Suppose the minimum is set at $55 million and a given team is spending $40 million in year one. To meet the threshold it may have to hire players it does not really need or pay them excessive salaries. Alternatively, suppose the same team has invested heavily in its player development and is stocked with a strong, young group of players. In year one its payroll might be below the threshold, but in years two through four, as its players become eligible for arbitration and free agency, the payroll might rise well above the minimum. These and other situations argue for the importance of a flexible minimum payroll; for example, the payroll might be defined as a three-year average and include all player development expenditures, not just expenditures on the major league roster.[60] But the 2002 accord has no minimum payroll at all; nor does it have any other effective incentives for revenue-receiving teams to spend the transfers on their players.

Of course, the argument that the team receiving the transfer knows best what it needs to spend the money on makes some sense. Resources generally will be allocated more efficiently if done on a decentralized, market-oriented basis. Minimum payrolls impose a centralized decision and are likely to result in some resource misallocation (although in this case MLB purportedly seeks a nonmarket outcome of greater parity).

The problem with this logic, however, is that it fails to address the issue for which the revenue sharing system was created: competitive balance. The high marginal tax rates on low-revenue clubs (discussed earlier) and the consequent disincentives to spend the transfers on player payroll suggest that decentralized decisionmaking will lead to little improvement in the competitive performance of low-revenue clubs. A reasonable compromise might have been to impose a graduated tax on teams whose payrolls fell below a defined minimum. The tax rate would rise as teams fell further below the minimum threshold.[61]

In a characteristic obfuscatory comment on the Fox Sports network, Commissioner Selig defended the absence of a salary minimum this way: "One of the myths that surrounded all this is that owners haven't invested the money they got in revenue sharing. In the agreement, there is specific language drafted by both the clubs and the [MLBPA] that the money must be spent on their franchise and on players, and it's going to be enforced and … it's going to be enforced by me."[62] First, one of the biggest offenders in the previous revenue sharing system was Selig's own team, the Milwaukee Brewers. Selig's comment seems structured to take possible heat off his own team. Second, Selig said he would enforce the owners' agreement to spend the revenue transfers "on their franchise and on players." Spending money on their franchise potentially can include any operating cost (such as front office salaries, ballpark enhancements, and team promotion) or interest expenses (on which Devil Rays owner Vince Naimoli suggested he would spend the transfer). There's no guarantee here that competitive balance would be aided. Further, without a specific formula and methodology, how will Selig know how the transfers are being spent?

From the perspective of improving competitive balance, there is some better news in the new labor agreement. In addition to the marginal tax rates, the total amount of the tax is also a relevant factor that will influence teams' willingness to spend on players. Owners never know with certainty what a player will contribute to team revenue. At best, they estimate a player's contribution, which is really a modal point on a probability distribution. Players perform differently from year to year based on myriad personal and team factors. Signing expensive players is risky, and high-revenue teams are generally better able to absorb the risk. As more revenue is transferred away from the top teams, they are likely to exhibit more cautious behavior in signing players and the bottom teams with augmented revenue are more likely to accept additional risk.

The approximate net contributions (preceded by a minus sign) or receipts for 2003 under the new system are shown in tables 5-4 and 5-5. The Yankees' revenue sharing burden, which was approximately $28 million in 2001, would rise to $46 million in 2003, $47 million in 2004, and $49 million in 2005 and 2006. The Mariners would be the second highest payors, with their net contribution rising from $17 million in 2001, to $28 million in 2003, and to $29 million in 2005 and 2006. That is, the Yankees would contribute almost $20 million more than the second highest contributor— a severe burden to be sure, but not as onerous as the nearly $90 million the Yankees would have paid if the owners' original proposal had succeeded. The heavy tax on the Yankees helps to explain why only that team's ownership voted against the new collective bargaining agreement. If the owners wanted to single out Steinbrenner with their new system, they appear to have succeeded.

At the bottom, the Expos (assuming they will still exist) continue to be the largest net recipient, with their take increasing from around $28 million in 2001 to $31 million in 2003, $33 million in 2004, and $35 million in 2005 and 2006. The Twins, still based on 2001 revenues, are the second largest net recipients, with their take rising from roughly $18 million in 2001 to $23 million in 2003, $24 million in 2004, and $26 million in 2005 and 2006. The

Table 5-4. *Revenue Sharing Results for 2003 under the New Agreement*

Millions of dollars

Team	Revenue share	Luxury tax	Total
Anaheim	12.53	0.00	12.53
Arizona	−3.78	0.00	−3.78
Atlanta	−15.72	0.00	−15.72
Baltimore	−8.44	0.00	−8.44
Boston	−23.69	0.00	−23.69
Chicago Cubs	−7.33	0.00	−7.33
Chicago White Sox	−2.29	0.00	−2.29
Cincinnati	15.86	0.00	15.87
Cleveland	−18.95	0.00	−18.95
Colorado	−6.55	0.00	−6.55
Detroit	9.05	0.00	9.05
Florida	20.71	0.00	20.71
Houston	−3.23	0.00	−3.23
Kansas City	18.68	0.00	18.68
Los Angeles	−10.68	−0.32	11.00
Milwaukee	8.16	0.00	8.16
Minnesota	22.64	0.00	22.64
Montreal	31.35	0.00	31.35
New York Mets	−24.46	0.00	−24.46
New York Yankees	−45.81	−9.49	−55.30
Oakland	14.55	0.00	14.55
Philadelphia	14.23	0.00	14.23
Pittsburgh	8.29	0.00	8.29
San Diego	11.20	0.00	11.20
San Francisco	−5.49	0.00	−5.49
Seattle	−27.89	0.00	−27.89
St. Louis	−9.69	0.00	−9.69
Tampa Bay	13.61	0.00	13.61
Texas	−10.47	−2.52	−12.99
Toronto	13.59	0.00	13.59

Notes: These are estimates based on 2001 revenues and 2002 forty-man rosters.

Negative numbers indicate the team is a net payor. Positive numbers indicate that the team is a net recipient.

Marlins follow close behind the Twins as the third largest beneficiary. Relative to the last agreement, the Expos, Twins, and Marlins gain only between $2.5 million and $4.3 million each in the first two years of the agreement; the Expos' increase eventually rises to $7.5 million in 2005 and 2006. In contrast, the *extra* burden on the Yankees will be $21.5 million by 2005 and 2006 (not including the luxury tax).[63]

Table 5-5. *Revenue Sharing Results Compared, 2001–06*

Millions of dollars

Team	2001	2003	2004	2005	2006
Anaheim	9.83	12.53	13.23	13.92	13.92
Arizona	−4.36	−3.78	−4.51	−5.24	−5.24
Atlanta	−9.32	−15.72	−16.79	−17.87	−17.87
Baltimore	−6.81	−8.44	−9.48	−10.53	−10.53
Boston	−16.75	−23.69	−24.65	−25.61	−25.61
Chicago Cubs	−7.50	−7.33	−8.08	−8.82	−8.82
Chicago White Sox	−3.32	−2.29	−2.89	−3.50	−3.50
Cincinnati	12.40	15.87	16.90	17.94	17.94
Cleveland	−13.20	−18.95	−20.10	−21.23	−21.23
Colorado	−6.51	−6.55	−7.45	−8.35	−8.35
Detroit	8.49	9.05	9.40	9.76	9.76
Florida	18.26	20.71	21.91	23.12	23.12
Houston	−4.88	−3.23	−3.90	−4.57	−4.57
Kansas City	16.00	18.68	19.91	21.15	21.15
Los Angeles	−8.47	−10.68	−11.58	−12.48	−12.48
Milwaukee	1.21	8.16	9.34	10.51	10.51
Minnesota	18.38	22.64	24.41	26.19	26.19
Montreal	27.65	31.35	33.34	35.32	35.32
New York Mets	−15.68	−24.46	−25.55	−26.63	−26.63
New York Yankees	−27.39	−45.81	−47.33	−48.85	−48.85
Oakland	10.83	14.55	15.81	17.07	17.07
Philadelphia	10.81	14.23	15.15	16.07	16.07
Pittsburgh	1.93	8.29	9.52	10.75	10.75
San Diego	9.40	11.2	11.64	12.08	12.08
San Francisco	−6.81	−5.49	−6.10	−6.72	−6.72
Seattle	−17.24	−27.89	−28.69	−29.48	−29.48
St. Louis	−7.44	−9.69	−10.49	−11.29	−11.29
Tampa Bay	8.51	13.61	14.02	14.42	14.42
Texas	−7.53	−10.47	−11.33	−12.18	−12.18
Toronto	9.50	13.59	14.33	15.06	15.06

Notes: These are estimates based on the level and distribution of teams net local revenues in 2001. These results do not include the impact of the luxury tax. It is noteworthy that, in addition to the fourteen net recipient teams, all of whom see their transfers augmented under the new plan, five of the net payor teams see their contributions diminish. The extra burden falls almost entirely on the top six revenue teams (Yankees, Mariners, Mets, Red Sox, Indians, and Braves), and of course, as discussed in the text, within this group the Yankees take the biggest hit.

It is difficult to imagine that the modest increases at the bottom will engender appreciably different team behavior in the labor market, particularly given the problem with the marginal rates discussed above. The Kansas City Royals are the fourth largest net recipient, and *USA Today Sports*

Weekly cited Royals owner David Glass telling his front office shortly after the agreement that they should be prepared to "slash payroll this winter."[64] Other reports state that Glass ordered a $10 million reduction in team payroll for 2003. At best, one would anticipate, some of the low-revenue teams may make an extra effort to re-sign more of their young talent.[65]

Thus the Yankees shoulder a very hefty additional burden while the teams at the bottom enjoy a relatively modest gain. The Players Association's resistance to the revenue sharing and luxury tax increases was largely out of concern for their impact at the top. Steinbrenner has been a pacesetter in the players' market. If his resources are diminished, the players are concerned that Steinbrenner will no longer push the salary envelope. When Steinbrenner lifts the salary scale at the top end, the middle and lower-end salaries generally follow upward, enabling the players' salary share to keep up with revenue increases. Of course, Steinbrenner is also concerned about his new tax burden, and this is why he asked his lawyer, David Boies, to look into bringing a legal claim against Major League Baseball. Steinbrenner's dismay could only have been deepened when his team was whipped by the Anaheim Angels—net revenue recipients of nearly $10 million in 2001—in the 2002 American League Division Series.

There will also be appreciable burdens for the Red Sox, Mets, and Mariners. They are the collateral damage for the assault on the free-spending Yankees. Red Sox owner John Henry stated in early October 2002 that he expected the new agreement to impart a substantial deterrent to payroll spending by the high-revenue teams:

> The Red Sox would have preferred a less onerous structure while still moving a quarter billion dollars per year. Almost 60 percent of the bill for this tidal wave of dollars is going to be paid by four teams. That seemed onerous to us. . . . There is no doubt in my mind that the monetary demand for free agents and arbitration-eligible players is going to drop this year. . . . I think this is a real plus for baseball.[66]

Thus, if the agreement is to have an impact on competitive balance, it is likely to show up via payroll compression at the top rather than payroll elevation at the bottom.

There is another approach to revenue sharing that would obviate the incentive problems of the new system. If the revenue sharing tax were based on *potential* rather than *actual* revenues, there would be no incentive issues.

Potential revenues (analogous to the economist's term *rent*) would be defined by the size and conditions (such as stadium age and lease terms) of a team's market. The larger the metropolitan area, other things equal, the larger the potential revenues.

A straightforward econometric technique could be used to estimate potential revenues. The basic idea is to estimate the relationship (via an equation) between team revenues and win percentage, using controls (dummy variables) for each market. Then, using the estimated equation, assume that a team's win percentage is .500. The predicted revenues will yield potential revenue for each team when its performance is average. The tax would then be applied to this (average) potential revenue. If the team performed above average, it would still pay the same tax as if it were at .500. That is, there would be no penalty (its tax would not go up) for performing well. Conversely, if it performed poorly, its tax would not go down; that is, there would be no incentive to perform poorly, as there is in the current system.[67] Weak teams from large markets, such as the Phillies, Tigers, and Blue Jays, would no longer qualify for handouts. The main drawback to such a system from the owners' perspective is that it would provide much less drag on player salaries than a tax on actual revenues,[68] but this could be dealt with more straightforwardly and appropriately through the luxury tax.

Another advantage to using potential, instead of actual, revenue is that it would skirt the problem of accounting gimmickry. As we saw in chapter four, through related-party transactions and other mechanisms, teams can (legally) manipulate their reported income. MLB has hired Pricewaterhouse-Coopers to oversee team revenue reporting, but the controls so far have not been effective. The Players Association is unlikely to call for more rigorous controls because it is in its interest to have teams pay a low revenue sharing tax. Since higher tax rates increase the incentive to hide revenue, it is likely that—absent new controls—accounting legerdemain will intensify under the new basic agreement. (The contributions and marginal rates calculated above assume no additional revenue shuffling by the teams.)

Luxury Tax

The sharpest struggle during the 2002 negotiations was over the luxury tax on high team payrolls. Even here, however, both sides agreed early on that there would be such a tax, and the only issues were the tax rate and the applicable payroll threshold. These realities suggested that common ground was attainable. The idea behind the luxury tax was that it would be a less draconian and more flexible version of a salary cap. A hard cap prevents a team from spending over a certain amount on the players. A luxury tax discourages, but allows, expenditures above a certain level.

Not only do teams have vastly different market endowments (population, corporate base, stadium age), but owners have different maximization strategies depending on the relationship between the ball team and an owner's other assets. These differences caused payroll differentials to explode after the mid-1990s, leading the owners to insist that a tax be levied in the name of improving competitive balance. The owners' initial proposal was that the portion of forty-man roster payrolls above $98 million be taxed at a rate of 50 percent. The players countered that they were philosophically opposed to the tax, but that position soon morphed into one where they would accept an initial threshold of $137.5 million and a tax rate of 15 percent.

Significantly, as noted above, in the 1996 basic agreement the two sides had agreed on a luxury tax of 35 percent for the top five teams in 1997 and 1998 (and 34 percent in 1999), and the tax had no discernible effect on salary growth. Don Fehr argued that the earlier luxury tax was phased out as revenue sharing was phased in, and this was crucial because it is the joint impact of the two policies that matters. Fehr also noted that the earlier tax did not have a fixed numerical threshold, so it constituted a moving target that was harder for the clubs to anticipate and react to.[69] For each of these reasons, Fehr said that with the proposed increase in revenue sharing the players could not abide a substantial luxury tax this time.

In the face of Fehr's resistance, the owners lowered their proposed rates and raised their threshold. The final system, which is much closer to the players' position and is less onerous than the 1997–99 system, is depicted in table 5-6. The payroll threshold begins at $117 million in 2003 and rises to $136.5 million in 2006. The tax rate increases from 17.5 percent for first-time offenders to 30 percent for second-time consecutive offenders and to 40 percent for teams that cross the payroll threshold three years in a row. Given the negligible effect of the 1997–99 luxury tax, it is hard to imagine that the new system will provide much drag on high-end payrolls.[70]

Nonetheless, some owners may use the tax—low as it is—as a pretext for cutting payrolls. Rangers owner Tom Hicks, for instance, pledged that his team would never pay a luxury tax, meaning that his team payroll would always be below the threshold. This is precisely the signaling effect that the

Table 5-6. *Luxury Tax Thresholds and Breach Rates, 2003–06*

Year	Threshold (millions of dollars)	First breach (percent)	Second breach (percent)	Third breach (percent)
2003	117.0	17.5	…	…
2004	120.5	22.5	30.0	…
2005	128.0	22.5	30.0	40.0
2006	136.5	No tax	30.0	40.0

Source: *Sports Business Daily,* September 4, 2002, p. 8.

owners seek. If the tax were to have such a prohibitive impact, then its significance would be the same as a salary cap. It is more likely, however, in the context of the still enormous revenue disparities, the different owner objective functions, and the structure of the new luxury tax, that the policy will be little more than a nuisance to a few top teams.

Another factor that might diminish the tax's impact is the possibility of payroll manipulation. Straightforward manipulation, such as employing large signing bonuses or restructuring contracts to make salaries jump one year and fall the next to avoid consecutive breaches, won't work. This is because signing bonuses will count the same as salary, and salary will be computed as the average annual compensation over the life of the contract.[71] Yet, what is to stop Steinbrenner from transferring $5 million of Bernie Williams's salary to a "personal services" contract with the YES network or Red Sox owner John Henry from signing Jeremy Giambi to a modest baseball salary plus a guaranteed executive or broadcasting job at NESN after he retires? A similar cap-evading strategy was employed by the NFL Denver Broncos' owner, Pat Bowlen, in signing John Elway to his last contract. Instead of paying Elway a higher salary, he offered to sell him a share of the team at a discounted price.

The Yankees will have a strong incentive to use their YES network in creative ways to reduce player payroll. If the team stays at its $171.5 million annual forty-man payroll, it will pay luxury taxes of $9.5 million in 2003 (and a total revenue sharing and luxury tax of $55.3 million) and $14 million in 2006 (for a total bill of $62.9 million).[72]

Two additional provisions regarding the luxury tax are also to the union's liking. First, if the two sides do not agree on a new contract for the 2007 season, the 2003–06 contract would remain in effect but without any luxury tax. This provision provides an additional incentive to the owners to bargain constructively for a new deal.[73] Second, if a team does not pay a luxury tax in 2005, it does not pay any tax in 2006, no matter how high its payroll might go in that year. This provision would allow a team that was below the threshold in 2005 to load up on payroll in 2006 without penalty.

Other Considerations

One significant change was made in amateur draft policy. A team that is unable to sign a first-round pick is given an extra first-round pick in the same position the following year.[74] This will help low-revenue clubs (which are more likely to lose their first-round picks).

The two sides agreed in concept to introduce an international draft, but they could not agree on the implementation details. A joint committee will study implementation with the hope of putting it into practice in June 2004. It is disappointing that other balance-enhancing prospective reforms (such as giving additional draft picks to low-revenue teams, instituting a professional player draft,[75] and allowing the trading or selling of draft picks) were not carried out.[76]

(Interestingly, after the Yankees won their fourth consecutive World Series in 1939, the owners of American League clubs passed a rule intended to break the Yankees' victory string. The rule barred each year's pennant winner from buying, selling, or trading any player within the league during the following season. The Tigers edged out the Bronx Bombers for the 1940 pennant and the owners repealed the rule, only to see the Yankees storm back with a vengeance to win the next three pennants in a row. Maybe the rule worked!)[77]

The owners' requested changes in the arbitration system were not accepted. The system will remain unchanged. Debt limits will be set in line with team EBITDA (earnings before interest, taxes, depreciation, and amortization) with a three-year grace period, rather than the 60/40 system that Selig attempted to install. Neither long-term player contracts nor deferred compensation will count as debt under the new system.[78] The two sides did, however, agree that player deferred compensation must be fully funded within eighteen months of the year in which it is earned.

Contraction is tabled until 2006. If the owners decide to contract for the 2007 season, the MLBPA agrees not to bring an NLRB challenge and not to undertake or encourage an antitrust complaint. However, in order to contract for 2007, the owners must take a vote between April 1, 2006, and July 1, 2006, and must notify the players of their intent (and provide a 2007 playing schedule) by that latter date. Further, the owners agree that any effort at contraction will not involve more than two teams and that the Players Association will have full rights to bargain over the effects of contraction.

As mentioned earlier, the two sides also agreed to improve the players' benefit plan (with the owners' annual contribution increasing from $70 million to $115 million) and to raise the minimum wage from $200,000 to $300,000. Finally, the players agreed to testing for anabolic androgenic steroids throughout the agreement.[79]

Assessing the Accord

The 2002 agreement is the product of compromise. The owners' original revenue sharing plan called for the redistribution of $250 million annually under the straight-pool system. The players called for a redistribution of $184 million under the split pool. The final compromise on this issue is considerably closer to the owners' position: roughly $255 million to be redistributed at full implementation (with lesser amounts in 2003 and 2004) under a system that is three-quarters straight and one-quarter split pool. The final compromise on the luxury tax, however, is much closer to the players' position. The threshold rises from $117 million to $136.5 million, and the rates vary from 17.5 percent to 40 percent, depending on the number of transgressions.

The agreement is likely to produce some modest changes in the desired direction. Over the agreement's four-year period, close to $1 billion will be shifted from the top to the bottom teams. It will be surprising if this does not level performance outcomes somewhat, mostly by blunting the top rather than lifting the bottom.

As shown in table 5-7, the new system (at full implementation) places a proportionately larger burden on the top quartile of teams (whose tax share rises from roughly 67 percent under the old system to 72 percent under the new one) and provides a proportionately smaller gain to the bottom quartile (whose share of proceeds falls from roughly 70 percent to 63 percent). The middle two quartiles benefit disproportionately from the new system.[80]

Table 5-7. *Revenue Sharing Systems Compared*

Millions of dollars

	Total redistributed	By quartile[a]			
		1st	*2d*	*3d*	*4th*
New system (2005)	253.35[b]	−182.15	−71.2	+89.15	+154.2
Share (percent)		71.9	28.1	36.6	63.4
Old system (2001)	168.24	−112.52	−55.7	+50.37	+117.87
Share (percent)		66.9	33.1	29.9	70.1

Source: Estimates based on MLB data.

a. With thirty teams, the quartiles are divided as follows: eight teams in each of the first two quartiles (together they include the sixteen payors) and seven teams in each of the bottom two quartiles (together including the fourteen recipients).

b. This total includes $10 million collected equally from each team for the discretionary fund. The recipients' total is $243.35 million because it is not determined how this $10 million will be distributed.

MLB will generate in excess of $15 billion in revenue over the period, so the new revenue sharing schemes will redistribute less than 7 percent of the game's resources. Because of this and because of the incentive problems discussed, the procompetitive balance effect is likely to be minor.

Some salary restraint is also likely to flow from the new agreement. Marginal tax rates in the neighborhood of 37 to 47 percent, along with the luxury tax, will deter salary growth. The new debt rule (connecting allowable debt to team cash flow), to take effect in 2006, along with new financing requirements for deferred salary, should further retard player salaries.

Factors outside the agreement, however, are likely to inhibit salary growth even more. The recessionary economic conditions, along with the stock market's travails and the bleak financial fortunes of several team owners whose other investments have foundered, probably provide a more powerful deterrent to salary growth than anything in the new agreement.[81] The widespread introduction of well-educated, business-minded managers into teams' front offices as well as the increased use of statistical analysis to assess player potential may also help to put a damper on salary growth. Also, MLB is unloading some top talent from the Expos (currently owned by MLB), and the increased availability of star Japanese players will help to retard free-agent bidding.

Further, insurance companies are making it more difficult and costly to insure the value of long-term player contracts. Not only have premiums increased, but companies are limiting contract coverage to three years and declining to insure certain body parts for previously injured players. These constraints likely will put an additional damper on lucrative long-term deals.[82]

The industry's finances, as analyzed in chapter four, are more a distributional than an aggregate issue. The new revenue sharing transfers will help modestly to alleviate this imbalance.

Baseball has experienced a lack of performance parity since the mid-1990s. Something needed to be done, but the magnitude of the problem is several orders below the dire characterizations of Selig. Selig in 2001 referred to the Oakland A's as an aberration. What were the Oakland A's in 2002, or the Minnesota Twins in 2002? String together a few aberrations and pretty soon you have an incipient dynasty.

The success of the Twins and A's notwithstanding, the correlation between payrolls and on-field success has been too strong to ignore.[83] Although the new labor agreement will contribute mildly to rectifying the imbalance, the financial trajectory of the industry is likely to contribute even more. Central fund revenues (which are divided equally among the teams) should experience solid growth during the course of the agreement.[84] There is an automatic step-up in the national television money, sponsorship revenues have soared, baseball's Internet income is projected to reach $100 million net by 2005, and international revenues have grown handsomely.

Simultaneously, the low-revenue Padres, Reds, and Phillies will be playing in new stadiums, and there are likely to be new challenges to the ability of cable companies to pass along sports programming costs to consumers, perhaps resulting in lower local cable revenues. This tendency is seen most clearly in the shutting down in November 2002 of Paul Allen's regional sports channel, which had been formed to carry the NBA's Portland Trailblazers. Local cable distributors were unwilling to pay the rates that Allen sought. And although there was an additional motivation involved, Steinbrenner's difficulty in getting Cablevision to put his YES network on expanded basic at $2 per subscriber is another case in point. Together these forces are bound to produce some additional leveling in the distribution of club revenues.

Amelioration notwithstanding, it is difficult to imagine that the distributional and financial tensions that were perceived to afflict the industry in 2002 will disappear by 2007. And additional tensions may emerge, as clubs

in the larger markets encounter new problems and those i
may face the renewed prospect of contraction. There is I
the game will need other changes to avoid another labor
frontation next time.

What Have We Learned?

Two themes seem to repeat themselves in baseball's collective bargaining: owner discord and distrust between players and owners. In 2002, it may have appeared to many observers that the owners had discovered a new unity. Any perceived unity, however, was only skin deep. Commissioner Selig imposed a gag order on the owners and threatened fines of up to $1 million for owners who spoke publicly about the collective bargaining process or the game's economics.

There is ample evidence that there was as much dissension this time as ever. For instance, one anonymous medium-market club owner told the *Illinois Daily Herald* in late July 2002:

> You think this is funny but this is how Bud operates. He tells 30 own-
> ers 30 different things and then slaps a gag order on us and threatens
> us with a million-dollar fine so that the players don't find out we all
> hate what's going on. We're supposed to be unified? That's laughable.
> Lift the gag order again, and you'll see how unified. Now, on top of
> everything else in Montreal, the [former Expos] minority owners have
> filed racketeering charges against Bud and [Marlins managing gen-
> eral partner] Jeff [Loria], and if the books of every team are exposed
> during that legal fight, you can say goodbye to Bud and any deal with
> the players. This is more dangerous than you can imagine. Bud is play-
> ing with fire here and we're all getting burned. I'm convinced Bud got
> his contract extension by threatening 10 of us, making promises to
> the other 10 and loaning money to the last 10. This thing is on the
> track headed for a disaster, and Bud is right there in the front of the
> train conducting the whole operation."[85]

In a moment of public candor, Selig told the Associated Press after the owners voted 29 to 1 to ratify the new labor deal: "I'm not going to suggest to you today that there are not clubs with very different views, but at some point you have to come together."[86]

Some have characterized the group of thirty owners as a three-headed monster: the big-revenue owners who want less revenue sharing, no luxury taxes, and accommodation with the players; the low-revenue owners who want more revenue sharing, high luxury taxes, and a tough stance toward the players; and the middle-revenue owners who want various permutations in between. Of course, ownership strategies and synergies differ, as do owner ideologies and personalities, and these differences create still more subdivisions among the owners.

It is only a small exaggeration to characterize the beginning of each collective bargaining period as follows. The owners meet to discuss what changes they want to make to the game's economic system. They can't agree on basic changes, let alone a farsighted, comprehensive plan for the game's future. After hours or days of discussion they discover that they all agree on one thing: they'd like player salaries to be lower; and it is this lowest common denominator that forms the basis for the collective bargaining proposals. Before 2002, these proposals often came in the form of a demand for a salary cap, along with various side demands, such as raising the service limit for arbitration eligibility.

Other than the 1972 strike that affected the regular season for nine days, all subsequent work stoppages in baseball ensued from owner demands for change. Since the players won free agency in 1976,[87] during each contract negotiation they have been confronted by an ownership demand that free agency be abridged in one way or another. The owners always came to the table without a cohesive vision for the industry but with a demand for unilateral sacrifice by the players. In practice, as implemented by the commissioner's office, the subtext was often to break the union. Along the way, the owners cried poverty as the players experienced ownership collusion and saw franchise values rising.

In the 2001–02 round of negotiations the divisions among the owners were reflected in Selig's on-again, off-again approach to bargaining. After receiving the blue-ribbon panel's report in July 2000, Selig delayed for almost a year before beginning informal discussions with the players. This delay can be understood in part as an effort to develop a unified bargaining position among the owners. In the spring of 2001, Selig authorized Paul Beeston to begin informal negotiations with the players—which the players say were advancing very constructively—but Selig abruptly terminated the negotiations without explanation or notice to the players. One could attribute this erratic behavior to a peculiar personality trait of the commissioner, but more likely it was a reflection of dueling ownership groups putting pressure on the process.

With ownership trying to hold its ranks together, its public posture becomes stiffer and its claims more exaggerated. Player distrust becomes more entrenched, such that even if the industry were actually in desperate financial straits the Players Association would not believe it. The owners present partial financial information, but it is not sufficiently extensive or transparent to persuade anyone outside the choir. The media, in turn, tend to choose sides and see the issues as black or white.

Herein lies one of the reasons why a salary cap is a nonstarter in baseball negotiations. The Players Association says it doesn't want a system that precludes owners from paying players as much as they want to pay them. True enough, but it is also true that players fight for mechanisms that will prevent the salary share in revenues from slipping. Players, for instance, defend the high-revenue teams, because these teams are seen as the trailblazers for the salary scale. By leading the way in signing the star players to stratospheric contracts, the high-revenue teams are the ones that ensure salaries will rise with team revenues. But if the players are concerned that the salary share in revenues might fall, why not buy into a salary cap system as long as the established player share were high enough?

One major reason is distrust. Salary caps by definition give players a share of revenues. If players don't trust the owners' revenue numbers, then they can never get to the point of negotiating about what the share of revenue should be. To get beyond this obstacle, owners need to acknowledge the revenue shuffling that goes on and provide full transparency in their financial reports to the players.

A second reason, from the players' perspective, is that a cap system needs a mechanism to curtail runaway owner profits when revenue growth exceeds the inflation rate. If team revenues are growing at, say, 10 percent and inflation is 2 percent, with a constant player share, profits will experience explosive growth. Assume that industry revenues in year one are $4 billion and the salary share is 60 percent, or $2.4 billion. Also, assume that nonsalary costs are $1.4 billion, leaving a profit of $200 million. Now, if revenues and player salaries grow at 10 percent a year for four years, in year five revenues will be $5.86 billion and salaries will be $3.52 billion (still 60 percent of revenues). However, if nonsalary costs grow at the rate of inflation, they will be $1.52 billion in year five and profits will be $820 million. That is, profits will have grown more than fourfold over the four-year period, or at an annual rate of 42.3 percent.

This runaway profit phenomenon will occur whenever revenue growth is significantly above the underlying rate of inflation and the salary share is fixed. In the ten years between 1992 and 2002, the revenue of all of the big four team sports leagues grew many times faster than the rate of inflation. Once again, designing a mechanism to allow the salary share to rise in such circumstances (preventing runaway profits) requires confidence in the financial numbers that ownership shares.

The long-standing experience of deception and distrust requires that owners work proactively to bring the players aboard. When Selig pretended that he was being forthcoming with MLB's financial numbers in December 2001, he convinced some journalists and many members of the public. But he failed to convince most members of Congress and certainly failed to convince the Players Association. Indeed, Selig instructed his labor negotiator, Rob Manfred, to send the Players Association a letter warning them that they could not comment on the numbers Selig was providing to Congress.

The appropriate relationship between owners and players is one of partnership. For partnership to work, the owners must undertake vigorous and consistent efforts to involve the Players Association in strategic and financial planning. These changes will demand new, strong leadership and open communications.

Of course, partnership is a two-way street, and a new attitude will also be needed from the Players Association. The union has wrapped itself in the ideology of the free market for good reasons. Open competition among the teams for players' services has been a boon for salaries. But the baseball industry itself is a cartel, and the players as well as the owners have been the beneficiaries of monopoly power.[88]

As noted in chapter three, monopoly sports leagues need some internal restraints on open competition among the teams in order to attain a necessary modicum of competitive balance and to be successful. Those restraints include the players' market. In an industry where the range from top to bottom team revenue grew from $30 million in 1989 to $208 million in 2001, and where some owners develop important synergies between the team and related businesses that might be worth tens of millions of dollars annually, there is a potentially reasonable case to be made for an effective luxury tax on high team payrolls.

This case is bolstered by the possibility of the winner's-curse phenomenon. The winner's-curse hypothesis says that if five owners—all operating on essentially the same information—bid $4 million for a player and a sixth owner bids $5 million, the latter will get the player but the weight of the evidence suggests that the player is only worth $4 million. In this case, the intensity of the competition has led the sixth owner to overbid for the player's services.[89] (Of course, it is also possible that the sixth owner is right and the others were wrong, or that the player has a higher value to the sixth owner.)

While a new attitude from the union will be needed, the initiative must rightfully come from the owners. Former MLB commissioner Fay Vincent wrote in 2002: "Baseball's biggest problem today is the same as it was when I came into the game fifteen years ago: The leadership in baseball thinks the players' union is the enemy. I believe they have it completely wrong: The players' union protects the owners from themselves."[90]

CHAPTER SIX

The Stadium Issue

Between 1989 and 2001 sixteen baseball-only stadiums were
built for major-league teams. During the previous thirteen
years, none had been built.[1] The total cost of the sixteen new facilities was $4.9 billion in current dollars, with an average development
cost of $306 million. Of the $4.9 billion, $3.27 billion, or 66.7 percent, came
from public coffers.[2] If the anomalous and largely privately financed PacBell
Park in San Francisco is left out, the public share rises to 70.7 percent. In late
2002, three more stadiums were under construction and five additional
ones had been proposed.

Public financing for these baseball stadiums has been facilitated by the
ability of most local governments to issue federal-tax-exempt bonds to help
pay for construction. This exemption permits the issued municipal bonds
to carry an interest rate roughly one-third lower than it would otherwise be.
By allowing this exemption, the federal government reduces the debt service
or financing costs for stadium bonds and thereby subsidizes stadium construction, the economic benefits of which go overwhelmingly to team owners and players. The present value of the federal subsidy on a $225 million
stadium financed with thirty-year tax-exempt bonds has been estimated to
be between $47 million and $94 million.[3] This estimate implies that the
present value of the federal government subsidy to the construction of the
sixteen major league ballparks built since 1989 lies between $683 million
and $1.37 billion.

On reflection, stadium construction is a curious activity for the federal
government to subsidize. MLB, like other team sports leagues, is a monopoly. As a monopolist, it artificially reduces the number of franchises relative

to the demand for franchises from economically viable cities. With excess demand for teams, cities are thrust into competition with each other to obtain or retain a team. This competition leads cities to offer public funds for facility construction and more favorable lease terms. The greater the competition, the more financing and the more concessionary the lease terms the city must offer.

Naturally, smaller cities have to offer more subvention than larger ones. It would make little sense for John Henry, for instance, to threaten to move his Red Sox out of Boston. Boston is the nation's six largest media market. It has more than 4,600 businesses with more than 100 employees (ranked sixth nationwide). It has a rich baseball culture and a storied ballpark. If Henry were to threaten, Boston would have little cause to worry. Kansas City or San Diego would have more cause.

George Steinbrenner, of course, once threatened to leave New York, but, Rudy Giuliani notwithstanding, the city has not yet built the Yankees a new stadium.[4] The Yankees are still in the Bronx. In any event, by subsidizing stadium construction, the federal government also encourages U.S. cities to compete with each other to host Major League Baseball. Even if one believed that baseball would be economically or socially beneficial to an area, there is no general reason for the federal government to support one city's bid over another's. From the country's perspective, it is a zero-sum process—what is one town's gain is another's loss.

Most stadium projects pass through a similar political process. A team owner proclaims that his team needs a new stadium to remain competitive in the league.[5] The need is sufficiently dire, says the owner, that he or she will have to consider moving the team if public financing for a new facility is not forthcoming.

In April 2001, Commissioner Selig added a new twist to this scenario by sending a letter to a Florida state senator, Alex Villalobos, threatening that without public financing the Marlins might either be moved or eliminated. Selig's letter read in part as follows: "This current plan [about to be voted on by the state legislature] provides a final opportunity for the Marlins to remain in South Florida. . . . The Marlins would be a prime candidate for contraction or relocation. Bluntly, the Marlins cannot and will not survive in South Florida without a new stadium."[6] The threat of contraction may be less risky than a threat to relocate because it does not directly implicate the local owner as the perpetrator and thereby alienate the local fan base.[7]

Once the demand for a new facility has been made public, it is relatively simple to line up support from local beneficiaries: contractors, construction companies, construction unions, architectural firms, bankers who hope to float the bonds, lawyers who work for the bankers, and assorted business groups who expect to benefit privately from stadium construction. With an important part of the private sector mobilized, the team owner and his allies then turn to key politicians for support. Along the way a public relations campaign is mounted.[8] Part of this campaign is the hiring of a large consulting firm (such as KPMG or Deloitte & Touche) to produce an economic impact study of a new ballpark. These reports employ an inappropriate methodology, based on antiquated input-output models and unrealistic assumptions, to project the effect of a new baseball facility. Invariably, they conclude that hundreds of millions of dollars and thousands of jobs would be generated annually from the project.

When stadium projects are submitted to referendum, the vote is usually close. Indeed, if the vote were not close, then the stadium proponents would have done a poor job estimating the public's willingness to support the plan. For instance, if a proposal to build a new stadium with $100 million in public funding were approved with 60 percent of the vote, then the proponents would have underestimated the public's willingness to subsidize. They might have been able to request $150 million and win the referendum with only 51 percent of the vote.

Given that these votes are generally tight, the swaying of a few percentage points of voters to one side can be decisive. Thus, to be effective, the economic impact reports by consulting firms do not have to convince many people.

The Economic Impact of New Ballparks

There are very few fields of economic research that produce unanimous agreement. Yet every independent economic analysis on the impact of stadiums has found no predictable positive effect on output or employment.[9] Some studies have even concluded that there is a possible negative impact.[10] Why?

Despite the enormity of its cultural presence, baseball is still a relatively small business. Yearly average team revenues in MLB are approximately $112 million. For a medium-size city like St. Louis, the baseball team accounts for around 0.3 percent of local economic activity; for a large city like New York, a baseball team contributes only 0.03 percent of economic output. Teams typically employ between 70 and 130 people in their front offices. Beyond this, they hire 1,000–1,500 day-of-game personnel who work in unskilled, low-wage, temporary, part-time jobs. It is problematic to attribute even these jobs to the sports team, however.

Apart from their relatively small size, there are three main reasons why professional sports teams do not promote economic development: the substitution effect; extensive leakages; and, the likely negative effect on local government budgets.

The Substitution Effect

The vast majority of consumers has a largely inflexible leisure budget. If a sports team moves to town, the money one spends taking the family to a game typically is money that is not spent at a local bowling alley, golf course, restaurant, concert hall, or theater. The net effect on spending in the metropolitan area then is zero, or very close to zero. Although sports teams may relocate the spending and economic activity within an urban area, they are not likely to add much to it.

The main exception to this logic is when a team attracts people from out of town to its games. Some teams have claimed that as many as one-third of its fans come from outside the metropolitan area. The Baltimore Orioles, for instance, have claimed this, but a Virginia group trying to bring a team to the Washington, D.C., area commissioned a study in 2001 that found the share coming from the greater D.C. area was only 13 percent. Unlike some other such analyses, this study provided details of its methodology, and its sampling technique appeared to be appropriately random.[11]

Indeed, the experience of major league teams in the various sports leagues suggests that between 5 and 20 percent of fans are from "out of the area."[12] Of course, this range depends on how one defines the area. A strict definition of urban limits, and hence a smaller radius around the stadium or arena, implies a larger percentage from outside the area. A combined MSA (metropolitan statistical area), which includes several counties, implies a smaller proportion of fans from outside the area. Thus the smaller the radius chosen for a promotional study, the great the amount of "new spending."[13]

Further, there is considerable evidence that most out-of-state fans at most sporting events do not come to town *because of* the game.[14] Rather, they are in town for business reasons, to see family, or for other leisure activities. If they were not at the game, they would spend their money on other entertainment in the same city. So their disbursements in and around the ballpark substitute for other local spending. Also, they may be guests of a local business or family who pays for the tickets and concessions, in which case there still is no new money attracted from outside the area.

Some stadium proponents have also argued that the local sports team attracts visiting media personnel from other cities. This, of course, is as true for journalists as it is for television or radio reporters and team members themselves. But there is generally no net contribution here, because the inflow is offset by a similar outflow of team members and media personnel when the local team plays away games.

In addition to attracting some new spending from out-of-state fans, professional sports teams receive distributions of national television contracts and other funds from their central league office. To the extent that these funds remain in the local economy, additional new local demand may be attributed to a sports team. As I explain next, however, there are substantial leakages that retard or negate this effect.

Leakages

Approximately 53 to 55 percent of MLB team revenue goes to player compensation at the major league level. Thus when a team's revenue rises by $10 to $50 million as a result of playing in a new facility, the majority of the added revenue goes to the players. The remaining 45 to 47 percent goes to the owners and to help defray additional costs, if any, associated with the new facility. The impact of this spending on local economies depends on how much of it is respent locally and how much leaks out to other areas.

First, with average player salaries of $2.4 million, most players and owners face the top federal marginal tax rate (38.6 percent),[15] plus an additional 1.45 percent in Medicare tax.[16] Thus over 40 percent of their incremental income leaks directly from the local economy to Washington, D.C. Second, high incomes also lead to higher savings rates, especially for players, whose incomes are sensibly viewed as transitory. Most of these savings leak out of the local economy and into the world's money markets. Third, more often than not, players do not live year-round in their team's local community, and frequently owners do not either. Their families and principal homes are elsewhere.[17] Even if they do live locally, their high incomes allow them to travel extensively and own a home or homes elsewhere. Thus a large share of their spending takes place outside the team's host city. Fourth, prices for food items at a ballpark or arena are considerably higher than at normal retail establishments, and a large part of this price differential is siphoned off by the facility concessionaire company, which more often than not is based elsewhere. Fifth, 11–12 percent of team revenues on average go to player development for the teams' minor league systems. Generally, this money is spent outside the major league team's host city.

Contrast these leakages from sports expenditures with those from entertainment dollars spent at locally owned businesses, such as bowling alleys, theaters, or restaurants. The proprietors of such businesses likely face a lower marginal tax rate than either owners or players, have lower saving rates, and do the bulk of their spending in the local metropolitan area. These leakages mean that the vaunted multiplier from expenditures at a baseball stadium is much lower than at other leisure venues. It is likely that the appropriate baseball-expenditures multiplier is close to 1.2; in contrast to the 2.5 to 3.0 figure often used in the promotional impact studies performed by consulting companies.[18]

Budgetary Impact

Because sports facilities are not expected to generate additional net output in a metropolitan area, they cannot be counted on to augment tax collections. Indeed, public expenditures occasioned by operating a sports facility generally exceed the revenue generated by it. To assess the budgetary impact of a new facility, however, it is necessary to know its financing and lease terms.

If the financing burden is large and is borne primarily by public coffers, and if the lease terms are concessionary to the team, then the public obligation for debt service, infrastructure maintenance, environmental remediation, incremental sanitation and security expenses, probable cost overruns, forgone property taxes, and subsequent facility enhancement is likely to generate a substantial budgetary hole in the municipal, county, and/or state accounts. Where state funding is involved, getting the necessary votes for a stadium in one district often requires logrolling to garner support for dubious projects elsewhere in the state, thereby increasing the real cost of stadium construction. Such budgetary gaps must be filled with decreased government services or higher taxes, either of which will produce a drag on the local economy.

Unfortunately for host cities, the monopoly status of the major team sports leagues has enabled the teams to drive impressive bargains in negotiating financing and lease terms. Even as baseball stadiums have grown more and more expensive, in some cases costing more than half a billion dollars, public contributions to construction costs have continued to average nearly 70 percent. Quirk and Fort, after studying twenty-five facilities built between 1978 and 1992, concluded that the host cities provided each team with an average operating subsidy of $7 million per year.[19] In none of the cases did the host city receive a positive net operating income from the facility. The perverse influence of the 1986 Tax Reform Act on lease terms (detailed in chapter seven) and the escalating costs of recent facility construction suggest that the size of these subsidies has only grown since 1992.

Promotional economic impact studies often claim that the actual construction of the sports facility provides a positive economic stimulus. The problem with this contention is that the funds to build the stadium or arena have an opportunity cost. If the construction is funded by the city, then the city must raise the money via higher taxes or reduced services. Spending on construction thereby causes lower spending by the government in other areas or lower disposable household income. If stimulating a local economy were so simple, every municipal government could guarantee full employment with a public works program that hired workers to dig huge holes in the ground and then hired other workers to fill the holes. Only when some of the funding comes from state or federal coffers can the city expect a net job gain from facility construction, and in this case the gain would come at the expense of worker layoffs elsewhere in the state or country.[20] This reasoning, based on both multiplier and budget impact analysis, is consistent with the results of empirical studies that fail to detect any discernible positive effects on local economic growth associated with a sports facility or a team.

Another common contention is that sports facilities "put a city on the map." Cities with major league teams are shown periodically on national or international television. The result, it is said, is increased tourism and business. While the claim is theoretically plausible in part, there is no empirical evidence to back it up.

The part of the contention that is not plausible is the notion that businesses will relocate to the city because it becomes "big league." Sound businesses move in search of a more qualified or less expensive labor force, a convenient location for inputs or sales, a good infrastructure, a sound fiscal environment with a favorable tax policy, attractive government services, cutting-edge research laboratories, good schools and hospitals, and appealing cultural opportunities. The latter may include local theater, opera, symphony, parks, art museums, universities, or sports teams. If the first half-dozen or so items are equivalent between two cities, then the business may look at cultural amenities and consider sports. It does not seem plausible that the presence or absence of sports teams would be a decisive location factor for more than a few companies. There is no systematic evidence that business relocations follow sports teams.

Other Effects of Stadium Construction

Income Redistribution

Some have characterized publicly financed stadiums as massive reverse Robin Hood schemes. The single largest source of public financing has been the sales tax. Since 1990 the sales tax has accounted for 29 percent of the public funds going to baseball stadium construction.[21] The sales tax is regressive, falling disproportionately on lower-income families.

New stadiums generate tens of millions of dollars for teams annually. More than half of this goes to the players, and a good share of the balance goes to the owners. That is, this extra revenue—which comes disproportionately from lower-income families—ends up in the pockets of millionaires, or in some cases billionaires.

Further, new ballparks are gentrified. They cater especially to higher-income groups with their club seats, luxury suites, restaurants, and other amenities. Public money builds the parks, and the team, in turn, charges higher ticket prices to the public. In 2002, according to *Team Marketing Report*'s annual survey, it cost an average of $145 to take a family of four to the ballpark.

Core Redevelopment

Potentially there is also some good news. Even though it is difficult to justify new stadium construction on economic growth grounds, such construction could facilitate efforts to redevelop an urban core. Many downtown areas in U.S. cities were devastated by the suburbanization trend that began in the 1950s. In an effort to revitalize their central city and restore an aura of cultural vibrancy, many municipal governments have subsidized efforts at economic development in the city's core. Sports facilities are often part of this strategy.

Since it is possible for sports facilities to rearrange economic activity within an urban area, such strategies seem plausible. The impact of the sports stadium alone on the rest of an urban core, however, is likely to be small. A stand-alone baseball park with eighty-one games a year is unlikely to induce many rational independent retailers to invest in adjacent businesses. This is particularly so for the modern ballpark, whose raison d'etre is to capture as much of the fans' spending within the confines of the stadium as possible. Therefore, it is necessary to plan the surrounding activities with appropriate synergies, and usually this calls for other public investment projects.

Cultural Enrichment

Cities do not build downtown playgrounds and public parks because they believe that jobs will be created or that incomes will be elevated. They build them to enrich the cultural life of their citizens.

Ballparks, by helping a city attract a new or retain (or improve) an existing team, may serve a similar function. A baseball team in town generally brings pleasure to a significant share of the population. Part of this population pays to see the team play at the ballpark; another part pays to watch it on cable; another enjoys watching it for free on off-air television or listening to it on the radio. Still another and larger part of the population enjoys reading about the team in the newspaper, hearing about it on the news, or talking about it at the watercooler at work or at cocktail parties.

Some may argue that this is low-brow entertainment, or worse, a mind-dulling waste of time. But pleasure is pleasure and is in the eye of the beholder, not some cultural critic. Insofar as part of this amusement comes without the public's paying for it, the public benefits from an externality.

Other members of the public are intense fans. Even though they have to spend $145 or more to take their family to a game, they may derive $300 worth of satisfaction from the activity. These people are experiencing a consumer surplus. Having the ball team in town makes this possible.[22]

Still another possible justification for public expenditures on a facility is that a ballpark (and team) may bring public goods benefits to a community—

that is, benefits from which it is impossible to exclude any individual. In the case of a stadium these benefits may include self-image enhancement for a city or greater community cohesion.

The prospective existence of externalities, consumer surplus, and public goods benefits provides a justification for some public financial support. Properly, before allocating such funding, a stadium should be compared with other projects with similar potential to create direct or indirect benefits for the community. However, it is important to recall that, unlike the benefits of a public park or art museum, the financial benefits from a new ballpark are privately appropriated. While some public funding may still be justified, it is not that portion of support that follows from MLB's ability to thrust cities into competition with each other. I return to this matter in chapter seven.

Finally, it should be emphasized that new stadiums do not automatically produce more revenue for a team. New stadiums only represent the potential for new revenue. For this potential to be realized, the team must sell tickets, concessions, signage, and so on. Whether it succeeds will depend in part on its marketing efforts and skills and in larger part on the playing field success of the team. A star player generally attracts more fans to the ballpark, because of both his personal achievement and the improved performance of the team. If these additional fans pay more for their seats in a new park, spend more on concessions, and stimulate more company advertising, then the value contributed by this player (his marginal revenue product) increases. With a new ballpark, therefore, team ownership should be able to bid more aggressively for talent and improve the quality of the team.

Herein is the potential for synergy between a new stadium and team quality. If this potential is realized, the new stadium will provide a significant revenue boost for the team that lasts several years. If the ownership, however, stands on its heels and expects revenues to pour in without improving team quality, it is likely to experience what the Detroit Tigers, Milwaukee Brewers, and Pittsburgh Pirates did in the second year of their new facilities. The first year, fans were attracted by curiosity about the new stadiums. By year two, the stadiums themselves were insufficient to keep them coming.

It also warrants mentioning that where a team lies in the stadium construction cycle affects team quality and revenue. The Baltimore Orioles were first in the present stadium cycle with Camden Yards in 1992. Because they were the first example of the new retropark in downtown, there was more curiosity and attention—including extensive interest from outside the Baltimore–Washington, D.C., area. Also because they were first, the additional $30 million or so in revenues the team received enabled it to develop a competitive edge. As other teams added stadiums, they were simply catching up to the Orioles, not stepping out in front. For all of these reasons, a new stadium is not a panacea for a team's economic woes.

CHAPTER SEVEN

What Is to Be Done?

It is not always best to let things be, though it is probably easiest. Major League Baseball is a monopoly: it is the only provider of top-level professional baseball in the country.[1] Economists believe that this condition leads to a number of undesirable outcomes: lower output, higher prices, indifferent service to the consumer, and inefficiency.

The general remedy that economists propose for such a condition is either divestiture (breaking up the monopoly into more than one firm) or, in the case of clear economies of scale, regulation. Of course, in the general case, the industry would not also benefit from a presumed antitrust exemption. The U.S. House of Representatives and Senate have been prompted to consider public policy remedies for baseball more than sixty times since 1950, sixteen times since 1990.[2] Congress has never acted to either regulate or break up MLB. With one minor exception, it has also never acted to take away baseball's presumed antitrust exemption.

In this chapter I discuss what a rational public policy toward the professional baseball industry might look like. In doing so, I consider public subsidies for stadiums, tax issues, cable and broadcasting policy, and antitrust/regulation matters. I conclude with some proposals for ways MLB might more effectively self-regulate.

Before embarking on this course, however, it is good to remember that in the past rational public policy toward baseball has been impeded by "rational" politics—that is, politics where politicians act in their own best interest. Recall the poignant and prescient comments of Representative Emanuel Celler, the chair of the early 1950s House committee investigating the baseball antitrust exemption: "I want to say . . . that I have never known, in my 35 years of experience, of as great a lobby that descended upon the House than the organized baseball lobby. . . . They came upon Washington like locusts."[3]

What was true five decades ago is just as true today. In 2001, MLB had a full-time lobbying organization that spent $1.2 million.[4] In addition, during the summer of 2001, as the owners were developing their contraction plans, MLB established a political action committee (PAC). Among those who received $1,000 checks from the PAC were four members of the Senate Judiciary Committee: Orrin Hatch, the committee's top Republican; Michael DeWine, the top Republican on the antitrust subcommittee; Jeff Sessions (R-Ala.); and Richard Durbin (D-Ill.). MLB's PAC also gave $1,000 to each of two members of the House Judiciary Committee: Henry Hyde (R-Ill.) and Robert Wexler (D-Fla.).[5]

Moreover, as sports franchises have skyrocketed in value, today's owners tend to be some of the wealthiest and more powerful individuals and corporations in America. As such, directly and through PACs, baseball ownership has important and close ties to members of Congress and, needless to say, to the man in the Oval Office.

Put this together with the emotional attachment that many members of Congress have to the game and the fact that in the past most of the congressional issues connected with baseball affected only one or two cities at a time (such as expansion or team relocation), and it is not surprising that Congress has not acted to curtail MLB's monopoly powers.[6] Attacking MLB's presumed exemption has been perceived as a no-win situation for members of Congress. On the one hand, there is little to gain in constituency support, and on the other hand there is the risk that an alienated MLB establishment would be less willing to retain a team in or introduce a team to a member's district or to provide a member with box seats for a high-profile game.

The one exception to congressional passivity was the 1998 Curt Flood Act, which lifted MLB's antitrust exemption as it applied to collective bargaining. In this case, both the barons of baseball and the union supported the bill. It was agreed in the 1996 collective bargaining accord that both owners and players would support this partial lifting on the theory that it might make the sport's labor relations less tumultuous. It could do so by giving the Players Association another weapon besides the strike in the

event that owners attempted to impose unilateral restraints
labor market.

The NFL, for instance, avoided a longer work stoppage i
the players decided to go back to work and to bring an antitru
the owners around the Plan B free-agency system the owners had imposed.[7]
In order to do this, the NFL Players Association had to decertify itself as a
collective bargaining unit and bring the suit as an association. After many
years, the players eventually prevailed. The judge found Plan B to violate the
antitrust laws and told both sides to negotiate a new, less restrictive agreement. The new agreement, which has been fundamentally in place ever
since, was introduced in 1993.

Thus the Curt Flood Act did give the MLBPA another weapon, but it is
not one that it finds very attractive to use. To bring an antitrust suit, the
union first would have to decertify,[8] and then might have to wait several
years while the litigation played out.[9] If the judge found in the union's favor,
the union and owners would then have to negotiate a new agreement. In the
interim, the owner-imposed system would be operative. Since the average
career length in MLB is approximately five years at the major league level,
such a prolonged process might affect most, if not all, of the average player's
career span. The union might also make itself vulnerable to owner machinations when it attempted to recertify after the antitrust suit was concluded.
The Curt Flood Act, therefore, is only a very modest step toward helpful
public policy.

While most baseball issues taken up by Congress have been local in
nature, MLB sometimes seems to do its best to agitate the whole country at
once. The announced intention of the owners to contract by at least two
teams—postponed until 2006 by the 2002 collective bargaining agreement—has the potential to mobilize members of Congress from a dozen or
more states. Why? First, MLB did not announce which teams would be
eliminated, but it did announce that there were a dozen or so candidates.
Second, if an MLB team is eliminated, then its five or six minor league affiliates will eventually be eliminated as well, affecting still more cities and
states. Third, if MLB eliminates (instead of relocates) weak franchises, then
it means certain cities that want a team won't get one. Baseball's contraction
gambit, then, has the potential to arouse enough members of Congress to
undo the historical record of inaction.

The threat of baseball's ninth work stoppage in 2002 similarly generated some attention in Congress. Senator Arlen Specter of Pennsylvania sent a letter to Judiciary Committee chair Patrick Leahy on August 29, 2002, calling for a hearing to review baseball's presumed antitrust exemption if the players went out on strike. Senator Specter's letter read in part as follows: "There is no doubt that a strike would be Major League Baseball's way of saying let the public be damned. Baseball . . . has risen to its lucrative heights as a result of the exemption under the anti-trust laws. . . . If baseball is determined to kill the goose that lays the golden egg, Congress should send a clear message to the owners and players for a plague on both your houses."[10] Chairman Leahy has indicated an interest in pursuing the matter even though a strike was narrowly averted.

Thus MLB has mismanaged itself into a position where Congress might be willing to enact some meaningful public policy reforms. Whether it does so will in large measure be determined by what its members hear from their constituents. Fans groups are already mobilized and making more noise than ever before. If the Players Association mobilizes its membership to lobby as well, the presumed exemption may become vulnerable to legislative action.

Further, as detailed in chapter two, the judicial status of baseball's presumed antitrust exemption remains ambiguous. Since 1990 the judicial rulings on the status of MLB's exemption have resolved little: one state ruling and one federal ruling have held that the exemption applies narrowly to the old reserve clause and to no other aspects of the industry, and one state and one federal ruling have held that it applies broadly to the entire business of baseball. Together the rulings cover only three of the eleven judicial circuits in the United States, leaving ample ambiguity in the status of the scope of MLB's exemption in the remaining circuits.

With such uncertainty, it is riskier for MLB and its teams to make long-term decisions. For instance, can MLB prevent a team from relocating, can MLB contract, or can MLB impose onerous internal tax rates on rich teams to redistribute revenues without fear of a successful antitrust suit? Owners and potential owners are less likely to invest in franchises, not knowing whether they will be able to move their team (or if they do move, how much MLB might charge them for the privilege), and not knowing their ability to sign independent sponsorship contracts or to retain locally generated revenue. More than ever before, baseball's antitrust status demands clarification.

For each of these reasons, it is no longer a foregone conclusion that Congress will remain inert when it comes to baseball. In this context, the intellectual arguments for a new public policy become more pertinent.

Public Policy toward Stadiums

Baseball's monopoly allows it to artificially restrict the number of franchises and to treat cities without teams as assets of the league. As a consequence, cities and states compete against each other, leading to exorbitant stadium-financing packages and sweetheart leases. Further, when state governments become involved in financially supporting stadium construction, they often must simultaneously support parallel pork projects elsewhere in the state to secure the necessary votes in the legislature.

Fledgling efforts by cities to cooperate in forming a sports-host cartel have foundered. The incentives to cheat on any such cartel are too strong to preserve concerted behavior. In effect, absent effective national legislation, cities are on their own. On their own, cities have attempted to include lease provisions that deter team relocation and provide a more equitable sharing of the facility returns. But usually only the largest cities have sufficient bargaining leverage to accomplish part of these aims. Often, clauses requiring a team to play out its entire lease have escape provisions, such as attendance thresholds or state-of-the-art stadium modernization requirements.

Still other cities in recent years have included lease provisions that require the team to share either profits or capital gains with the public entity upon future sale of the franchise. While it is too early to tell how these sharing provisions will work out, the teams' ability to manipulate their books does not augur well for the public coffers. Other cities have liquidated damages provisions in their leases requiring the teams to reimburse the city for tens of millions of dollars if they vacate their facilities before a lease expires. These provisions, though, also often come with qualifying covenants.[11]

Some leases grant the city, or an investor group approved by the city, the right of first refusal to buy the team before it is sold or relocated. A potential problem here is the price. If an owner wants to move a team from city A to city B (or to sell the team to someone who will move it), it is because the team is worth more in city B. This might be because city B is building a new facility with strong revenue potential and favorable lease terms and/or city B possesses more auspicious demographic, geographic, or economic characteristics. If the team is worth, say, $100 million more in city B than in city A, then at what price does one offer the team to city A? If it is at the market price (the franchise value in city B), then city A or an investor in city A would be foolish to pay $100 million more for the franchise than it is worth in city A. If it is at an arbitration-determined value of the franchise value in city A, then it will be below the market price and the owner is being deprived of his property rights. The typical provision stipulates a market price criterion and thus provides little protection to the existing host city.

Another possible defense for cities attempting to hold on to a franchise is the invocation of eminent domain. Eminent domain is the power of government to take (condemn) private property for public use, with just compensation to the owner. This defense was attempted both by the city of Oakland when the NFL Raiders moved to Los Angeles in 1982 and by Baltimore when the Colts moved to Indianapolis in 1984. In the former case, the California Court of Appeals ruled that condemnation of a football franchise would violate the commerce clause of the U.S. Constitution.[12] In the latter, the condemnation was upheld by the Maryland Circuit Court, but the Colts then removed the action to the U.S. district court, which ruled that Baltimore no longer had jurisdiction because the team had moved out of the state by the time the condemnation was declared. Eminent domain, while not constitutionally impossible for sports teams, does not appear to be a promising vehicle for cities to use to retain their baseball teams.[13]

Of course, the Minneapolis Sports Facilities Commission, as described in chapter one, was successful in preventing the contraction of the Twins for the 2002 and 2003 seasons. Here the combination of a specific performance clause in the contract and the threat that MLB might have to open the details of its financial records and contraction deliberations to the public were enough to prompt baseball to wave a white flag. Tight contract language seems to have helped Minnesota in this instance, but it is not clear whether the stadium authority would have prevailed under different circumstances.

While one may legitimately question the costs and benefits to a particular metropolitan area of attracting a professional sports team, there appears to be no rationale whatsoever for the federal government to subsidize the financial tug-of-war among the cities to host ball clubs. If there is a global welfare gain from the relocation of a team from city A to city B (because city B may be larger or wealthier or have more avid sports fans), then city B ought to be able to pay for that gain without a subvention from Washington, D.C.

It appeared back in 1986 that Congress had convinced itself of the irrationality of allowing a tax exemption from the interest on municipal bonds for stadium construction projects. The 1986 Tax Reform Act had a provision that stipulated that the interest exemption would not apply to facilities where more than 10 percent of the bond debt service was financed from private sources (that is, from revenues generated at the facility). The apparent intention of this provision was to cease providing federal subsidies for sports facilities when the teams were privately owned. As Senator Patrick Moynihan of New York stated: "Congress intended to eliminate the issuance of tax-exempt bonds to finance professional sports facilities as part of the Tax Reform Act of 1986."[14]

The provision, however, was replete with loopholes that have allowed almost complete circumvention of its intent. The 10 percent on private financing applied only to annual funding flows; it did not apply to capital raised up front. Thus if the stadium authority were to receive, say, 40 percent of gross concessions revenue of $25 million per year ($10 million), then the resulting $10 million would count toward the 10 percent limit. If, however, the concessionaire instead paid the stadium authority or the team $60 million up front for the concession rights over a ten-year period, then this sum would not apply to the private funding limit. The same reasoning applies to naming rights, long-term luxury and club box leases, pouring rights, permanent seat licenses, and so on.[15] Further, if the lease provided that instead of paying rent (which would count toward the limit), the team paid for facility maintenance, then again there would be no offset against the limit. Along with still other loopholes, the 1986 tax reform provision allowed teams to receive ever more favorable leases without rental payments and with less or no sharing of stadium-generated revenues.

Senator Moynihan, cognizant of this irony and concerned about the prospect in the mid-1990s that New York City might build a $1 billion-plus new stadium for the Yankees, introduced bill S.1880 in June 1996. The bill would have eliminated the tax-exempt financing for professional sports stadiums. The bill did not make it out of committee.

Other congressional initiatives to regulate the abuses in this area do not inspire confidence. The first round of "city relocation and fan protection" bills came in 1984–85, pursuant to the relocation of the Oakland Raiders and the Baltimore Colts. One of these bills contained a provision to create a federal sports arbitration board that would preside over issues of team relocation and sale. The same bill would have exempted the NFL from its provisions if the league expanded by two teams and placed one of them in Baltimore, thus laying bare the parochial impulse behind the bill. None of the 1984–85 proposals came to a vote on either the House or the Senate floor. Similarly, the 1995–96 round of congressional initiatives was inspired by the departure of the Cleveland Browns to Baltimore. U.S. Representative Louis Stokes from Cleveland and Senator John Glenn of Ohio introduced a bill that would have granted the NFL an antitrust exemption for franchise relocation matters and established a right of first refusal for the host city. The exemption was intended to give the NFL clearer power to thwart team movement, but it ran the risk of ultimately giving the league greater bargaining leverage over cities. The first-refusal provision did not deal with the franchise price issue (discussed earlier) in a manner that would protect the existing host city. U.S. Representative Martin Hoke, from another Cleveland district, proposed a bill that would have allowed teams to move but would have obligated the league to restore a team within three years to the bereft city through expansion or relocation of another franchise. It also extended a limited exemption to the NFL for relocation issues. As with earlier initiatives, Congress never voted on any of these bills

Congressional initiatives have been plagued by local chauvinism and myopia. The sponsors invariably are reacting to a team movement problem in their state or district and opportunistically seize the occasion to posture in defense of their constituents. The remaining members of Congress are reluctant to support the measure, largely because they want to remain in the good graces of the sports leagues so that they themselves, their districts, and their states will be treated kindly by the leagues.

While it is arguable that there could be a small gain in net global welfare when a team relocates from a smaller to a larger city, it is clear that proper public policy should be oriented toward promoting an increase in the supply of baseball franchises so that all economically viable cities have a team. The best way to accomplish this is discussed shortly. Absent a successful policy to increase the supply of teams, it is appropriate for Congress to take up again the issue of the federal subsidy for stadium construction through the municipal exemption. Stadiums may generate positive externalities, consumer surplus, and public goods benefits for the residents of an area. Similar to a museum or a public park, these externalities might justify a level of public subsidization, even though in the case of a stadium the financial benefits are appropriated privately.

There is, however, no reason for the federal government to subsidize a process that picks one city over another. Thus it would be desirable for a new version of the Moynihan bill to be considered and passed.[16] Moreover, at the end of 2002, nineteen of baseball's thirty teams had new stadiums (or stadiums being built) that benefited from the federal tax exemption. The new bill should therefore provide similar treatment for the eleven teams that have not had a stadium built since 1989. Those teams should be grandfathered for a period of up to five years. The principal goal here is to remove this exemption before the next round of stadium construction begins, which, if the past is an indication, should be around 2020.

At the local level, stadium subsidies are a matter of preference. The important point is that residents should understand that there is no generalized economic benefit from stadium construction (see chapter six). If the city provides a construction subsidy, it is only appropriate for it to be based on the expected consumption benefits that it will provide to residents.

Further, local governments need to bargain hard around lease provisions, especially concerning clear guarantees of tenancy and sharing of capital gains accruing to team ownership. Ultimately, the ability of many cities to strike a fair bargain will rest on other public policy measures that ensure adequate league expansion over time. Finally, as discussed in chapter two, cities' interests can also be protected by requiring MLB to allow municipal ownership of its franchises.

Tax Policies

Thanks in part to Bud Selig's successful tax case against the IRS, owners of sports teams are able to use their franchises as tax shelters.[17] Under IRS policy, owners are allowed to presume that up to 50 percent of the price they pay to acquire a team's assets may be attributed to the value of the players' contracts. Owners can then amortize this value over three to five years. Thus, for example, if a baseball team sells for $400 million today, the owner may amortize half of this, or $200 million, between 2003 and 2007. Each year the owner could claim a $40 million amortization charge, sending the team's book profits well into the red. Using rules that apply to various

orms, such as subchapter S, the owner can then take the book
eam and transfer it to his or her individual tax returns, thereby
s or her taxable income.[18]

economic point of view, this tax shelter makes little sense. First,
it is apparent that the largest share of franchise value derives from the
monopoly rent, which is generated by belonging to MLB and the exclusive
territorial rights membership confers, rather than from the players' contracts. Second, baseball players do not depreciate as a machine does. In fact,
most players reach their years of peak performance after the midpoint in
their careers. That is, through on-the-job training they appreciate, rather
than depreciate, in value for more than half of their time in the majors.[19]

Third, baseball players do not produce a net income stream (and asset
value) for their team unless the additional revenue they generate for a team
is greater than their compensation. In this sense, a baseball player should no
more be considered a depreciable asset for a team than a factory worker is
for a manufacturing company.[20] Fourth, a player can be replaced simply by
promoting a player from the minors. If anything, the depreciable investment in players should be the amount spent on player development in the
minor leagues for those players who make it to the majors.[21] Expenditures
on player development, however, are already expensed (deducted as costs),
so it would be double-counting to amortize them as well.

Rational tax policy, therefore, would eliminate this shelter for owners of
baseball (and other sports) teams.

Broadcasting and Cable Policies

Technological and regulatory change has proceeded so rapidly that it is difficult to define an optimal public policy for baseball telecasting. Nonetheless, certain basic principles do support the welfare of the consumers.

One core issue here is the migration to cable (and to satellite) of both
local and national broadcasting. This migration results in fewer games
being available on free television, higher prices over time, and sometimes
no games being available at all (when programmers and distributors cannot come to terms). The latter indignity befell 2.9 million New York City
households served by Cablevision in 2002, when the cable distributor
refused to carry the Yankees' YES network on its expanded basic package.
A related issue is that distributors (cable companies) often bundle sports

programming into the expanded basic package, compelling non–sports fans to pay for it. The high monthly rights fees charged by the sports channels for expanded basic carriage ($1.50 to $2.50 per month per subscriber), albeit lucrative for the teams, make it more difficult for sports fans to pay their monthly cable/DBS bills, and non–sports fans are paying dearly for others' obsessions.

As discussed in chapter two, the 1961 Sports Broadcasting Act (SBA) permitted the packaging of league games to national broadcasters for over-the-air free television. This packaging involves individually owned teams coming together to form a television cartel that sells national broadcasting rights. The SBA makes this activity legal for free television. It does not, however, make it legal for services that charge a fee, such as cable or satellite television, or for eventual streaming over the Internet. Hence, if MLB's presumed antitrust exemption were narrowed or eliminated, MLB's deals with ESPN (presently worth around $142 million yearly) and with DirecTV (*Extra Innings*) could be challenged on antitrust grounds.[22]

If these challenges were successful, the alternative would be for individual teams or groups of teams (such as divisions within each league) to sell their games for national television. The outcome would be more games and cheaper prices.

A related issue is the league's granting of exclusive broadcast territories to its teams. These exclusive territories were held to be illegal in 1953 in *U.S. v. NFL*, but they are still maintained by every league. Without them, each game would potentially have two broadcasting sellers, and the resulting competition would bring prices down. It would also significantly diminish the advantage of big-city teams by compelling them to share part of the rent generated by their market.

As discussed earlier, in 1984 a Supreme Court decision forced the NCAA to end its cartelization of college football television rights. The result was a dramatic increase in the number of games broadcast as well as lower rights fees paid by the broadcasters.[23]

Naturally, if revenue that is now part of MLB's central fund becomes team- or division-specific revenue, the result could be increasing inequality in revenue across the teams—a problem that MLB is presently trying to resolve. The best way to deal with this problem would be for the league to mandate that some high percentage of these new revenues be shared leaguewide, even though they are contracted by decentralized units (teams

Table 7-1. *Structure of MLB's National Media Income, 1997–2000*

Millions of dollars

Income source	1997	1998	1999	2000
Domestic television and radio	329	317	340	513
Foreign rights	17	19	29	37
Superstation	48	51	53	53
Copyright royalty arbitration panel[a]	36	71	87	41
Total	429	458	509	645

Source: *The Owners' Box,* Offering Memorandum for Sale of the Boston Red Sox, May 2001, p. 57. The MLB's DirecTV revenue from its *Extra Innings* package appears to be subsumed under the "domestic television and radio" category. Unlike the NFL, MLB's direct broadcast satellite package had a slow start. Whereas the NFL's package generated upward of $140 million for the league in 2001, MLB's package appears to have generated less than $20 million.

a. This panel distributes to programmers revenue generated by payments from use of the compulsory license by transponder companies.

or divisions). This would be a version of the model MLB currently uses with the Braves/TBS and the Cubs/WGN.[24] Of course, if, as part of this change, the leagues were not allowed to grant teams local broadcasting monopolies, then the resulting rent-sharing would also serve to level revenue inequalities (see table 7-1).

In the cases of the Braves and the Cubs, it is clear that additional broadcasting of games becomes available to fans. Out-of-market fans would be more likely to be able to watch their favorite team and do so at a lower price. The appropriate public policy to stimulate such an outcome would be to revoke or reduce the scope of baseball's presumed antitrust exemption.

The migration to cable in local contracts is also a significant issue. A team's motivation to move to cable is straightforward: cable produces two income streams—advertising and carriage fees; broadcast television produces only advertising. In recent years, the perceived popularity of sports programming has led teams or their cable affiliates, first, to insist that their games be carried on the expanded basic rather than the premium tier, and second, to raise the monthly charge for carriage on the basic tier. If a team can choose between selling its games on a premium tier to 5 percent of the cable households in a given area for $10 a month and on the expanded basic tier to all cable households for $2 a month, its choice is obvious. In a market of 5 million cable households, the former yields $2.5 million monthly and the latter, $10 million. Also, if the game reaches more households, the

Table 7-2. *Baseball's Migration to Cable, 1987–2002*

	Broadcast		Cable	
Year	Total games	Average games per team	Total games	Average games per team
1987	2,098	80.7	914	35.1
1991	2,039	78.4	1,144	44.0
1996	1,835	65.5	1,287	50.9
1997	1,668	59.6	1,737	62.0
1998	1,655	55.2	2,058	68.6
1999	1,646	54.9	2,187	72.9
2000	1,571	52.4	2,246	75.0
2001	1,507	50.2	2,417	80.6
2002	1,380	46.0	2,478	82.6

Sources: *Broadcasting and Cable*, July 29, 2002; Andrew Zimbalist, *Baseball and Billions: A Probing Look into the Big Business of Our National Pastime* (Basic Books, 1994), p. 157.

team can charge substantially higher prices for the more than sixty advertising spots available per game. Moreover, if the team owns the cable station, it is more likely to be able to receive twelve months, rather than seven (the length of the baseball season) of subscriber revenue.

Table 7-2 depicts the steady trend toward cable-ization of the game at the local level for the fifteen years from 1987 through 2002. In 1987 the average team had 80.7 games shown locally on broadcast television and 35.1 games on cable. By 2002 these numbers had practically reversed, with 46.0 games on broadcast television and 82.6 games on cable. The trend shows signs of continuing. On September 5, 2002, the Red Sox announced that they would broadcast only twenty-eight games over the air in 2003, in contrast to seventy in 2002; and that the number of NESN telecasts would rise to 122, up from 85 in 2002.[25] In turn, the Red Sox raised the fee they charge cable compaies for NESN by 40 to 70 cents per month in 2003.[26] Teams that control their own cable outlet, as do the Red Sox, also have the ability to shelter income from MLB's increasingly costly revenue sharing system. This provides yet another impetus toward cable-ization.

This migration to cable has brought ever higher local media revenues to MLB teams. Together these revenues grew from $116.9 million in 1985 to $342.1 million in 1990 and to approximately $655 million in 2002—and these are only reported revenues.[27] As we saw in chapter four, teams that own their cable or broadcast television station can shuffle revenues away from the team. Within this local media revenue total, cable has played a larger and larger role. Team revenues from local cable deals grew from roughly $200 million in 1999 to $275 million in 2000 and to $350 million 2002—an annual growth rate of 20.5 percent over the past three years.[28]

It is little wonder that baseball teams have found the lofty payoffs from cable to be irresistible. Of the 9,924 cable systems in the country, fewer than 100 have competition from another system in their area. The 1996 Telecommunications Act deregulated rate-setting in the industry beginning on April 1, 1999 (except for the stripped-down basic tier), on the theory that there would soon be stiff competition in all areas. The competition was to come from the act's relaxation of the prohibition against telephone companies offering cable service (and against cable companies offering telephone service), as well as from the growth of direct broadcast satellite (DirecTV and EchoStar). But competition from the telephone companies has not materialized.[29] Satellite services provide some modest competition (today there are roughly 68 million households subscribed to cable and 14 million subscribed to satellite), but satellite is not available or feasible in all areas, and the product it offers can differ substantially from that of cable. The outcome of rate deregulation and ineffective competition in most areas has been rapid price increases in cable services.[30]

To a large degree, these increases have been pushed by the higher prices being charged by sports programmers (the national cable stations—such as ESPN or TBS—and regional sports networks). The programmers, in turn, are selling the output of games from teams that have territorial exclusivity in different media markets conferred upon them by monopoly sports leagues.[31] In most areas there is only one regional sports network. We have, then, a monopoly (team) selling to a monopoly (programmer), which then sells to a monopoly (cable company), which then sells to the public. Of course, in a few areas the industry is not a monopoly but a duopoly with considerable market power, and in some areas there is vertical integration among the team, programmer, and distributor. Whatever the permutation in a given city, the consumer is playing against a stacked deck.

Because of the rapidly transforming technological landscape, it is not a simple matter to prescribe specific public policies. It is clear, however, that the FCC needs to take additional measures to promote competition in the delivery of cable and satellite (and other video programming) services to communities. It is also clear that technology provides consumers considerably more options than are being made available by cable and satellite companies. There is, for instance, no good reason why a New York Mets fan should be obliged to pay several extra dollars a month for an expanded basic package to watch the New York Yankees, or vice versa, or why someone who is not a baseball fan should have to pay to watch either team.

The monopoly cable distributors are bundling. While in some instances bundling is an acceptable restraint of trade (especially when there is competition, so the consumer can choose whether to buy the bundle), in others (where there is little or no competition) it is not acceptable. If each area of the country had at least two competing cable companies and one offered the regional sports network in its expanded basic package and the other did not, then the bundling in the cable package might be less problematic. Given that there is no such competition and that technology allows de-bundling, the appropriate public policy is to ensure that several de-bundling options be made available to the consumer. Different bills promoting such a policy or other forms of rate regulation are being introduced or contemplated in the U.S. Congress as I write in October 2002.

Regulation and Antitrust

Competition is the driving force of capitalism. Without it, capitalism founders. Public policy should be geared to promoting competition in all industries unless a strong case for exception can be made.

Over the years MLB has offered several arguments in defense of its league's presumed antitrust exemption. First, until 1977 MLB maintained that the player reserve system was essential to preserve competitive balance in baseball and that the exemption permitted the industry to maintain this labor market restriction. But the reserve system affected whether monopoly rents went to the owners or the players. It did not equalize the distribution of player talent. In fact, with free agency it became more expensive to hold together a winning team and easier for a weak team to turn around its fortunes. Thus after the reserve system was eliminated, competitive balance in baseball actually improved. So much for defense number one.

Second, MLB asserted that it did not need to be regulated administratively or subjected to competitive pressure because it self-regulated effectively through its independent commissioner. The commissioner's power to act in the game's best interest, the argument went, was the only stewardship needed to prevent exploitation of the consumer or dynamic inefficiency. To be sure, commissioners had a small degree of wiggle room until the dismissal of Commissioner Fay Vincent in 1992. But it was only very modest wiggle room. The few commissioners who tried to exercise true independence were usually dispensed with in short order by unappreciative owners. Since 1992, however, the commissioner has been an owner. Any claim that Selig behaves as anything other than a CEO strains credulity.

Third, the owners have claimed that MLB is not really a monopoly and that the absence of profitability proves it. Rather, this argument goes, baseball is one of many games in the sports industry and one of an even greater number of companies in the entertainment industry. All these companies compete for the entertainment dollar. This argument is bogus from an economic point of view and from the perspective of the Antitrust Division of the Justice Department. All retail industries in the country compete in a general sense for the consumer's dollar. Every $40 I spend on a shirt is $40 I do not have available to spend at the ballpark, but this reasoning misses the point. The issue is how closely two different goods substitute for each other (or, in economics jargon, what is their cross-elasticity of demand). If baseball can raise its prices by 5 percent or more (above competitive levels) and still see its profits rise, then, by the Justice Department's criterion, baseball is sufficiently different from other entertainment products to be considered a separate market.[32]

Regarding the industry's purported lack of profitability, as detailed in chapter four, the continuing rise in franchise values and an understanding of the industry's accounting practices and company interlocks challenge this claim. If baseball teams as a group do not earn monopoly rent (above market rates of return) on strictly financial terms, it is because (a) the indirect or nonfinancial returns are not being measured, (b) the monopoly rent has already been capitalized in a higher franchise value, or (c) the industry is being mismanaged.

Fourth, baseball needs to restrain trade in order to preserve competitive balance. For instance, without the ability to sign national television contracts, revenue distribution in MLB would grow still more unequal. The exemption allows MLB's thirty teams to join together as a television cartel to sell national broadcasting rights, but also to sell national cable and satellite rights. Yet, as already explained, MLB could allow individual teams or divisions to market national video rights and then have a policy to tax away the lion's share of the revenue thereby generated; or MLB could relax its policies regarding territorial exclusivity for its teams.

In any event, MLB does not need a blanket antitrust exemption to carry out policies in furtherance of its competitive strength as an industry. Only unreasonable restraints of trade are illegal. Rule-of-reason judgments allow industries to engage in ancillary restraints. Competitive balance is a prerequisite for a successful team sports league in the long run. Therefore, restraints that promote competitive balance are potentially acceptable in a court of law, as long as they are the least restrictive way of accomplishing the goal. Baseball does not need its blanket exemption if any of its restrictions are procompetitive and serve consumers' interests. Moreover, without a special blanket exemption, MLB would still be protected by the 1961 SBA. The NFL has no special exemption, and it certainly has managed to avoid competitive imbalance.

Fifth, the owners aver that the presumed exemption allows MLB to better control franchise movement. The fact that no team has moved since 1972 is testimony to this control. At one level, this is probably a correct assertion; the presumed exemption has prevented at least one MLB team from moving over the past three decades.

MLB, however, does not need an antitrust exemption in order to prevent team relocations. As explained, MLB could do so under a rule-of-reason analysis, as the NFL has successfully done on occasion. Further, the commissioner's office has not refrained from threatening host cities again and again that a team will move (to a vacant, viable market) if it does not get funding for a new stadium. And the commissioner's blue-ribbon panel has recommended that MLB follow a more lenient relocation policy. More recently, of course, the commissioner's office has added the threat of contraction.

MLB still derives leverage to extract public stadium subsidies from its artificial restriction on the number of franchises. Were there two competing baseball leagues, this leverage on cities would evaporate.

It is not clear that it is always appropriate to prevent a team from relocating. If fans in one city where a team is already located have less interest in and less ability to support the team than fans in another city without a team, then aggregate consumer welfare would be maximized by allowing the team to move. The caveats here are two. One, a comparative assessment of two cities should not be based on short-term factors. For the most part, baseball cities are made, not born. There were years in the 1970s when

Commisioner Selig probably would have deemed the New York Mets and Yankees suitable candidates for relocation or contraction. Between 1969 and 1975 the Yankees' season attendance never surpassed 1.3 million, and in one year, 1972, it did not crack the 1 million mark. Between 1976 and 1984 the Mets' attendance was below 1.5 million every year, and in two years the team failed to draw 750,000. If contraction had been on the table in the late 1980s, prime targets would have been the Atlanta Braves, Cleveland Indians, and Seattle Mariners. Two, before moving, teams should have to fulfill the remaining years (or pay the indemnity) on their lease obligation. The optimal policy might be one that allows the city to protect its investment with a tight, long-term lease (say thirty years). If, when the lease expires, it makes economic sense for the team to stay, it does so. If not, it goes to another city.

In the NFL when teams have moved away from long-standing host cities, those cities have mobilized to bring a team back (St. Louis, Cleveland, Baltimore, and Houston), and often by compelling the league to expand. In the NBA, Charlotte has had its team restored, and as I write, it appears that Los Angeles will soon be awarded an NFL expansion franchise. The same could happen in baseball. Team movement, then, can create the necessary political pressure and lead to expansion. For all of these reasons, giving MLB an antitrust exemption to preserve team stability makes little sense. The key to defending the legitimate rooting and economic interests of cities is to follow a policy that undermines MLB's ability to artificially limit the number of franchises—either by failing to grow adequately over time, or worse, proposing to reduce the number of teams.

Sixth, MLB has claimed that an exemption is needed to maintain its minor leagues. As explained in chapter two, MLB's minor league baseball is premised on a labor market restriction: amateurs are signed via a draft that requires them to bargain with only one club and, once they sign, to belong to that club for up to seven years. Were MLB to lose its presumed exemption, the present system would not automatically implode. A minor leaguer would have to bring litigation to challenge its restrictive practices. In this event, MLB could attempt a rule-of-reason defense. If the challenge were successful, then MLB's present system would have to change. But it is not clear that this would be undesirable.

There are presently five independent minor leagues. Without an exemption, affiliated minor league clubs may lose their ties to the major league team, but they would not necessarily disappear. To be sure, there is no guarantee that if MLB retains its presumed exemption the number of affiliated teams would remain the same. To cut costs, MLB has reduced the number of minor league teams in the past; it has also indicated an interest both in reducing subsidies when the present minor league agreement expires in 2004 and in carrying fewer teams.

Further, if minor leaguers did not "belong" to a particular major league club, then it is likely that competitive balance among major league teams would improve. Major league clubs would draft players out of the minors, not out of college and high school.[33] These players would be more developed and their potential talent level more knowable. The reverse-order draft would confer a larger advantage on the low-finishing teams than the present amateur draft does.

The point here and elsewhere about lifting the presumed exemption is that it would permit judicial review of baseball's policies and actions. When MLB claims that the minors as currently structured are necessary or that contraction by two teams is imperative, as long as MLB is presumed to have a blanket antitrust exemption there is no (or limited) judicial review.[34] Without review, there is no permitted discovery of facts and there is no analytical challenge of baseball's assertion. Without an antitrust exemption, the plaintiff's lawyer can conduct discovery of the relevant information and present an analysis to be heard by an independent judge and/or jury. Given that MLB is not regulated and faces no competition (it is the only top-level professional baseball league in the United States), the opportunity for judicial review would provide the only chance to limit the potential abuse of its monopoly powers.

An alternative in theory is to regulate the baseball industry. Such regulation could take a variety of forms and could be directed at several distinct elements of the industry, such as the schedule, the number of franchises, the number of games on cable, labor relations, team movement, and others. After the experiences of 1994–95 and 2002, many fans would probably like to see a mandatory cooling-off period for baseball labor disputes, followed by compulsory mediation and, in the event that mediation fails, compulsory arbitration.[35] Needless to say, baseball is not as crucial to the operation of the economy as the railways or the airways, but for large sections of the country it is culturally central. Many believe that the sport played an important role in lifting the country out of the doldrums after September 11, 2001.

In 1972, a Republican senator, Marlow Cook of Kentucky, introduced the first legislative effort to regulate the sports industry through the creation of a federal sports commission. In presenting his bill, Senator Cook stated:

> The primary purpose of the Commission, therefore, is to provide the sports fan with a voice in the operation of that system—a voice that has hitherto been ignored. . . . It is inevitable that certain protests will be made during the course of these hearings that the area of sports is one that should remain free of governmental interference. I would hope that those witnesses will consider the idea that it may be preferable to spare the world of sports the embarrassment and turmoil of constant litigation and conflict.[36]

Senator Cook never satisfactorily explained how the fans' interests would be represented on his commission. His bill never made it out of committee.

In a less heavy-handed approach, Steven Rifkin in 1974 suggested the creation of a national sports council of experts that would periodically recommend legislation to Congress.[37] An advantage of having a national sports council is that, as a standing body of experts, the council could periodically propose needed legislation as the sports industry evolved and its issues changed. The council would have the power to subpoena league documents, but Congress would retain ultimate legislative authority.

Whatever the appeal, a national sports council or broader regulation is difficult to imagine in the present U.S. political environment. Not only does regulation run counter to the prevailing ideological current, but the reality of partisan politics in the United states raises many warning flags about how regulation would function. Most regulatory bodies in the United States have been subject to lobbying pressures from the organized groups within an industry. For baseball, it is likely that team owners and the Players Association would have a more powerful influence than fans or cities.[38] This problem would limit the effectiveness of either a regulatory body or an advisory sports council (whose impact would ultimately depend on legislative action).[39]

Further, it does not appear that baseball reaps any significant economies of scale from operating as a thirty-team enterprise that it would not reap as two fifteen-team enterprises. Without such economies, a major argument for regulation, as opposed to antitrust action, evaporates.

In a concurring opinion to the 1972 *Flood* decision, the chief justice of the U.S. Supreme Court wrote, "It is time the Congress acted to solve the problem."[40] Nothing has transpired in the ensuing thirty years to lessen the veracity of that appeal.

In 1979 the National Commission for the Review of Antitrust Laws and Procedures recommended the following regarding antitrust immunities:

1. Free Market competition, protected by the antitrust laws, should continue to be the general organizing principle of our economy.

2. Exceptions from this general principle should only be made when there is compelling evidence of the unworkability of competition or a clearly paramount social purpose.

3. Where such an exception is required, the least anticompetitive method of achieving the regulatory objective should be employed.

4. Existing antitrust immunities should be reexamined.

The commission went on to make it clear that the burden of proof "to show a convincing public interest rationale" lay with those seeking to create or maintain an antitrust exemption, and, further, that "the defects in the marketplace necessary to justify an antitrust exemption must be substantial and clear."[41]

There is, then, a compelling case for Congress to lift the ambiguity over the scope of baseball's presumed exemption and resolve it in favor of judicial review and competition. It would, at least, provide a check on MLB's not infrequent arrogance and mismanagement.

Lifting the exemption, however, does not guarantee competition in the industry; it just allows for judicial review and potentially puts a check on restrictive behavior. Competition itself would go a long way toward resolving many of the problems discussed in this book. Thus it would also make sense for Congress to contemplate a more radical policy: forced divestiture of MLB into two leagues.[42]

With divestiture, MLB would be broken up into two competing business entities. The entities would be allowed to collaborate on playing rules and to engage in interleague and postseason play, but they would not be able to divvy up metropolitan areas, establish common drafts or players' markets, or collude on broadcasting policy, among other things. Under these circumstances neither league would be likely to vacate an economically viable city, and if one did, the competing league would be likely to jump in. Other consumer-friendly consequences would flow from such an arrangement, and lower local, state, and federal subsidies would scale down team revenues, owner profits, and player salaries. But competition would compel more efficient management practices, and teams would remain solvent, albeit with reduced cost structures.

Significantly, most, if not all, of MLB's competitive-balance issues would be resolved. With two competing leagues, not only would presently unoccupied cities find themselves hosting teams, but some present host cities might find an additional team or two in their market. If sharing the New York City market with the two existing teams offered better prospects for a franchise than, say, having New Orleans to itself, New York City might once again have three (or more) baseball teams. If the Yankees and Mets had to share New York with additional teams, much of their competitive advantage over smaller markets would disappear.[43] Indeed, with competition over time one would expect teams to allocate themselves across the country so as to equalize the expected incremental revenue from each venue. A competitive league would obviate many of the artificial internal restrictions that often create perverse performance incentives.

It is not fortuitous that the commissioner's blue-ribbon panel and former commissioner Bowie Kuhn recommended that baseball consider putting a third team in New York. The implied expansion or reallocation of teams is a more desirable policy for dealing with competitive balance issues than is an internal system of progressive taxes on revenue.

Rather than relying on the sound judgment and beneficence of baseball's barons, competition between leagues would accomplish the expansion/reallocation automatically. Just as McDonald's and Burger King rush to beat each other to any viable strip mall, each league would rush to fill a potential baseball market before the other. With competing leagues, it is inconceivable that the nation's capital and eighth largest media market would be without a Major League Baseball team for over thirty years.

One potential downside to divestiture is that competition between two leagues will tend over time to strengthen one league and weaken the other. The weaker league may see some of its franchises fail and may eventually be absorbed by the stronger league. The first result would be instability, and then the possible reassertion of monopoly. This possibility, however, seems both remediable (divestiture could be legislated again in the future) and a modest price to pay given the expected benefits of competition.

Self-Regulation

I have argued that proper public policy should not be deferred in the hope that baseball's commissioner will begin to enact enlightened, proconsumer policies. Given baseball's missteps and the increasing inaccessibility of the sport to young and low-income Americans, growing grassroots pressure has a chance of awakening Congress from its baseball slumber.

With or without congressional action, baseball needs to think seriously about self-improvement. The sport's fan base is forebodingly geriatric. Little League participation is declining, even with an expanding population. Baseball needs to undertake more youth initiatives. It would do well, for instance, to start some World Series games before 8:08 P.M. eastern time and maybe even bring some weekend day games back. Even if this hurt short-term television ratings, it would promote a youth following and the long-term health of the game.

Stadium gentrification in the 1990s fit nicely with the protracted economic boom and the burgeoning stock market bubble. There was plenty of corporate cash to pay for luxury boxes, club seats, catering, signage, and sponsorships at the ballpark. Baseball, however, cannot rely entirely on the corporate dollar to keep it afloat in the long run. Its long-run strength is in a mass fan base. Some students of the game's history have suggested that baseball became the national pastime back in 1882, when the fledgling American Association charged 25 cents for a ticket, half the price charged by the National League at the time, and brought the working classes to the ballpark, for which it was roundly criticized by National League president William Hulbert.

This mass base must be cultivated, not assumed. In 2002, according to Team Marketing Report, a family of four spent $145.26 on average to attend a major league game, a 67.5 percent increase from ten years earlier. Teams would be well advised to have thousands of seats available for under $10, to offer family specials weekly, to allow fans on the field after games, to open ballparks in time for home-team batting practice, to encourage players to become involved in community events, to arrest the migration of telecasting to cable/satellite, and so on. A balance needs to be struck between short-term gain and long-term success.

On the labor front, MLB escaped by the skin of its teeth in 2002. Absent new public policy initiatives, MLB will need to tweak its revenue sharing system to provide clear incentives to build a winning team. Effective management is a sine qua non of team success. Competitive balance can be further advanced with new draft rules giving preference to small-market clubs and by placing an additional team in certain large markets. Even more important, MLB needs to avoid work stoppages, or even close brushes with stoppages, like the plague. They kill fan interest and undermine the stability needed for lucrative television contracts and corporate sponsorships.

The best way to avoid these confrontations in the future is for baseball to establish an owner-player partnership. Partnership is built on trust, and trust is built on openness and communication. Hall of Famer Dave Winfield, writing in the *New York Times* in October 2002, put it this way:

> Until trust develops between players and owners . . . there will be no long-term growth or development in Major League Baseball. This mistrust needs to be dealt with or it is just going to fester. Without that trust, baseball will not move forward.
>
> Collective bargaining alone will not lead the way. Any piecemeal strategy to address the problems is only a temporary solution.
>
> Baseball needs a breakthrough, a complete paradigm shift from business as usual.[44]

Bud Selig's behavior since 1999 serves as an antimodel. He established a *unilateral* owners' commission to study baseball's problems. He then waited at least fifteen months after the commission's July 2000 report before formally opening collective bargaining negotiations in January 2002; and it was not until December 2002 (one month after the old agreement expired) that he put the owners' substantive demands on the table. Before beginning substantive negotiations, he announced his intention to eliminate two teams and eighty union jobs, dismissed the one person in his office who had the best communications with the Players Association, announced he was going to implement an antiquated, inoperative team debt rule that amounted to a back-door salary cap, proposed the creation of a $100 million fund to be used at the commissioner's discretion, and put new demands on the bargaining table that went well beyond what was recommended by his blue-ribbon panel. These are not measures conducive to building a partnership and a cooperative relationship; they are antagonistic measures whose misguided and ultimately unfulfilled purpose was to gain the upper hand in negotiations.

Instead, the next commissioner might consider doing the opposite. Long before the new collective bargaining agreement expires at the end of 2006, the commissioner would be well advised to establish a *bilateral* study commission to examine how the agreement has affected baseball's competitive balance and financial performance. The joint study committee ought to help establish a common understanding of the dimensions of the game's economic problems.[45] Soon after the work of the commission is completed, it is important for talks between owner and player representatives to commence. Throughout this period, it is imperative that full financial information be shared and that the commissioner's office take no unilateral action.

A commissioner's ability to behave in such a straightforward, rational, and open way will depend critically upon the degree of cohesion and cooperation among the owners. When Bud Selig in 2001 first had Paul Beeston negotiate informally with players and later shut down those discussions, it is likely that at least two different groups of owners were in conflict about how to proceed. One group became better organized and ascendant when it did not like the news it was getting about the informal talks.

Baseball's new revenue sharing and luxury tax will impose additional burdens on the high-revenue teams. It is not improbable that this will engender some new tensions and may even produce litigation. When the dust settles, however, baseball will have a system in which the economic circumstances of the teams are more closely shared. One can only hope that this will allow for more unity among the owners, which, in turn, with strong leadership, will promote a more reasoned, balanced, and long-term approach to managing our national pastime.

There is no reason, however, for public policymakers to sit back and hope that baseball's barons will finally get it right. Consumers need an industry that is subject to judicial checks and competitive pressures. Only then will baseball fans be able to put the traumas of the 1990s and early 2000s behind them and utter freely the simple and enduring exhortation: May the best team win.

The 2003 Season

There's an old baseball saying: *plus ça change, plus c'est la meme chose.* Yogi Berra didn't say that, but Major League Baseball's 2003 season proves that a good adage dies hard. Once again, there were eight months of great baseball and more-competitive-than-usual races to the postseason. With two weeks left in the season, there were fully fifteen teams with a chance to make the playoffs. When the regular season ended, both the Cubs and the Red Sox found themselves still playing.

The possibility of a Cubs–Red Sox match up in the World Series sent playoff television ratings soaring. The hapless Cubs were last crowned world champions in 1908. The Bosox hadn't achieved that distinction since 1918, when team owner Henry Frazee was in the throes of trading Babe Ruth, Carl Mays, Herb Pennock, Waite Hoyt, Sad Sam Jones, Bullet Joe Bush, Wally Schang, and Everett Scott (and losing general manager Ed Barrow) to the Yankees.

Ultimately, the curses of the goat and the Bambino prevailed, and television ratings returned back to earth for the World Series matchup between the Marlins and the Yankees. The lowly Marlins had reached the .500 mark only twice in the team's eleven-year history, in 1997 and 2003. In 1997, the wild card Marlins went on to win the World Series. As wild card entrants again in 2003, they needed only six games to knock off the mighty Yankees. The Marlins won their second World Series without ever winning a division championship. An appealing storyline to be sure, but it was the third lowest rated World Series ever, posting an average rating of 12.8.[1]

Commissioner Selig was quick to take full credit for the competitive pennant races and the modest lift in postseason ratings. These salubrious outcomes, Selig declared, resulted directly from the wild card and revenue sharing systems, which were his babies. His modest words were as follows: "I don't want to toot my own horn. But everything I have tried to do the last 11 years worked wonders this year."[2]

Baseball, of course, was the last of the U.S. team sports to adopt a wild card ticket to the playoffs. Selig may have done some politicking to win its final approval, but many owners wanted it and Selig can hardly lay claim to inventing the concept.

Revenue sharing is a far more complicated and troublesome story. It might be prudent for Selig to be a bit more diffident about soliciting attention to the design and implementation of baseball's revenue sharing system. He was careful, however, not to take credit for the second consecutive year of falling attendance, the failed plan to spice up the All-Star Game, or the messes in Montreal and Milwaukee, among other curious happenings.

Revenue Sharing

The 2002 collective bargaining agreement provided for augmented revenue sharing. As discussed in chapter 5, the central purpose of the sharing was to transfer money from the top half to the bottom half, in order to enhance competitive balance among teams. The design of the system was flawed in a few ways. First, teams in the third revenue quartile receive proportionately more in transfers than teams in the bottom quartile. Thus teams like Selig's Milwaukee Brewers benefit relatively more than teams like the Tampa Bay Devil Rays.

Second, the implied marginal tax rate on teams in the bottom half rises above 45 percent. That is, every time a team's revenue grows by $1, it receives approximately $0.45 less in revenue sharing. This rate is simply too high if the goal is to induce low-revenue clubs to spend transfers on improving team on-field performance.

Third, absent adequate incentives, the system would benefit from a (flexible) minimum payroll requirement before teams receive transfers, as recommended by the commissioner's own blue-ribbon panel. It has none.

Instead, the plan substitutes exhortation and a weak enforcement mechanism that is under Selig's control. The new collective bargaining agreement reads:

> Accordingly, *each Club shall use its revenue sharing receipts . . . in an effort to improve its performance on the field. The Commissioner shall enforce this obligation* by requiring, among other things, each Payee (recipient) Club, no later than April 1, to report on the performance-related uses to which it put its revenue sharing receipts in the preceding sharing year. Consistent with the authority under the Major League Constitution, the Commissioner may impose penalties on any Club that violates this obligation.[3]

Selig appears to have done preciously little enforcing. During 2003, five of the seven bottom-payroll teams actually lowered their opening-day payrolls by a total of $62.6 million, despite receiving $63.1 million in revenue sharing transfers. Selig's family team, the Milwaukee Brewers, was one of the worst offenders. The Brewers reduced opening-day payroll from $52.7 million in 2002 to $40.6 million in 2003, finishing the season with the second lowest average player salary in Major League Baseball. This parsimony was in spite of the facts that (a) the Brewers' net revenue sharing grew from $1.5 million in 2001 to $9.1 million in 2002 to an estimated $18.35 million in 2003, and (b) they were playing in a new stadium, financed with some $400 million of public funds.[4]

If the competitive pennant races in 2003 were the product of MLB's new revenue sharing system and luxury tax on high payrolls, then team payroll disparity should have been reduced. That is, these reforms were intended to lower the high payrolls and raise the low ones, thereby promoting greater parity in spending and balance on the field. The evidence is to the contrary. The range from the bottom to the top team payroll increased from $91.55 million in 2002 to $130.1 million in 2003. Nor was it just the disparity between top and bottom teams that grew; the standard deviation of team payrolls jumped 11.8 percent in 2003.[5] Payroll differences generally account for between 20 and 50 percent of the variation in team performance. Good management, good team chemistry, and good luck are always important. It was these latter factors, rather than the narrowing of payroll differentials, that serendipitously produced MLB's competitive pennant races in 2003.

The Mess in Milwaukee

While Bud Selig was acting commissioner, between 1992 and 1998, he still apparently remained actively engaged in managing the affairs of the Milwaukee Brewers. Indeed, MLB agreed to allow him to open a satellite commissioner's office in Milwaukee. According to *Milwaukee Magazine*, as late as 1996 Selig was pulling a full-time salary from the Brewers of nearly half a million dollars. Michael Megna, who appraises sports franchises and has done work for the Brewers, stated: "Selig was trying to wear too many hats and was too ambitious."[6]

During this time Selig was lobbying the Wisconsin state legislature for funding for a new ballpark—a ballpark he once said the team would build with its own funds. He told politicians and fans that the Brewers would be able to build a competitive team if they had a new stadium. Ultimately, the team arranged a sweetheart deal for itself.

The retractable-roof stadium itself was to cost $250 million, $90 million of which would be contributed by the Brewers. According to a May 2002 report by the Wisconsin Legislative Audit Bureau, as of the end of 2001 the total cost for the project, including infrastructure, was $424 million.[7] The Brewers' share remained at $90 million. Of this, the Brewers received a twenty-year naming rights deal from the Miller Brewing Company for $41.1 million.[8] Another $50 million came from low-interest loans from the local chamber of commerce, the Milwaukee Economic Development Corporation, and two Milwaukee foundations. Subsequently, the quasi-public Stadium District took over between $36 million and $41 million of these loans. In 2002 the Stadium District swapped these loans (which were debt held by the Brewers) for a reduced obligation to cover certain stadium costs. Thus of the $50 million that the Brewers borrowed, the team will only be responsible for paying back around $10 million.

For their modest contribution, the Brewers got the following. First, the chamber of commerce guaranteed that the team would sell at least 10,000 season tickets during 1995–97 and at least 12,000 beginning in 1998, with up to a $6 million annual payment for any shortfall. Second, the team has a state-of-the-art, retractable roof stadium, with over $4 million in furnishings for team offices out of public funds, at a yearly rent of only $900,000. Third, the team keeps all revenue generated at the stadium, including naming rights, premium seating, catering, signage, and even non-baseball events. Fourth, the Stadium District pays $1.75 million annually into a renovation and improvement fund for the ballpark.

In addition, the Stadium District paid $3.85 million per year to help defray the stadium operation and maintenance costs of repairs, uniforms, cleaning, utilities, insurance, as well as salaries and benefits for seasonal employees. These costs are almost universally defrayed by the team in other cities. The Stadium District's annual payment was ended in 2002 in exchange for canceling the team's roughly $40 million debt.

The public's largesse and Selig's representations notwithstanding, the Brewers only got worse in their new facility. The team descended from a lowly average of 76.5 wins per year during 1996–99 to a woeful average of 64 wins during their three years in Miller Park, 2001–03. The team has not achieved a winning season since 1992 and has not made it to the postseason since 1982.

As if this were not discouraging enough to their fans, the Brewers announced that the payroll budget for 2004 was going down again, this time to around $30 million. Moreover, their own projections showed that the team budget for payroll and player development would stay flat between 2004 and 2006, despite estimated increases in net revenue sharing receipts from $18.35 million in 2003 to $21.45 million in 2006.[9] Their newly hired chief executive officer, a highly respected Milwaukee businessman named Ulice Payne, expressed displeasure with the falling payroll and was shown the front door. His separation settlement with the Brewers was estimated to be worth $2.5 million.

All hell broke loose in Wisconsin. Tommy Thompson, by this time the U.S. Secretary of Health and Human Services, was Wisconsin's governor when the stadium deal was signed in 1995. He asserted: "The Brewers made it clear that if we built a modern, state-of-the-art stadium, it would provide them with the resources to field a winning baseball team. . . . The Brewers need to put an end to the games. They need to invest in a winning team."[10]

State Senator Mike Ellis declared: "The Seligs just scammed the living dickens out of the people of this state." And Milwaukee Mayor John Norquist bluntly stated: "The Brewers have an ownership problem." Fifty-four state legislators signed a letter demanding that the Brewers open their books to the Legislative Audit Bureau.

Meanwhile, the Brewers' acting president, Rick Schlesinger gave an interview to the *Milwaukee Journal-Sentinel* and allowed, "I can tell you that I had a couple of meetings with Ulice, Quinn [the chief financial officer] and the commissioner."[11] The only problem is that the commissioner has held his 30 percent ownership in a blind trust since 1998 and is supposed to have nothing to do with team management. Further obscuring the demarcation between the commissioner's office and the Brewers' ownership, Major League Baseball took out a full-page ad in the *Journal-Sentinel* to tell its readers that Selig had received the "Recognition of Goodness Award" from the Jewish Foundation for the Righteous.[12]

When he was selling baseball's new revenue sharing plan to the owners and players, Selig repeated his mantra that fans in all cities needed to have "hope and faith" in the prospects for their team at the beginning of the season. It is a lovely thought—one that is quite alien to the people of Milwaukee.

As for Selig himself, the heat apparently became too much. On January 16, 2004, he announced that his family was putting its share of the Brewers up for sale. His statement included the following sentiment: "It is time for me to sever my ties with the Milwaukee Brewers. [It is] in the best interests of the game."[13] One can only wonder why it took him twelve years (he became acting commissioner in 1992) to realize that there is a conflict of interest in being both an owner and the commissioner.

Montreal

The Expos still count Montreal as their home (most of the time, anyway). The racketeering suit by the former Expos minority partners against Jeffrey Loria and MLB is still in process.[14] No one—not Washington, D.C., not Northern Virginia, not Portland, Oregon—has produced an offer with sufficient public funding for a new stadium. And even if someone had, the racketeering litigation could put a stop to any sale of the team. Scheduling for another twenty-two games in Puerto Rico was held up for months, as Major League Baseball and the Players Association negotiated over playing conditions and financial compensation to the Expos players for splitting their home season.

The Expos suffer from what I shall now coin "Brewers' syndrome": increasing revenue sharing transfers and decreasing payroll. Their opening-day payroll in 2003 was $52 million; it figures to fall below $45 million for 2004, despite the receipt of revenue sharing transfers in excess of $35 million.[15] At one point, the commissioner's office held the Expos' payroll budget hostage until the players agreed to play in Puerto Rico again.

The Expos, of course, share another characteristic with the Brewers: Selig family control. As commissioner, Selig has the ultimate say over budget matters for the team as long as it continues to be owned by MLB. With any luck, the racketeering case will settle and MLB owners can look forward to a capital gain when the Expos are eventually sold and moved.

Minnesota and Miami

As discussed in chapters 1 and 2, Selig wanted to eliminate the Minnesota Twins in 2001. Yet in both 2002 and 2003 the Twins made the playoffs. Now, the Brewers' general manager, Doug Melvin, said that his team was using the Twins as its model. What he meant was that they were going to try to build a winning team on a low payroll—Melvin neglected to mention that the Twins increased their opening-day payroll from $40.2 million in 2002 to $55.6 million in 2003.

The tables certainly seemed to have turned since 1997, when Selig told the *Minneapolis Star Tribune:* "Unless somebody else has a different idea, a new stadium is the only option to keep the Twins economically viable. . . . I have to say to you very candidly: We cannot and will not consign a team to failure that can't make it."[16]

The Twins are still playing in the 1982 Metrodome, but Selig is taking his candid message to another town with a successful team: Miami. Back in April 2001, Selig wrote a Florida state senator that "the Marlins cannot and will not survive in South Florida without a new stadium." Then, after game three of the 2003 World Series was delayed for 39 minutes by rain (causing the TV ratings to drop from 14.6 before the delay to 10.8), Selig declared, "They need a domed stadium here because they do get a lot of rain, whether it's 4 o'clock, 5 o'clock or 7 o'clock."[17] Interestingly, the Marlins had only one rained-out home game throughout the 2003 season, while the Yankees had four home rainouts. Had the World Series gone to a game seven, it would have surely been rained out in New York. Perhaps the commissioner would, then, have called for a dome over Yankee Stadium.

Oakland and *Moneyball*

The Oakland Athletics is another team that has achieved relative success in recent years on a modest payroll and in an old stadium. Selig was out in Oakland prior to the 2003 season, lecturing at a Bay Area baseball luncheon about the importance of a new ballpark for the Oakland A's: "It's a high priority. . . . You don't want to consign any of your teams to failure. It goes back to what I say about hope and faith. Once you take hope and faith away, you have nothing. On April 1, if you have no chance to win, you've got a problem. So the stadium debates become very crucial."[18]

As Selig spoke these words, W. W. Norton was sending its soon-to-be bestseller *Moneyball,* by Michael Lewis, to the bindery. Lewis tells the story of how the Oakland A's became a successful team on a shoestring budget. According to Lewis, until the A's former general manager Sandy Alderson discovered the work of Bill James and other sabermetricians in the mid-1990s, baseball's system of player development, selection, and strategy was based on hackneyed folklore.[19] For instance, basic statistical analysis shows that on-base percentage (hits plus walks divided by at bats) is a far more important offensive category than batting average alone or slugging percentage (which gives two points for a double, three for a triple, and so on), yet most general managers paid little attention to it. Similarly, the standard fielding percentage statistic is a poor measure of defensive ability because it only records putouts, assists, and errors on balls that the fielder reaches, but gives no credit to a fielder with greater range or better positioning instincts.

Armed with a fresh arsenal of data and limited by a diminutive budget, Sandy Alderson created a new baseball culture in the Oakland A's front office and promoted a contrarian philosophy. He hired and schooled Billy Beane in the new system, which Beane, along with his hired hands from Harvard, developed further. Beane added some personal touches, and voilà, the Oakland A's found a way to win with little money.

Moneyball tells a fascinating story, but it is also misleading.[20] Lewis spends considerable time describing the Oakland A's picks in the 2002 amateur draft, but little time explaining how the major league rosters of the past three years were actually assembled. Clearly, the main explanation of the team's recent success lies in its superlative starting pitching. How these remarkably proficient hurlers were identified, obtained, and developed by pitching coach Rick Peterson remains largely untreated by Lewis.

According to various player development mavens, Beane wanted to sign Ben Sheets, but he didn't have the money, so he chose crafty southpaw Barry Zito instead. Tim Hudson, dominant right-handed starter, was identified by Oakland A's scout John Poloni, though Poloni is denigrated by Lewis in the book as the "fat scout."

The record was not much different for position players. Beane apparently persuaded Sandy Alderson to pass over Colorado slugger Todd Helton in 1995 in order to sign Ariel Prieto. In 2003 the Oakland A's won the American League West Division, despite ranking tenth out of fourteen American League teams in the supposedly crucial on-base percentage statistic. And Beane's proposition that it is safer to sign college graduates than high school players does not seem to have informed the Oakland A's selection of their strongest hitters in 2003, Eric Chavez (signed out of high school) and Miguel Tejada (signed at age seventeen out of the Dominican Republic).

The Alderson-Beane-James approach can clearly provide some new insights. Yet its ability to create a competitive advantage for a team is modest and will diminish as more teams hire statisticians to mine its potential contributions. Good scouting always has been and will be important—as will having lots of money.[21]

The Dodgers

Rupert Murdoch had already got what he wanted out of the Dodgers: control over the regional sports television market in southern California. In late 2003 he also got ownership of the leading satellite TV distributor in the United States, DirecTV. He can now concentrate on putting the finishing touches to his global satellite television system.

Murdoch chose Boston real estate developer Frank McCourt to be the next owner of the Dodgers. McCourt, however, while he has lots of prime Boston real estate, does not have the $430 million in cash needed to buy the Dodgers. So Murdoch's News Corp. reportedly arranged to loan McCourt $205 million until he sold some of his land. McCourt also arranged loans of $150 million from Bank of America and another $75 million from the MLB credit facility—which is to say that he planned to borrow the entire $430 million.

The owners claim that they have a 60/40 asset/debt rule in effect. If implemented, it would restrict McCourt's debt to $172 million. In the 2002 collective bargaining agreement there is also a restriction that by 2006 a team's debt (in excess of $25 million) cannot surpass ten times its EBITDA (earnings before interest, taxes, depreciation, and amortization).[22] The Dodgers have been reporting negative EBITDA for the past several years, and McCourt has stated that he expects operating losses for another two or three years, meaning that the team probably would be allowed only the $25 million debt exclusion.

In practice, the rule is implemented entirely at the discretion of the commissioner. The 60/40 rule has not been enforced since it was first introduced in December 1982. The existence of the rule, however, comes in handy as a pretext to tighten payroll budgets. Murdoch's News Corp. has a multibillion-dollar national TV contract with baseball, as well as local TV contracts with over twenty teams and MLB's Extra Innings package on DirecTV. It is likely for this reason that MLB was willing to look past the heavy debt load in McCourt's bid .

As McCourt's bid received increasing scrutiny in the press, Los Angeles real estate developer Eli Broad also offered $430 million for the team. Broad's offer entailed only minor recourse to debt. But Murdoch preferred McCourt's bid. One possible explanation is that Broad wanted to renegotiate the seriously undervalued long-term television deal between the local Fox regional sports channel and the Dodgers.[23]

Historically, the policy of MLB and the other sports leagues has been to favor local ownership. Murdoch's power, however, trumped history. MLB eventually modestly restructured McCourt's bid (approximately 90 percent was debt financed) and declared him the winner.[24] Not only did this please Murdoch, but it meant that the Dodgers' new owner was cash-strapped and therefore unlikely to put any upward pressure on players' salaries. To be sure, the *Los Angeles Times* reported that "people familiar with the initial business plan he [McCourt] submitted to major league baseball said he planned to model the Dodger payroll after the $65-million to $75-million neighborhood of the San Francisco Giants."[25]

Curiously, Selig told the Associated Press on January 16, 2004: "Rules are rules, and there are no exceptions. We have very stringent ownership rules, guidelines that we follow fastidiously, because if we don't in one place, then we aren't going to be able to in another." Sure, and Pete Rose never bet on baseball.

Labor Relations

Not surprisingly, the slower revenue growth in MLB and the 2002 collective bargaining agreement reversed baseball's upward salary spiral. Though the 2003 average salary edged up 3.3 percent above that of 2002, this was the result of built-in increases in preexisting long-term contracts.[26] As of mid-January 2004, among the 153 free agents who had signed new contracts, the average salary fell 26.6 percent. Final figures for the average salaries of all players in 2004 are not available as I write, but they are likely to fall.

The collective bargaining agreement contains at least five provisions that are helping to thwart salary growth: increased revenue sharing, with the marginal tax rate reaching above 45 percent; luxury taxes on high payrolls; a requirement that deferred salaries be fully funded within eighteen months; a new rule that limits team financial debt to a multiple of its EBITDA beginning after fiscal 2005;[27] and, a rule that restores a same round, same place draft pick in the following year to a team that fails to sign a pick in the present year.

Despite these negotiated provisions, the new restrictions and higher costs for player insurance imposed by the insurance companies, and the slower growth of MLB revenues, the Players Association has made it known that it is concerned about possible ownership collusion and has asked agents to gather any relevant information. It is impossible to know from the outside what, if any, coordination efforts were made by the owners. Given the collective bargaining agreement and the economy, however, it seems unnecessary to resort to such notions to explain the soft players market. A likely motivation for the union's position was not to uncover actual collusion but to deter its development—or even to give clubs pause before making lowball offers to players.[28]

The very use of the C word, however, threw cold water on the analysts who were proclaiming a new era of labor peace in baseball. More cold water came cascading down when the union nixed the possible restructuring of Alex Rodriguez's contract. With mounting losses from his investment company and an underperforming team, Rangers' owner Tom Hicks tried to trade the $179 million-plus and seven years remaining on Alex Rodriguez's contract to the Boston Red Sox for Manny Ramirez's contract ($97.5 million and five years remaining) and some cash. Commissioner Selig allowed the Red Sox to talk to A-Rod while he was still under contract with the Rangers, at the request of Tom Hicks.[29]

A-Rod and the Red Sox reportedly reached a deal that would have lowered his salary over the seven years by some $28 million in exchange for giving him increased marketing rights, converted deferred payments into a large signing bonus, and conferred the right to become a free agent every year after his first two seasons with the Sox. When contracts are restructured by changing or adding "special covenants" to the uniform players' contract, the collective bargaining agreement (article 2) provides that these covenants must "actually or potentially provide additional benefits to the Player." The agreement does not stipulate that these benefits must be only pecuniary.

In the past, the restructured contracts of traded players have been approved by the Players Association. It makes sense for the Players Association to perform an oversight role here, to make sure that there is no duress involved; for example, the original team threatens to bench the player unless he accepts a trade with a restructured contract.[30] In this case, the Players Association nixed the deal, arguing that it represented not a restructuring but a reduction in A-Rod's contract. Rob Manfred of the Commissioner's Office immediately challenged the right of the Players Association to determine whether the deal that A-Rod and his agent, Scott Boras, reached with the Sox was a net benefit to A-Rod. After all, in addition to the enhanced marketing and free agency rights, A-Rod would get to play for a competitive team and move to Boston, where his wife has an extensive network of family and friends.

Even though no duress was involved, the union convinced A-Rod that restructuring his contract as he intended would set a negative precedent for all union members. He withdrew his permission for the trade (he has a no-trade clause in his contract), and the Commissioner's Office decided not to arbitrate the matter without his support.[31]

Many were left scratching their heads over exactly whose interests the union was defending. A-Rod's $25.2 million average yearly salary is clearly an aberration—no other player has gone above $20 million, and currently the market for star players seems to have settled below even this level. If A-Rod's annual salary were reduced to $21.2 million, would it really have a negative impact on other players?

Moreover, many asked, why is it a bad precedent to have a player decide for himself whether there is a net benefit to a contract restructuring? If A-Rod wanted to make the deal, why did the Players Association think it knew better what was good for him? Isn't it a proper principle for each union member to be able to make this determination for himself?[32]

Leave it to the Yankees to trump the Red Sox and find a way to do a deal for A-Rod. Having shed nearly $15 million from their 2004 payroll due to the injury to Aaron Boone, the retirement from baseball of Drew Henson,

and the trade of Alfonso Soriano, the Yankees had just enoug
the required $15 million for 2004 (A-Rod is deferring $1 n
Rangers are picking up the balance of his salary). Still, the Y
man payroll for 2004 will likely finish up in the $190 million
the team will owe roughly $20 million in luxury taxes, in addi
$50 million in revenue sharing payments. It isn't cheap to play by the rules.

And related to the larger players market, remember all those years when owners proclaimed that they were forced to raise ticket prices because player salaries were skyrocketing? Now that payrolls are going down for many teams, can fans expect to see lower ticket prices? Maybe owners will instead acknowledge at last what economists have been saying all along: there is no direct link between player salaries and ticket prices.

Various and Sundry

The Fox Network, with a $2.5 billion, six-year television rights deal with MLB, had been pushing baseball to improve the falling ratings for its All-Star Game. Over the years, the midseason classic has become more and more of a media event, with carnival-like sideshows, and fans have responded accordingly, showing little interest in the game itself. This apathy was reinforced by the 2002 game, which was declared a tie by the commissioner because the teams had exhausted their pitching staffs.

So, in January 2003 the owners voted to oblige Fox—and make the All-Star Game meaningful again—or at least that's what they said they were doing (and told us so with a saturation campaign of TV advertisements). Henceforth, once permission was secured from the union, the league that won the All-Star Game would be the league with home-field advantage in the World Series. Now fans were supposed to care about the All-Star Game.

But does an all-star player from, say, the Rockies or the Pirates really care if the Marlins or the Braves have home-field advantage over the Yankees or the Red Sox in October? And if the players don't care, why should the fans? Sure enough, the fans didn't care. The All-Star Game's ratings were exactly the same in 2003 (9.5), as in 2002; the ratings even went down 11 percent (to 4.6) among the important eighteen- to forty-nine-year-old demographic. The whole commercial charade went for naught. Well, not exactly for naught; it served to reinforce baseball's fixation with short-term results at the expense of rational, long-term strategic development.[33]

This roundup of the 2003 season in the business of baseball would not be complete without a nod to the Tribune Corporation and its Chicago Cubs. The Tribune Corporation set up a new subsidiary, Wrigley Field Premium Tickets (hereafter Premium).[34] For the 2003 season, Premium purchased just under 12,000 tickets from the Cubs at regular prices, including 1,755 for the interleague series with the Yankees. Premium sold tickets with a face value of $45 for as much as $1,500 for the Yankees series. The extra revenue went on the books of Premium, not the Cubs. Tribune also apparently arranged for Premium to get free advertising on WGN during Cubs broadcasts—potentially further lowering the revenue attributable to the Cubs. Tribune attempted to justify this practice by arguing that Premium provided competition to other scalping agencies, thereby reducing the price of scalped tickets. Nice to know team ownership is looking after its customers.

Now What?

Shenanigans, missteps, and myopia notwithstanding, baseball marches onward. It is held together chiefly by three factors. First is popularity: the game is simply too deeply ingrained in our culture to be undone by mere mortals. Second is the powerful players union, which puts a check on many management excesses.

Third is mistrust: owners put up with Selig because without him they have only each other, and because each team wants to remain in his good graces. He, after all, approves or disapproves of contracts, trades, sales, and procedures. He also decides if team debt loads and uses of revenue sharing transfers are acceptable and has the power to fine owners who transgress. Not to be gainsaid, he wields a yearly $10 million fund that he spends at his own discretion.

The good news is that sensible, well-educated people are increasingly finding their way into teams' front offices, as well as into baseball's Internet arm, MLBAM. MLB's Japanese TV rights tripled in its new deal. And the industry will be nudged to greater efficiency as it faces indirect competitive pressures from the multitude of new entertainment options brought by the telecommunications revolution. In short, there's hope that things will eventually get better. For 2004, however, expect more of the same.

Notes

Preface

1. Dave Winfield, "Labor Deal Is Nice, but Peace Deal Is Needed," *New York Times,* October 20, 2002, sec. 8, p. 9.

2. Allen Barra, "Talk about Fan-Unfriendly," *New York Times,* September 29, 2002, sec. 4, p. 7.

3. While ratings for Fox's Saturday afternoon game of the week were down 3.8 percent from 2001, ratings for the important demographics of adults aged 18–34 and males aged 18–49 were each up over 10 percent. Ratings for FSN baseball broadcasts were up 4.4 percent. Ratings for ESPN Sunday and Wednesday night broadcasts were up 12.9 percent. Ratings for ESPN Monday night and weekday afternoon games were up 33 percent. Ratings on ESPN2 were also up 9.1 percent. Playoff ratings on Fox through the league championship series averaged 6.4, up 4.9 percent from the 6.1 ratings average in 2001. World Series ratings, however, were down 24 percent from 2001 and hit an all-time low. Most analysts attributed the decline to the fact that it was an all-California series, that the series began on a Saturday night, and that each game had a late start and long length. Baseball's television appeal appears to be becoming increasingly regional. See Bill King, "Final 2 Months Melt Fox's Ratings Gain," *Sports Business Journal,* October 7–13, 2002, p. 9; and *Sports Business Daily,* October 16, 2002, p. 9, and October 29, 2002, pp. 6–8.

Chapter 1

1. Fortunately for the commissioner, Doubleday and Wilpon were able to settle out of court within a few weeks of the Doubleday counterclaim. This claim alleged that Selig had presented phony financial figures about baseball to the Congress and that the so-called 60/40 rule was a salary cap in disguise. This is discussed in detail in chapter five. Doubleday also had a worthy gripe about the team assessment performed by longtime MLB financial consultant Robert Starkey. Starkey estimated

the team's value at $391 million when previous offers had already come in at $500 million or more, according to Doubleday. Starkey's methodology for arriving at this estimate appeared to be both inappropriate and prejudicial. For a discussion of his methodology and the Doubleday claim, see Andrew Zimbalist, "The Mets Are Worth More Than $391 Million," *Sports Business Journal*, August 19–25, 2002.

2. Economists refer to the type of monopoly that MLB experiences as a cartel. That is, baseball is an industry in which thirty separately owned businesses come together for business purposes and make joint decisions affecting the output levels and pricing of their product.

3. For an interesting perspective on the commissioner's office and the mission of Bud Selig, see Fay Vincent, *The Last Commissioner* (Simon and Schuster, 2002), chap. 9.

4. Don Walker, "Conflict Charge Irks Selig," *Milwaukee Journal Sentinel*, November 15, 2001, p. 1C.

5. This was the 2002 opening-day payroll for the Devil Rays, including the twenty-five-man roster plus three players on the disabled list.

6. Little League, for instance, was not introduced until just before the United States entered World War II.

7. Roger Maris's sixty-one home runs in 1961 were originally asterisked because baseball had just lengthened the season from 154 to 162 games. Ruth hit sixty home runs in 154 games.

8. The ability of individual players to excel, other things equal, would give a competitive advantage to teams with superstars. This factor by itself, other things equal, might exacerbate competitive imbalance. Similarly, contraction by itself might improve competitive balance. Either effect, however, would be diminutive relative to the potential impact of a properly designed system of incentives and revenue distribution.

9. This was an extension, signed in October 2001, for the 2002 season. It was one of three one-year options that extended through the 2003 season.

10. Buster Olney, "Budgets Will Be Stretched for Giambi and for Bonds," *New York Times*, November 20, 2001.

11. Quoted in *Sports Business Daily*, April 30, 2002, p. 11.

12. Of course, challenges could still be made by parties other than the Players Association.

13. The same is true of another member of the Red Sox hierarchy, George Mitchell, whom Selig had appointed to his blue-ribbon panel.

14. For one such account, see Vincent, *The Last Commissioner*, p. 282.

15. As it happened, in addition to the RICO lawsuit and litigation between the Mets co-owners (which was settled at the end of August 2002), Steinbrenner hired lawyer David Boies to prepare a suit against MLB in the event that its ultimate revenue sharing and luxury tax plan proved too onerous for the Yankees. These matters are discussed in chapter five.

16. Henry, Lucchino, and Werner are sharp businessmen and excellent baseball people. In their first year in Boston they were superb. It is the process and the motives, not the outcome of ownership, that are being questioned in this case.

17. The sale of the Red Sox was part of the three-way transfer of teams that is an aspect of the complaint in the RICO litigation brought against Selig and present Marlins owner Jeffrey Loria. The suit claims that Selig and Loria defrauded the former minority owners of the Expos (consisting of some of Canada's largest companies, including Seagram, Loblaw, Fairmont, and BCE) by diluting their ownership shares through deception and undermining plans to rebuild the Expos' franchise. In the end, there was a three-team ownership change wherein Loria sold his Expos to MLB for $120 million (and received a loan from MLB for $38.5 million), with which he bought John Henry's Marlins for $158.5 million, enabling Henry to purchase the Red Sox. Apparently, making these transactions together secured for Loria and Henry the benefit of avoiding any capital gains tax under section 1031 of the Internal Revenue Code, which exempts the exchange of "like kind" assets. For a more detailed discussion of this RICO suit, see Paul Weiler and Gary Roberts, *Sports and the Law* (West Group, 1998), chap. 7 supplement to the 2003 edition.

18. Cable television has three general tiers of service: stripped-down basic, which includes local over-the-air stations plus the local cable access channel; expanded basic, which includes the stripped-down basic channels plus several dozen national cable channels and superstations; and premium, which includes special pay channels such as HBO, Showtime, regional sports networks, and others.

19. The New York Yankees and the NBA's New Jersey Nets together formed a holding company in July 1999.

20. YES could also anticipate approximately $15 million in production and front-office costs in 2002.

21. The Dolan family owned 24 percent of Cablevision's stock but controlled 75 percent of the voting rights as of September 2002.

22. The channel coverage and price are for service in Brooklyn and the Bronx. This expanded basic service includes Fox Sports New York and MSG Network as part of the package at $43.95.

Chapter 2

1. Gerald Scully, *The Business of Major League Baseball* (University of Chicago Press, 1989), p. 33.

2. Lee Lowenfish and Tony Lupien, *The Imperfect Diamond: The Story of Baseball's Reserve System and the Men Who Fought to Change It* (Stein and Day, 1980), p. 106.

3. Harold Seymour, *Baseball: The Golden Age* (Oxford University Press, 1971), p. 243.

4. Quoted in Lowenfish and Lupien, *The Imperfect Diamond*, p. 103.

5. Ibid., p. 106.

6. *Federal Baseball Club* v. *National League*, 292 U.S. 200 (1922).

7. *Marienelli* v. *United Booking Offices*, 227 F. 265 (S.D.N.Y. 1914).

8. The first radio broadcast of the World Series occurred in 1921, the year before the *Federal Baseball* decision. The method of broadcasting clearly involved interstate commerce. In the 1921 World Series the New York Yankees played the New York Giants. The sports editor of a Newark newspaper reported the games from a telephone in the Polo Grounds in Manhattan to WJZ, a Newark, N.J., station, which repeated the information over the air, the radio waves reaching back across the New Jersey–New York border into Manhattan and the Bronx.

9. Quoted in Walter Champion Jr., "Baseball's Third Strike: Labor Law and the National Pastime," *Pennsylvania Law Journal @ Reporter 4,* no. 20 (May 25, 1981), p. 2.

10. *Tolson* v. *New York Yankees*, 346 U.S. 356 (1953).

11. *Radovich* v. *National Football League*, 352 U.S. 445 (1957). Two years earlier the Supreme Court held that the exemption did not apply to the sport of boxing in *U.S.* v. *International Boxing Club*, 348 U.S. 236 (1955).

12. The NFL estimate includes revenue from the contract with DirecTV to telecast NFL Sunday Ticket. Stephen Carr and Timothy Cummins ("Professional Sports Franchises Still Present Unique Valuation Problems," *Valuation Strategies*, November– December 2001) estimate the NFL's total national TV rights fees in 2002 at $2.475 billion, or $79.8 million per team.

13. Quoted in Lowenfish and Lupien, *The Imperfect Diamond*, p. 207. Also see Charles Korr, *The End of Baseball as We Knew It: The Players Union 1960–1981* (University of Illinois Press, 2002), for an interesting discussion of the Flood exchange with MLB, based on previously undisclosed documents from the Players Association.

14. *Flood* v. *Kuhn et al.*, 407 U.S. 258 (1972), p. 744.

15. Ibid., p. 743. Somewhat ironically, this repudiation of the logic of the 1922 decision actually complicates efforts by state attorneys general to hold baseball accountable to state antitrust laws today.

16. Quoted in Marvin Miller, *A Whole Different Ballgame: The Sport and Business of Baseball* (Birch Lane Press, 1991), p. 142.

17. Arguably, the scope of the exemption was also called into question in two earlier cases, each citing the Blackmun decision in *Flood* to the effect that the business of baseball is exempt only insofar as it involves activities that are central to the "unique characteristics and needs" of baseball. In *Postema* v. *National League of Professional Baseball Clubs*, 799 F. Supp. 1475 (S.D.N.Y. 1992), the court held that baseball's exemption does not apply to action taken with respect to umpires. In *Henderson Broadcasting Corp.* v. *Houston Sports Ass'n.*, 541 F. Supp. 263 (S.D. Tx. 1982), the court held that the exemption does not apply to local radio broadcasting.

18. Padova based this upon five arguments: the repeated referencing of the reserve clause in connection with the exemption in Blackmun; the standard use of *stare decisis* in the United States as applying to both the rule and the result of a case;

the imperative to construe antitrust exemptions narrowly; the *Flood* court's clear repudiation of the grounds for the Holmes decision in *Federal Baseball*; and the more limited interpretation given to Blackmun's decision in *Postema* and *Henderson*.

19. Interestingly, Don Fehr, head of the Players Association, commented in 1994 that the players would not go out on strike if the union were empowered to bring an antitrust complaint against the owners. He said without that potential legal defense to protect their interests, the only defense the players had was to strike. He made no similar pledge in 2002, when the players did have the legal defense available due to the Curt Flood Act. It should be noted, however, that when Fehr made that pledge in 1994, the Supreme Court's decision in *Brown* had not yet been made. Hence, Fehr's expectation in 1994 may have been that the union itself could have brought an antitrust claim against the owners without having first to decertify itself. For an interesting discussion of some of the legal nuances of the *Brown* decision, see William Gould, "Baseball and Globalization," *Indiana Journal of Global Legal Studies*, vol. 8 (2000), pp. 85–120.

20. *Patterson* v. *McLean Credit Union*, 491 U.S. 164, 172 (1989), cited in Stephen Ross and Bruce Smith, Brief of *Amici Curiae*, Consumer Federation of America and American Antitrust Institute in Support of Appellant and in Support of Reversal, *MLB et al. v. Robert Butterworth* (11th Cir. 2002).

21. The beginning monthly salary of $850 has been stuck at that level since the 1980s. After their first year, Class A players' monthly salaries range from $1,100 to $1,200; Class AA players', from $1,400 to $1,600; and Class AAA players', from $2,300 to $3,000 (not counting veteran minor leaguers who previously played under major league contract, whose monthly salary range is generally $7,000 to $10,000).

22. Each major league team has an active roster of twenty-five players. The forty-man roster includes all players (generally, fifteen of whom play in the minors) who are on major league contracts and can be called up in the case of injury or after August 31, when the major league active rosters expand to forty.

23. Labor unions by their very nature are combinations in restraint of trade: a union forces an employer to bargain with a group of workers rather than with individual workers. Labor unions thus would violate the Sherman Act of 1890. The Clayton Act of 1914, however, explicitly exempts labor unions from the provisions of the Sherman Act. This is known as the statutory exemption. The so-called nonstatutory exemption evolved not from legislation but from court decisions. It holds that trade unions can exchange (in arm's-length bargaining) free labor market rights for other benefits. Thus, by union shop precepts, a trade union can bargain over general conditions for entering the shop. Player drafts fit this category. Under the nonstatutory exemption, a players' union can bargain away competition among teams over amateurs entering the major leagues directly in exchange for other desiderata in the collective bargaining contract.

24. Of course, there are also some veterans who play in the minor leagues. They, too, are generally interested in resurrecting their major league careers.

25. In June 2002 there were five established independent minor leagues functioning: the Atlantic League, the Northern League (with eastern and central divisions), the Western League, the Central League, and the Frontier League.

26. The UBL partners, who included the present author, called in some of the country's leading antitrust lawyers to discuss the possibility of legal action. They were told that the liability case was strong and that the damages case was uncertain. In any event, pursuing the matter would likely have cost tens of millions of dollars and taken several years. The partners, who were seeking to create competition for MLB by founding a league based on sounder principles, opted to fold operations rather than enter a legal battle.

27. Rozelle and Tagliabue quoted in Paul Weiler and Gary Roberts, *Sports and the Law: Text, Cases, Problems* (West Group, 1998), p. 556.

28. *Chicago Pro. Sports Ltd. Partnership* v. *NBA*, 808 F. Supp. 646, 649–50 (N.D. Ill. 1992); and *Shaw et al.* v. *NFL* (E.D. Pa. 2000). Also see letter from Charles Rule, assistant attorney general, Antitrust Division, U.S. Department of Justice, to the Hon. Howard Metzenbaum, chair, Senate Subcommittee on Antitrust, March 30, 1988.

29. MLB's contract with Fox might also be vulnerable without the exemption, since the network carries some of its national games on Fox's cable affiliates.

30. It is intriguing to recall that, despite its presumed exemption, MLB had many more team relocations than the other leagues in the 1950s and 1960s. It is, then, perhaps a touch disingenuous for MLB, since the controversy over the Raiders' move, to associate its exemption with franchise stability.

31. Here I assume that this expression of demand flows from a representative political process and is not distorted by wealth effects.

32. Arguably, a preferable outcome would be for MLB to add an expansion team to Washington, D.C. The prospective move of the Montreal franchise to Washington, D.C., or elsewhere in late 2002 was being held up by the RICO suit filed against MLB and Jeffrey Loria by the former Canadian minority owners of the Expos. Part of the argument made by the plaintiffs in this case is that Montreal was a good baseball city in the past—outdrawing the Yankees in several years between 1969 and 1991—and it is only because of negligent and ineffective ownership that local support for the franchise has drifted to its present nadir. See the Complaint in *BMO Nesbitt Burns Inc. et al.* v. *Jeffrey H. Loria et al.* (S.D. Fla. 2002).

33. See written testimony of Attorney General Bob Butterworth, Senate Judiciary Committee, February 13, 2002.

34. Cited in Weiler and Roberts, *Sports and the Law*, chap. 7.

35. *Sullivan* v. *NFL*, 34 F.3d 1091 (1st Cir. 1994). This was a jury verdict in a somewhat quirky trial. For more discussion of the antitrust aspects of the ban on municipal ownership, see Stephen Ross, "Antitrust Options to Redress Anticompetitive Restraints and Monopolistic Practices by Professional Sports Leagues," *Case Western Reserve Law Review*, vol. 23, no. 1 (2001), pp. 133–71.

Chapter 3

1. Richard Levin and others, *The Report of the Independent Members of the Commissioner's Blue Ribbon Panel on Baseball Economics*, July 2000, p. 7.

2. The standard deviation of win percentages is a measure of dispersion. For a given year, it is equal to the square root of the difference between each team's win percentage and the average win percentage (.500) squared, divided by the number of teams.

3. The idealized standard deviation is that which would obtain in a league with perfect equality in playing strength across teams for any given length of season. In a league of perfect parity, the standard deviation of win percentages would be $\sigma = 0.5/\sqrt{N}$, where N is the number of games each team plays during the season.

4. The gini coefficient is a measure of inequality. The higher the coefficient, the greater the inequality.

5. The Herfindahl-Hirschman index of championship concentration is also employed by some.

6. A standard measure of excess tail frequency would compare the percent of teams lying outside two or three standard deviations from the mean (of win percentages) to the percent that would obtain were there perfect parity of playing strength among the teams.

7 . Many sports economists have used the concept of an idealized standard deviation of win percentages. Statistically, it makes sense to compare this number with the actual standard deviation of win percentages because it standardizes for the length of a sport's season. The problem with this index of competitive balance, however, is that fans do not experience it directly. If a fan of the Carolina Panthers is told that he shouldn't be distressed that his team won only one game in 2001–02 because the sample of games was too small to reveal the true strength of his team, it is not likely that he would be comforted.

One meaningful way to distinguish among balance measures is to test how effective they are as predictors of attendance, controlling for relevant factors. In a 2002 article, Brad Humphreys suggests a new index of competitive balance and then tests its explanatory power; see Humphreys, "Alternative Measures of Competitive Balance in Sports Leagues," *Journal of Sports Economics*, vol. 3 (May 2002), pp. 133–48. Humphreys reasons that fans care as much about performance mobility of teams over time as they do about the imbalance across teams in a particular year. He devises a metric that reflects both these criteria and finds that it explains more of the variation in baseball attendance over the past 100 years than do alternative measures of balance.

8. Again, this argument follows that of Humphreys, ibid.

9. These significant correlations exist despite the New York Rangers, who seem to have done their best to destroy the link between payroll and performance. Their $67.3 million payroll in 2001–02 was the highest in the NHL, but they managed only a .439

win percentage and eighty points. Were the highest payroll team also a top-performing team in hockey, as the Yankees are in baseball, these correlations would be still stronger. An additional problem in hockey is that players do not become unrestricted free agents until after they have reached thirty-one years of age. Hockey is a physically punishing sport, and few players remain at the top of their game in their early thirties. Thus, relying upon free-agent purchases to develop a competitive club is a riskier proposition in the NHL than in MLB.

10. An r of .363 ($r^2 = .132$) means that in a simple regression of team performance on team payroll, the variance in team payroll explained 13.2 percent of the variance in team win percentage.

11. If win percentage is regressed on a team's payroll relative to the league average payroll in each year, the r-squared in the different sports in recent time periods is as follows: MLB, .22 (1980–2001); NBA, .16 (1986–2000); NHL, .11 (1990–98); NFL, .05 (1989–2000); England's Premier League, .34 (1974–99); Italy's Serie A, .56 (1988–99). See Stefan Szymanski, "The Economic Design of Sporting Contests: A Review," unpublished manuscript, Management School, Imperial College, London, October 2002.

12. The data were obtained from the National Hockey Players' Association (NHLPA). I also ran the regressions using the NHL point system (based on two points per win and one point per tie) instead of win percentages. The correlations were a bit stronger, but revealed an identical pattern.

13. Further, the NBA, by a considerable margin, has the highest ratio of actual to idealized standard deviation of win percentages among U.S. leagues.

14. The NBA has experienced earlier periods of single-team dominance as well, but not since the 1960s did a team repeat three years in a row as champion. Between 1959 and 1966 the Boston Celtics won eight consecutive championships, then lost in 1967, but won again in 1968 and 1969. What is notable about the Chicago Bulls' dominance during the 1990s is that it occurred during the salary cap era.

15. The player stability associated with the Bird exception may be diminished with the harder caps at 55–57 percent from the new escrow system that took effect in 2001–02, and at 60.1 percent from the prohibitive luxury tax that took effect in 2002–03. See Andrew Zimbalist, "Labor Relations Heating Up in the NBA," *Sports Business Journal*, November 11–17, 2002.

16. The other U.S. team sport leagues also employ a reverse-order draft. To avoid the possibility that poorly performing teams perceive an incentive to lose games during the latter part of the season in order to gain a higher draft pick, the NBA instituted a modification of the standard reverse-order picking system. In the NBA system, all teams that do not qualify for the postseason enter a lottery to determine the order of picks among them. In recent years, the NBA has further adjusted its system to give lower-finishing teams a higher probability of success in the lottery.

17. Levin and others, *Report of the Commissioner's Blue Ribbon Panel*, p. 7.

18. The PL was so named in 1992–93. Before that it was simply called Division I, and today's Division I was called Division II, etc.

19. Another aspect of this story is that the PL shares very little television revenue.

20. This is in contrast with an $r = .48$ in U.S. baseball during the period 1980–2000, the highest correlation for any U.S. league by a significant margin. The PL is also characterized by a relatively low standard deviation of win percentages of .11, and with thirty-eight games per regular season, an extremely low ratio of actual to idealized standard deviation of 1.22.

21. For an excellent discussion of Man U and other aspects of the English soccer industry, see Stefan Szymanski and Tim Kuypers, *Winners and Losers: The Business Strategy of Football* (Penguin, 2000). Also see Roger Noll, "The Economics of Promotion and Relegation in Sports Leagues: The Case of English Football," *Journal of Sports Economics*, vol. 3, no. 2 (2002), pp. 169–203.

22. This improvement in balance since the 1950s is also clearly reflected in the standard measure of concentration of first-place finishes. The Herfindahl-Hirschman index of concentration of first-place finishes fell in the American League from 0.66 in the 1950s to 0.29 in the 1960s, 0.18 in the 1970s, and 0.11 in the 1980s; in the National League it fell from 0.44 in the 1950s to 0.19 in the 1960s and to 0.12 in the 1980s (Humphreys, "Alternative Measures of Competitive Balance"). Because of the length of its season, baseball still has a lower standard deviation of win percentages than the other major team sports in the United States. If one adjusts for the length of the season, baseball falls in the middle.

23. Humphreys's competitive-balance ratio (CBR) is the standard deviation of a particular team's win percentages over time averaged across teams for a particular period divided by the yearly standard deviation of win percentages across a league averaged over the same time period.

24. *MLB Updated Supplement to the Report of the Independent Members of the Commissioner's Blue Ribbon Panel on Baseball Economics,* December 2001.

25. The top quartile refers to the top 25 percent of teams.

26. Commissioner Selig's office also has attempted to measure competitive imbalance in a different way. In a December 2001 poll of 1,000 fans, 75 percent agreed that there is a lack of competitive balance in the game, and 42 percent said they would be less interested in baseball if it were not improved. Even if the survey was conducted properly, it is not clear what "less interested" means in terms of fan behavior. Nor is it clear how much improvement fans want to see or what changes would constitute improvement.

27. Another anomaly in the 2002 postseason is that in the first round of the playoffs, using the forty-man payroll (as defined for the luxury tax), the lower-payroll club beat the higher-payroll club in each of the four division championships. As explained in the text, although abnormal, these 2002 results do not controvert the argument of a close statistical relationship between payroll and performance. Indeed, using the forty-man payroll data for 2002, the correlation between payroll

and win percentage remains positive and significant at the 1 percent level. Nonetheless, in 2002, the variance in payroll explains less than one-quarter of the variance in win percentage. Again, higher payroll raises the probability of success. It does not guarantee success.

28. Because win percentage is limited to be between 0 and 1, technically it is appropriate to use logistic regression. When this is done, the results on the significance of the relationship over the years are very similar.

29. Clive Granger, "Investigating Causal Relations by Econometric Models and Cross-Spectral Methods," *Econometrica*, vol. 37 (1969), pp. 424–38. Basically, the test involves exploring the lagged relationships between the two variables in question. The Granger method and its application to MLB during the period 1980–2000 are presented in Stephen Hall, Stefan Szymanski, and Andrew Zimbalist, "Testing Causality between Team Performance and Payroll: The Cases of Major League Baseball and English Soccer," *Journal of Sports Economics*, vol. 3 (May 2002), pp. 149–68. Some of the results presented in this latter article are discussed in the text.

30. In fact, if analyzed using the standard deviation of win percentages as the gauge, baseball's competitive balance showed a gradual, secular increase between 1903 and the 1980s. Before 1965, this increase in balance is most likely attributable to greater talent compression. See the discussion in chapter one. The drop in the standard deviation of win percentages was particularly sharp after the introduction of the reverse-order amateur draft in 1965; it fell from .087 and .080 in the American League and National League respectively during the period 1953–1964, to .069 and .071 from 1965 through 1976.

31. These numbers are pre-revenue sharing. Levin and others, *Report of the Commissioner's Blue Ribbon Panel*, p. 17; and *MLB Updated Supplement to the Report*, p. 24.

32. Clemens's contract gave him the option of playing for the Yankees in 2003. He could take the option to play or take a buyout of his contract. Either way he would get paid $10.8 million. If he took the buyout, he would become a free agent and could re-sign with the Yankees (or another team) as a free agent for additional pay. The benefit to the Yankees of this arrangement is that with a buyout Clemens's $10.8 million does not count toward team payroll in 2003; rather, it counts for 2001 and 2002, when there was no luxury tax. The salary structure also gives the illusion of Clemens's annual salary being approximately $10 million rather than $15 million and thereby bypasses issues with other pitchers on the team about their value relative to Clemens's. In the 2002 collective bargaining agreement, the owners and players have agreed to close what is now known as the "Clemens loophole."

33. Naturally, it is possible that players' use of steroids is contributing to the power surge. The record on the extent or impact of their use is not yet clear. It should also be pointed out, however, that outstanding pitching performances are also increasing.

34. This relationship was found to be statistically significant at the 1 percent level. Peter Fishman, "Competitive Balance in Major League Baseball," senior honors thesis, Department of Economics, Duke University, May 2002.

35. To be free agents, under existing MLB rules, Cuban defectors must first establish residency in a country other than the United States. If MLB's amateur draft is internationalized, Cuban players coming to the United States without first playing professional ball in a third country will no longer be able to attain immediate free-agent status. Among other things, then, internationalizing the draft might have the unintended consequence of making it easier for Cuba to keep its best players.

36. It is also true that certain preexisting opportunities were exploited for the first time. The Yankees' Alfonso Soriano at the age of twenty actually "retired" from Japanese baseball, allowing him to become a free agent for MLB. The Japanese league has since closed the "retirement" loophole. See Jeff Pearlman, "He's Arrived," *Sports Illustrated*, August 26, 2002.

37. Most teams have also established development camps in the Caribbean. According to one extensive study, the living and working conditions in many of these camps are deplorable, although they vary substantially. See Arturo Marcano and David Fidler, *Stealing Lives: The Globalization of Baseball and the Tragic Story of Alexis Quiroz* (Indiana University Press, 2003). At the start of the 2002 season, 26.1 percent of major leaguers came from outside the United States. Of those, 88 percent came from Latin America. Forty percent of first-year professional ballplayers came from outside the United States in 2002.

38. Under the 50 percent, straight-pool plan initially proposed by the owners in the 2002 collective bargaining negotiations, each team would have faced a marginal tax rate of 48.3 percent. If the 50 percent tax were applied on a split-pool basis, the marginal tax rate on the below-average-revenue teams would vary between 103 and 107 percent. That is, for every extra dollar such a team earned, its after-tax revenue would fall by between 3 and 7 cents.

39. I tested the following model with panel data separately for the periods 1950–65 and 1985–2000:

$$\text{ATT} = f\,(\text{WPC, WPC}_{t-1}, \text{PRICE, STAD, TEAM DUMMIES, TREND}),$$

where WPC is win percentage, WPC_{t-1} is win percentage lagged one year, PRICE is the average ticket price, STAD is a dummy variable equaling 1 if the team was playing in a stadium built within the previous three years, TEAM DUMMIES allow for team fixed effects, and TREND is a variable equaling 1 for the first year, 2 for the second, etc. The Cochrane-Orcutt iterative technique was used to correct for autocorrelation. The key results, which are robust for various specifications (including logs), are as follows:

	1950–1965	*1985–2000*
r^2	.51	.54
Estimated coefficient on WPC	2.40	3.33
t statistic on WPC	9.21	12.07
Estimated coefficient on WPC_{t-1}	0.27	1.75
t statistic on WPC_{t-1}	1.06	6.34

40. Of course, the effect in percentage terms is smaller. While one win during the first period raised attendance by 1.3 percent, one win during the second period raised attendance by 1.5 percent.

41. The economic and legal case for promotion/relegation is made cogently in Stephen Ross and Stefan Szymanski, "Open Competition in League Sports," *Wisconsin Law Review* (2002), pp. 625–55.

42. The 2002 basic agreement gives teams that are unable to sign a first-round pick in one year an additional pick in the first round the following year. Teams that lose a second-round pick get a sandwich pick between the second and third rounds the next year. These changes should provide modest relief.

43. To the extent that low-revenue clubs simply sell off their incremental talent acquired from new draft preferences, these teams will benefit financially from the preferences, but their relative on-field performance would experience little sustained improvement. If there were no market rigidities and these results obtained, the Coase invariance theorem would be supported. See Ronald Coase, "The Problem of Social Cost," *Journal of Law and Economics*, vol. 3 (October 1960), pp. 1–44.

Chapter 4

1. *Sports Business Daily*, July 11, 2002, p. 10.

2. Naimoli and Dombrowski quoted in ibid.

3. Selig quoted in Jason Reid, "Situation Not as Bad as Selig Described It," *Los Angeles Times*, July 12, 2002, p. Sports-1.

4. Leonard Koppett, "The Business of America's National Pastime Is Unpatriotic Obfuscation," *New York Times*, March 10, 2002, Sports, p. 11.

5. Thomas Boswell, "Honestly, Baseball Has Problem: Honesty," *Washington Post*, February 1, 2002, p. D1.

6. www.house.gov.judiciary/76556.pdf.

7. Fifty percent is the share the Internal Revenue Service (IRS) allows an owner to presume. Some owners in recent years have gone above the 50 percent threshold.

8. Various empirical estimates of player value tend to confirm this expected outcome. See, for instance, Lawrence Kahn, "The Sports Business as a Labor Market Laboratory," *Journal of Economic Perspectives*, vol. 14, no. 3 (2000), pp. 75–94; and Andrew Zimbalist, "Salaries and Performance in Major League Baseball," in P. Sommers, ed., *Diamonds Are Forever: The Business of Baseball* (Brookings, 1992).

9. It could be argued that in the majority of cases an MLB team does not own its minor league affiliates, but it has to pay the players on the roster nonetheless. Thus there is a cost to maintain the "perpetual asset." These expenditures on minor leaguers and player development systems (on average about $14 million per team per year) then could be viewed as an investment and amortized over time. Teams, however, expense these costs instead of treating them as investments to be amor-

tized. To be sure, generally teams also expense, rather than amortize, amateur signing bonuses.

10. An anonymous MLB executive interviewed by ESPN in early August 2002 said that MLB's aggregate operating loss in 2002 would rise to $450 million, but he provided no details. Since 2002 opening-day salaries were only 3.3 percent above than those in 2001, if operating losses go up at all mismanagement might have something to do with it. Clearly, all the talk of work stoppage during the season was not a favorable factor. Undoubtedly, U.S. economic conditions also played a role.

11. *Sports Business Daily*, July 3, 2002, p. 16.

12. Some reports suggested that MLB also withheld $210 million from the teams in order to accumulate cash to buy out the two teams scheduled for contraction. It is likely this is the same money that is referred to as the war chest for a work stoppage. And, as is argued in the text, it seems implausible that contraction was ever more than a ploy to gain bargaining leverage with the players and cities.

13. And of course the Internet investment was made with the expectation that it would enhance clubs' cash flow in future years.

14. It is not clear from Selig's report whether his revenue figure is also net of payroll luxury taxes, which were levied on the five highest payrolls during the period 1997–99. I will treat them as if they were netted out, which gives the benefit of the doubt to Selig for purposes of assessing the magnitude of these discrepancies. In any event, the total luxury tax collected during these years was small: $12 million in 1997, $5 million in 1998, and $11 million in 1999.

15. To do this, I use Selig's numbers to estimate team revenue sharing (and luxury tax) net contributions. These contributions equal total revenue minus total local revenue minus central fund receipts.

16. It is possible that this figure should be adjusted for the superstation payments that the Cubs make to MLB, which are probably on the order of $15 million annually. However, it is also likely that the *Broadcasting and Cable* figure is conservative. Kim McAvoy, "Yanks, Others Get in the Game," *Broadcasting and Cable*, April 1, 2002.

17. The reason the net tax is just under 20 cents is that the team gets back roughly one-thirtieth of every dollar it contributes.

18. Doug Pappas, "The Numbers: Local Media Revenues," *Baseball Prospectus*, December 2001.

19. Some of ESPN's games air on ESPN2, which has a lower penetration. As of mid-2002, TBS reached 87.2 million households (out of approximately 106 million television households in the country). This number implies that TBS reached close to 100 percent penetration of cable households, plus additional direct broadcast satellite (DBS) households and off-air households in the Atlanta area.

20. See, for instance, the *Newark Star-Ledger*, March 19, 2002; and Richard Sandomir, "Cablevision Is Holding Off on Carrying YES," *New York Times*, February 16, 2002, p. D8.

21. Under MLB's revenue sharing accounting rules, if a team uses cash for capital improvements in a stadium, such disbursements must be amortized over ten years.

22. Lest he be accused of being partial to his beloved Bronx Bombers, Giuliani made the same gift to the Mets.

23. Audited Combined Financial Statements, NESN, Years Ended December 31, 2000, 1999, and 1998. These statements were part of the documentary record established by the Massachusetts attorney general in 2002 during his investigation into the sale of the Red Sox.

24. According to the *Boston Herald* (August 10, 2002), the Sox plan to increase the number of games carried on NESN from 89 to 122, allowing them to have greater leeway in allocating media revenue through related-party transactions. NESN plans to substantially increase its monthly fee to cable companies in 2003. It is probable that most or all of this fee increase will be passed on to consumers.

25. Telephone conversation with the author.

26. Smiley had a year to raise sufficient capital to buy the team and came up some $50 million short. Huizenga eventually sold the team to John Henry, a Palm Beach commodities trader, minority owner of the New York Yankees, and future lead owner of the Boston Red Sox. Henry agreed to pay $150 million for the team and also to accept the status quo on the stadium lease as well as an extension of the contract with SportsChannel Florida.

27. Kim McAvoy, "Baseball Gets the Bucks," *Broadcasting and Cable*, April 2, 2001; and McAvoy, "Yanks, Others Get in the Game."

28. Team Marketing Report, *Inside the Ownership of Pro Sports* (Chicago, 2001), p. 61.

29. When Albert Belle's hip injury ended his career in 2002 with three years and $40 million left on his guaranteed contract, the insurance industry got a wake-up call. Premiums jumped from around $65,000 for a $20 million contract to $130,000. Teams responded by lowering the average share of a top player's contract that they cover by injury insurance from nearly 80 percent to between 40 and 50 percent. This keeps the teams' premium costs in a manageable range, but it also means that the teams absorb more of the injury risk to the star players. Insurance companies increasingly are reluctant to insure perennially problematic body parts of players. At the November 2002 GM meetings, insurance companies also indicated that they would no longer insure player contracts in excess of three years. Facility insurance also jumped appreciably following September 11, 2001. Sometimes teams cover these costs; sometimes they are covered by the quasi-public stadium authority. In 2002, facility property and liability insurance could run in excess of $2 million a year. See John Lombardo, "Belle Claim Takes Its Toll on Insurance," and Kim Nilsen, "Terrorism Coverage, Once Free, Now Major Cost," *Sports Business Journal*, September 23–29, 2002, pp. 21–26.

30. These shares are all based on the forty-man roster and include termination pay and prorated signing bonuses.

31. Quoted in *Sports Business Daily*, June 24, 2002.

32. Bill Shaikin, "Fox Reaches Dodger Goals," *Los Angeles Times*, December 13, 2001, p. Sports-8.

33. Personal communication, John Henry to the author, August 28, 2002.

34. According to Selig's blue-ribbon panel, of thirteen franchise sales between 1992 and 2000, if one includes the reported operating losses along with capital gains, five team owners lost money, three owners made a "modest" return, and five made a "substantial" return (Richard Levin and others, *The Report of the Independent Members of the Commissioner's Blue Ribbon Panel on Baseball Economics*, July 2000, p. 51). There are four problems with their analysis. First, they do not report the sale prices of the franchises or indicate that any adjustments were made to account for variations in the balance sheets. Second, there is no indication that they adjust for the tax-sheltering value of amortizing player contracts. Third, they uncritically accept the reported operating results of the teams. Fourth, they do not include all franchise sales during this period. One sale, for instance, that seems to be conveniently left out is that of the Angels. The Angels were purchased as an expansion team in 1960 for $2.1 million. They were next sold in 1996 for $120 million. Nonetheless, the point that there is no guarantee that there will be capital gains when an owner sells a team is certainly correct.

Rodney Fort's estimates are more conservative than John Moag's. Fort estimates that the average yearly rate of franchise appreciation based on sales in various decades is as follows: 1950s, 7.2 percent; 1960s, 6.0 percent; 1970s, 7.4 percent; 1980s, 7.9 percent; 1990s, 11.3 percent. Rodney Fort, *Sports Economics* (Prentice Hall, 2002), p. 389. For most decades, this appreciation rate is below that of the S&P 500 industrial common stocks, which, were Fort's estimates accurate, would not be surprising, since (a) there is more variability and risk in the return to common stocks, (b) there are more tax advantages to franchise ownership, and (c) there are higher nonpecuniary returns to franchise ownership.

Chapter 5

1. Reality is a bit more complicated than this common perception, as the text explains. The first bargaining agreement between the owners and the Players Association was in 1966. It occurred without a work stoppage and, significantly, converted the players' pension plan from contributory to noncontributory. MLB, however, did not recognize the MLBPA as the exclusive bargaining agent of the players until the 1968 agreement.

2. For an excellent treatment of Cannon's role in the early years of the Players Association, see Charles Korr, *The End of Baseball as We Knew It: The Players' Union, 1960–1981* (University of Illinois Press, 2002), chap. 1.

3. Quoted in James Edward Miller, *The Baseball Business: Pursuing Pennants and Profits in Baltimore* (University of North Carolina Press, 1990) p. 142. Also see the

discussion of Cannon in Marvin Miller's autobiography, *A Whole Different Ballgame: The Sport and Business of Baseball* (Birch Lane Press, 1991), pp. 6–8, 33–38, 65–66.

4. J. E. Miller, *The Baseball Business*, p. 142.

5. Don Drysdale, *Once a Bum, Always a Dodger* (St. Martin's, 1990), chap. 10.

6. Korr, *The End of Baseball as We Knew It*, chap. 5.

7. Koppett quoted in M. Miller, *A Whole Different Ballgame*, p. 222.

8. James Quirk, "The Reserve Clause: Recent Developments," in Michael Jones, ed., *Current Issues in Professional Sports* (Durham, N.H.: Whittmore School of Business and Economics, 1980), p. 114.

9. For more on MLB's final offer salary arbitration system, see, for one, A. Zimbalist, *Baseball and Billions: A Probing Look into the Big Business of Our National Pastime* (Basic Books, 1994), chap. 4.

10. For an excellent extended discussion of the Hunter case, see M. Miller, *A Whole Different Ballgame*, pp. 111–13, 227–34. For a different view of the same proceedings, see Bowie Kuhn, *Hardball: The Education of a Baseball Commissioner* (McGraw-Hill, 1988), pp. 139–43.

11. Until 1972 the owners required a player to have a signed contract in order to play. The challenge by McNally and Messersmith, therefore, would have been impossible before 1972 unless the player was willing to sit out a season. Donald Fehr, "The Relationship of the Baseball Players Association, Team Management and the League," in Jones, *Current Issues in Professional Sports;* and discussion with Marvin Miller.

12. There were actually three types of free agents delineated in the agreement. Reentry free agents were players with six years of service. Nontender free agents were players whose club refused to offer them a new contract under the 20 percent rule. Nonrenewal free agents were players who were granted their outright release. Reentry free agents were also subject to a repeater rule, which required five years to pass before a player could repeat as a free agent.

13. Of these, 111 players signed contracts for two years, 105 for three years, 21 for four years, 33 for five years, 10 for six years, and 1 for ten years.

14. *Official Baseball Guide* (St. Louis: The Sporting News, 1979), p. 314.

15. Robert Berry, William Gould, and Paul Staudohar, *Labor Relations in Professional Sports* (Auburn House, 1986), p. 68.

16. Korr, *The End of Baseball as We Knew It*, chap. 11.

17. Each owner collected $100,000 for each lost game on the policy.

18. M. Miller, *A Whole Different Ballgame*, p. 318.

19. Ibid., p. 298.

20. Paul Staudohar, *The Sports Industry and Collective Bargaining*, 2d ed. (ILR Press, 1989), p. 56.

21. Kenneth Jennings, *Balls and Strikes: The Money Game in Professional Baseball* (Praeger, 1990), p. 62.

22. The share of national TV revenue this represented fell from 33 percent to 17.4 percent, but the actual dollar contribution more than doubled.

23. Terry Pluto and Jeffrey Newman, *A Baseball Winter: The Off-Season Life of the Summer Game* (Macmillan, 1986), p. 304.

24. The order of the pick is in inverse order according to team standing.

25. John Helyar, "Playing Ball," *Wall Street Journal*, May 20, 1991, p. A12.

26. Quotes from Major League Baseball, Arbitration Panel, Decision on Grievance 87-3, pp. 10, 12.

27. Quotes from Major League Baseball, Arbitration Panel, Decision on Grievance 88-1, pp. 27, 9.

28. Option buyouts enable a team to buy itself out of the last option year of a contract; the share of new contracts containing such clauses fell by almost half. The number of new contracts containing performance bonuses fell from 272 in 1985 to 173 in 1986; the number with award and signing bonuses fell by over 50 percent; the number with no-trade clauses fell from 37 in 1985 to 17 in 1986.

29. Fay Vincent, *The Last Commissioner* (Simon and Schuster, 2002), pp. 281, 286.

30. According to *Newsweek*, February 19, 1990, p. 60, ticket sales and broadcast rights together came to 82 percent of total revenues in 1989. The 48 percent was to be applied to the salaries of all players on the active twenty-five-man major league roster plus the disabled list, not the forty-man roster (which includes players reserved by the major league team but playing in the minors or on the disabled list), as reported by Murray Chass, "Owners Offer Revenue Sharing Deal," *New York Times*, January 11, 1990.

31. For more discussion of these points, see Roger Abrams, *Legal Bases: Baseball and the Law* (Temple University Press, 1998), chap. 9.

32. MLB appealed the injunction to the Second Circuit Court of Appeals, but the Second Circuit affirmed Sotomayor's decision in September 1995. *Silverman* v. *Major League Baseball Player Relations Committee, Inc.*, 67 F. 3d 1054 (2d Cir. 1995).

33. Sotomayor's ruling was based primarily on whether certain items (for example, salary arbitration, ending the anticollusion clause, negotiating the clubs' ability to sign with individual players) were mandatory or permissible bargaining subjects. She ruled that these subjects all related to the wages of the players and were therefore mandatory. As such, management violated fair labor practices by unilaterally implementing changes in these matters.

34. In 1995, American League teams shared 20 percent of ticket sales with visiting teams, and National League teams shared 50 cents per ticket (or approximately 4 percent of the gate) with visiting teams. There was also a very modest sharing of revenues from local cable television contracts.

35. The apparent logic is that trade unions are by their nature restraints of trade and exist legally only because of the exception created by the Clayton Act. If unions exist only with the suspension of antitrust principles, then unions should not be able to avail themselves of antitrust protections. *Brown* v. *Pro Football, Inc.*, S. Ct. (1996). If nothing else, the ruling still allows antitrust challenges, but only after the union engages in time-consuming and wasteful bureaucratic procedures (decertifying and recertifying the union). In addition to the inefficiency involved, the union

is exposed to possible management manipulation to prevent recertification. For an interesting view of the complexities and legal ramifications of the *Brown* decision, see, for one, William Gould, "Baseball and Globalization," *Indiana Journal of Global Legal Studies*, vol. 8 (2000), pp. 85–120.

36. The panel did not state that this minimum should be a hard-and-fast requirement. Rather, it stated that incentives should be structured to "encourage" teams to meet this minimum.

37. Or, if they sign professional baseball contracts in an independent league, they can also sue (with likely success) to become MLB free agents the following year.

38. The panel report also proposed introducing a competitive balance draft wherein the bottom eight finishing clubs each year would be able to pick from eight playoff teams' minor league systems any players not on the forty-man roster. These picks would precede the Rule 5 draft each year.

39. Another intriguing proposal the panel made was to relocate a weak team to the New York City market. This proposal also gained the endorsement of former commissioner Bowie Kuhn and is supported by numerous team owners and executives. The dilution of the Yankees' and Mets' share of the country's largest media market would promote competitive balance. This and related ideas are discussed in chapter seven.

40. Naturally, Selig would have wanted to vet these proposals with the full ownership group. However, one would expect that while in gestation with the panel these ideas were being circulated and reformulated among all owners.

41. Talks between the two sides apparently commenced in September 2001, but they were sporadic and desultory and did not discuss the core issues.

42. According to Doubleday's counterclaim, Selig also included team stadium debt in liabilities, though it had not been counted in the original 60/40 rule implementation guidelines.

43. Although the land around Fenway would be worth roughly $75 million if sold in remediated condition on the open market, from the Red Sox's perspective it does not generate any revenue independent of the ballpark. The owners would be able to realize the value of the land only by moving the team to a new venue and selling the land. Even in that case, however, the money from the sale would probably have to be invested in the new site.

44. Robert Starkey, consultant to MLB, "New York Mets Valuation Analysis," April 12, 2002. Starkey actually misuses least squares regression analysis to generate a linear equation that he employs to value the Mets. The outcome is approximately equal to a 2.4 revenue multiple.

45. The counterclaim by Nelson Doubleday in his ownership dispute with Fred Wilpon was based in part on this relationship. See "Answer and Counterclaim" in *Sterling Mets Associates and Fred Wilpon* v. *Nelson Doubleday* (E.D.N.Y. 2002). It also appears to cite the wrong sale price for the Expos, which was reported in the press to be $120 million. However, it was also reported in the press that the Marlins' man-

aging general partner, Jeff Loria, received a $38 million loan from MLB that might not have to be repaid.

46. When players are paid in future years, they also generate revenue. This type of long-term contract does not accord with traditional notions of debt.

47. See analysis in *Moag & Company Industry Analysis* (Baltimore, Spring 2002).

48. "Answer and Counterclaim" in *Sterling Mets Associates and Fred Wilpon* v. *Nelson Doubleday*.

49. Ibid. The Doubleday counterclaim here seems to assume that the revenue multiple of two applies before revenue sharing. If it applies after revenue sharing, then the disparities would be smaller, albeit still large.

50. As I write in early October 2002, the framework for a new deal and a memorandum of understanding (MOU) have been agreed upon, but the actual collective bargaining agreement has yet to be written and signed. My knowledge of the agreement comes from press accounts, particularly those at the mlb.com site, in the *New York Times* and in *Sports Business Daily;* communications with some industry participants; the executed MOU of October 1, 2002; and an MLB document.

51. This is true if one considers the twelve lost days of early, voluntary spring training (before the start of exhibition games) in 1973 a lockout.

52. In practice, the Yankees would be entitled to receive back a small share of their revenue sharing payments. The share would be determined by whether a straight- or split-pool system was in effect. Because of the small redistribution to the Yankees, the net marginal tax rate would be slightly below 50 percent in this example. This matter is discussed in the text in more detail.

53. This is roughly $5 million above the estimate in table 5-2 because the numbers in the table are my estimates based on the figures Selig provided to Congress in December 2001. These figures came from the team's unaudited financial reports for that year. Apparently, the final figures suggested that total revenues rose by an additional $40 million or so, and the amount of redistributed revenue grew from $163 million to approximately $168 million.

54. This $10 million fund can be disposed of at the discretion of the commissioner within certain negotiated guidelines after consultation with the MLBPA. It is what remains of the owners' initial proposal to have a commissioner's discretionary fund of $100 million.

55. Although mlb.com reports that the total amount of shared revenue will grow from $258 million in 2005 to $301 million in 2006 (both based on 2001 revenues), the memorandum of understanding executed on October 1, 2002, makes it clear that the system will be at 100 percent implementation in both 2005 and 2006. Thus, assuming that the level and distribution of revenues is the same as in 2001, the amount of revenue sharing in 2005 and 2006 should be the same. Of course, the luxury tax contributions might differ, but this is a separate estimate.

56. These are estimates based on the level and distribution of 2001 net local revenues. Under the special central fund distributions in the new system, the sums are

based on each team's net local revenue over the three previous years. So, for instance, the 2004 distributions are based on revenues during 2001–03. Each year the revenue impact is one-third, but the yearly revenue enters into the calculation in three different years. This necessitates discounting the implied marginal rates. I have used 7 percent for a discount rate, as an approximation to the weighted average cost of capital in MLB. Another complicating factor is that over the four-year interval a team may pass from being a net recipient to a net payor, or vice versa. My estimates assume that no such jumps occur.

57. The marginal tax rate under the straight pool with a 34 percent nominal rate is 32.866 percent for all teams.

58. Quoted in *Sports Business Daily*, September 4, 2002, p. 22.

59. For luxury tax purposes, the forty-man payroll uses the average annual salary of players over the length of their contracts. Thus if a player in 2002 were in the first year of a four-year deal that paid him $10 million in 2002, $14 million in 2003, $18 million in 2004, and $22 million in 2005, his salary for luxury tax purposes would be recorded as $16 million in 2002, even though the team was paying him $10 million in that year.

60. The typical team spends around $14 million per year on its player development system.

61. This graduated tax would be imposed instead of simply disqualifying all teams that fell below the minimum from receiving any transfers. For example, if a team were below but within 10 percent of the minimum, it might lose 20 percent of its revenue transfers; if it were between 10 and 20 percent below the minimum, it might lose 40 percent; and so on. A similar graduated system could be applied for the payroll luxury tax. For an interesting related discussion, see Paul Weiler, *Leveling the Playing Field* (Harvard University Press, 2000), esp. chap. 18. Also see Stephen Ross, "Batter Up! From the Baseball Field to the Courthouse," *Cardozo Law Review*, vol. 23 (May 2002), pp. 1675–704.

62. Quoted in *Sports Business Daily*, September 12, 2002, p. 8.

63. Several low-revenue franchise owners had difficulty concealing their euphoria over the new agreement. The Royals, for instance, will see their yearly transfers rise from $16 million in 2001 to $21 million in 2006 (or more as MLB revenues grow, since these estimates are based on 2001 revenues). Since franchise values in MLB are roughly 2.5 times trailing revenues, when the Royals receive $21 million in transfers, not only will their bottom line be greatly helped, but the team's approximate franchise value will rise by 2.5 times $21 million, or $52.5 million. Further, if competitive balance improves in the game as a result of the agreement, one would expect baseball's popularity to grow and the Royals' value to be further lifted. It is the hope of a lifting-all-boats phenomenon that may mollify the opposition of high-revenue owners. Some owners look at the NFL experience, where competitive balance is very developed, to justify their expectations that all franchise values in baseball stand to gain appreciably.

64. The Royals already had the fifth lowest payroll in MLB in 2002. Bob Nightengale, "Beneath the Surface, Dissent Still Simmers," *USA Today Sports Weekly*, September 4–10, 2002, p. 41.

65. The Phillies, in the nation's fourth largest media market, appear to be embarrassed by their welfare riches. Their revenue sharing transfers, together with their approximately two-thirds publicly funded new stadium, appear to finally have awakened ownership from its prolonged slumber during the 2002–03 offseason.

66. Quoted in *Sports Business Daily*, October 2, 2002, p. 15.

67. There are, of course, some modeling issues, but they are straightforward. Using data from 1995 through 2001, I ran team local revenue on team win percentage, city dummies (leaving out the city whose team had the mean revenue), year dummies (omitting 1995), and a stadium age dummy. The results put the potential revenue of the Yankees at $64 million above the average, the Orioles $33 million above, the Indians $25 million above, the Red Sox $25 million above, the Braves $18 million above, the Expos $49 million below, the Twins $39 million below, the Pirates $29 million below, and so on. If negotiators deemed the modeling issues to be too problematic, a simpler measure of potential revenue could be employed instead. For instance, in the September 2, 2002, issue of *Business Week*, Michael Mandel ("Economic Trends," p. 26) developed the concept of a city's "economic base," which he defined as the total personal income of the city divided by the number of teams. The Yankees and Mets each had an economic base of $418 billion, while the average MLB team was in a city with an economic base of approximately $150 billion. Mandel's straight division by the number of teams suggests that two teams split a city's market in half. Econometric work suggests that an additional team in a market reduces the market by closer to 30 percent than 50 percent. An explanation for this is that two teams might intensify the baseball culture in a city and promote interest via rivalry.

68. For this reason, and because teams such as the Phillies, Tigers, Blue Jays, and Angels would be converted from net receivers to net payors, it would be difficult to garner the necessary ownership votes in support of the system. With strong and persistent leadership from the commissioner's office, however, such a system might eventually gain acceptance.

69. Of course, the opposite effect might also take hold; that is, when owners do not know the precise threshold, they may respond by becoming even more conservative. Further, as discussed, although the threshold was not stipulated in years two and three, under most circumstances it was calculable after the threshold in year one was defined.

70. The proceeds from the luxury tax will be spent as follows: 50 percent to the players' benefit plan, 25 percent to the Industry Growth Fund, and 25 percent to develop players in countries that do not play organized high school baseball and/or are being added to the first-year player draft.

71. As already noted, the new agreement also closes the so-called Clemens loophole.

72. One press report suggests that after all player performance bonuses were paid out in 2002 the Yankees' forty-man payroll grew to $175.3 million. *Sports Business Daily*, November 13, 2002, p. 12.

73. The NFL has included uncapped payroll in the final years of its collective bargaining agreements, providing a similar incentive. Some believe that it is partly for this reason that the NFL owners have always been anxious to extend the old contract two or more years before it expires.

74. A team that loses a second-round pick receives an extra pick between the second and third rounds of the next year's draft.

75. A variation on the theme would be to restructure the Rule 5 draft. Instead of letting teams protect forty players from the annual Rule 5 draft, they might be allowed to protect only the twenty-five players on the active roster plus an additional five to eight designated top prospects for a two-year period. Such a modification would further prevent the top teams from stockpiling good players. For additional discussion of this reform idea, see Ross, "Batter Up!"

76. The joint study committee is also charged with studying some of these draft reforms, however.

77. See Richard Tofel, "Change the Rules, but the Yankees Will Still Win" (http://online.wsj.com [September 10, 2002]).

78. EBITDA is to include revenue sharing. Teams in new ballparks will be allowed total debt equal to fifteen times EBITDA over the preceding three years (after a $25 million debt exclusion). Other clubs will be allowed an EBITDA multiple of ten.

79. This plan has come under sharp criticism for being insufficient. See, for one, Tom Verducci, "A Dopey Policy," *Sports Illustrated*, September 16, 2002, p. 27.

80. Proportionately, the third quartile (which includes Selig's Milwaukee Brewers) benefits the most.

81. To be sure, these outside financial difficulties may also curb the salary spending by some owners, such as Tom Hicks of the Rangers, whose investment firm, Hicks, Muse, Tate & Furst, reportedly lost some $1 billion in telecom and broadband investments in recent years and also invested more than $1 billion to develop a media empire in economic basket-case Argentina. Others in trouble include Larry Dolan of the Indians, whose family business, Cablevision, lost more than 90 percent in stock value during 2001–02; Ted Rogers of the Blue Jays, whose company, Rogers Communications, saw its shares lose over 70 percent of their value; Jerry McMorris of the Rockies, whose trucking company, NationsWay Transport, went bankrupt in 2000 and who could be personally liable for up to $12 million in unpaid wages; John Moores of the Padres, whose software company, Peregrine, fell in value from over $80 a share to below 30 cents a share; Vince Naimoli of the Devil Rays, whose company, Harvard Industries, was delisted from the Nasdaq, filed for bankruptcy, and tried to terminate Naimoli's $3 million consulting contract; and, of course, AOL/Time Warner of the Braves, whose stock fell from $60 to $13 a share during 2001–02. These owner financial woes are detailed in Sam Walker, "Barons of Base-

ball Strike Out," *Wall Street Journal*, August 2, 2002; and Dan McGraw, "Is Tom Hicks Going Broke?" *D Magazine*, July 2002.

82. See, for one, Murray Chass, "Insurance Costs Are Dictating 3-Year Offers," *New York Times*, December 1, 2002, p. 5.

83. It is a correlation that, despite the poor performances of the high-paid Mets and Rangers and the superlative performance of the low-paid Twins, continued to be positive and significant at the 1 percent level in 2002 (based on the forty-man season-ending payrolls).

84. This applies to all central fund revenues except those retained by the central office and those that are part of the new revenue sharing scheme.

85. Quoted in *Sports Business Daily*, July 25, 2002, p. 11.

86. Quoted in ibid., p. 13.

87. The winter of 1976 was the first free-agent market. It affected salaries for the 1977 season.

88. To clarify, financial rates of return in baseball will not necessarily be above competitive rates. That is, one might not perceive monopoly rents directly. One important reason for this is that the higher returns may already be capitalized in the value of the franchise. Thus higher absolute profits are divided by higher franchise values, yielding a more normal rate of return.

89. Jim Bouton's quip about high player salaries is appropriate here: "While it's true that the players don't deserve all that money, the owners don't deserve it even more."

90. Vincent, *The Last Commissioner*, p. 286.

Chapter 6

1. There were, however, two joint MLB/NFL facilities constructed: the Minneapolis Metrodome in 1982 and Joe Robbie Stadium in Dade County, Florida, in 1987.

2. These figures on stadium costs, private and public, come from Judith Grant Long, "Full Count: The Real Cost of Public Funding for Major League Sports Facilities and Why Some Cities Pay More to Play," Ph.D. dissertation, Harvard University, Department of Urban Planning, April 2002. This manuscript represents the most comprehensive, systematic, and up-to-date compilation and analysis of the issue of stadium costs available.

3. The amount depends on the prevailing market interest rates. Dennis Zimmerman, "Subsidizing Stadiums: Who Benefits, Who Pays?" in Roger Noll and Andrew Zimbalist, eds., *Sports, Jobs, and Taxes: The Economic Impact of Sports Teams and Stadiums* (Brookings, 1997), pp. 119–45.

4. As noted in chapter four, however, in his last weeks in office Rudy Giuliani single-handedly arranged for the Yankees and the Mets each to receive $5 million a year to study and design new ballparks.

5. There is a logic to this claim in baseball and hockey. A new stadium increases the potential value of a player's output, thereby justifying an owner's signing players to richer contracts and acquiring a more competitive team. This logic, however, applies only weakly in basketball and hardly at all in football, where there are salary caps. The harder the cap, the less the logic applies. In the NFL almost all the teams spend very close to the cap in every year. Teams can exceed the cap by paying out large signing bonuses that are then amortized over the nominal life of the contract. This strategy means a team can spend more than the cap in a particular year, but it then is restricted to spending less than the cap in subsequent years.

6. See the written testimony of Attorney General Bob Butterworth, Senate Judiciary Committee, February 13, 2002.

7. Not surprisingly, Bud Selig's threat turned out to be an empty one. Under the terms of the 2002 collective bargaining agreement, there can be no contraction, at least until 2007.

8. For a fascinating and detailed account of how these dynamics can play out at the minor league level, see Jim Bouton, *Foul Ball* (Public Affairs Press, 2003).

9. See Noll and Zimbalist, *Sports, Jobs, and Taxes*; and John Siegfried and Andrew Zimbalist, "The Economics of Sports Facilities and Their Communities," *Journal of Economic Perspectives*, vol. 14, no. 3 (2000), pp. 95–114.

10. See, for one, Dennis Coates and Brad Humphreys, "The Growth Effects of Sport Franchises, Stadia and Arenas," *Journal of Policy Analysis and Management*, vol. 14, no. 4 (1999), pp. 601–24.

11. Goal Group Consulting, L.L.C. et al., "Impact of a New Major League Baseball Team in Northern Virginia on the Baltimore Orioles," Chicago, May 30, 2001. The one-third claim was made in a study of the Boston Red Sox in connection to the former ownership's effort to inspire public funding for a new park. This claim is cited and used uncritically by C. H. Johnson Consulting in its report on the economic impact of a new Fenway Park on the Boston economy. The methodology employed to arrive at its estimate is not described. See C. H. Johnson Consulting, "Economic Impact Analysis of the Proposed Ballpark for the Boston Red Sox," Chicago, 1999.

12. Noll and Zimbalist, *Sports, Jobs, and Taxes*, chaps. 2 and 15; John Crompton, "Economic Impact Analysis of Sports Facilities and Events: Eleven Sources of Misapplications," *Journal of Sports Management*, vol. 9 (January 1995), pp. 17–29.

13. Conceptually, a benefit principle of taxation would imply that the delineated area should coincide with the tax jurisdiction that supports the construction and operation of the facility. Of course, sometimes a stadium is financed with a combination of city, county, state, and private money. In such circumstances it is appropriate to count people in proportion to the share of finances each jurisdiction contributes.

14. Noll and Zimbalist, *Sports, Jobs, and Taxes*, chaps. 2 and 15.

15. This rate applies through fiscal 2003 and will be phased down thereafter.

16. This rate is 2.9 percent on self-employment income.

17. John Siegfried and Andrew Zimbalist, "A Note on the Local Impact of Sports Expenditures," *Journal of Sports Economics*, vol. 3, no. 4 (2002), pp. 361–67.

18. See ibid. for an elaboration of this point. Interestingly, if one uses a narrow definition of local area that increases the amount of out-of-area spending, it lowers the amount of input purchases (and the multiplier) from the area. Some promotional impact studies have used a narrow definition for the purposes of estimating out-of-area spending and then a broader definition of area to estimate the multiplier.

19. James Quirk and Rodney Fort, *Pay Dirt: The Business of Professional Team Sports* (Princeton University Press, 1992), pp. 170–71.

20. If the local economy is at full employment before stadium construction, then the project will either attract new workers to the area or take the place of another project. It may also lead to higher wages and property values for some residents, thereby raising the cost of living for others.

21. Long, "Full Count," table 5-4, p. 123. The second most important source of funding is what Long calls "tourist tax revenues." Tourist tax revenues include rental car and hotel taxes. These revenues constitute 25 percent of public funds for post-1990 baseball stadiums, but they were the principal funding source for several facilities, providing 52 percent of the financing for Comerica Park in Detroit, 84 percent for Minute Maid Field in Houston, 60 percent for Safeco Field in Seattle, 76 percent for Tropicana Field in St. Petersburg, and 67 percent for the New Comiskey Park in Chicago. Many politicians promote these tourist taxes for financing new stadiums as falling on visitors, not local residents. Not so. Either the higher taxes deter travelers, business conventions, and other visitors, or they constitute an available source of revenue for general purposes (that is, an opportunity cost if employed for stadium building). Either way, they represent an economic cost to the local population. Nonetheless, this is not generally appreciated, so there is the illusion that tourist taxes fall on outsiders, and, accordingly, tourist taxes have become increasingly popular.

22. Of course, if a team is already located in the town and is not likely to move, that consumer surplus could be reduced by building a publicly financed stadium. If the consumer has to pay more for the seats but derives the same level of satisfaction, the consumer surplus is diminished.

Chapter 7

1. Tell that to a team owner and you will be told that it is nonsense. He or she will assert that baseball competes with the other sports as well as other forms of entertainment. Loosely interpreted, this is correct, but it is not what either the U.S. Department of Justice or antitrust economists understand by monopoly. A monopolist is a single producer in an industry. An industry is defined by the extent of substitutability between its output and the output of another industry. If the products

are highly substitutable and a small change in the price of one output significantly affects the price or quantity demanded of the other output, then the two products are probably in the same industry. Economists use the concept of cross-elasticity of demand to measure this substitutability. Because the cross-elasticity of demand is difficult to quantify in practice, the Antitrust Division of the Justice Department uses a different guideline to ascertain the closeness of two products: if a company can raise the price of its output by 5 percent or more (above competitive levels) and not reduce its profitability, then it is deemed to be in its own industry.

2. Rivkin states that between 1953 and 1972 Congress considered more than fifty separate bills related to baseball's antitrust treatment. Steven Rivkin, "Sports Leagues and Federal Antitrust Law," in Roger Noll, ed., *Government and the Sports Business* (Brookings, 1974).

3. Quoted in Jerome Ellig, "Law, Economics, and Organized Baseball: Analysis of a Cooperative Venture," Ph.D. dissertation, George Mason University, Department of Economics, 1987, p. 41.

4. While this sum is scarcely sufficient to hire a competent second baseman these days, it happens, given the paucity of MLB matters that come before the Congress, to be a reasonable sum to hire a professional lobbyist or two and adequate staffing, and rent an office in Washington, D.C.

5. "Political Cash Could Aid MLB in Contraction," *Sports Business Journal*, November 19, 2001.

6. The Players Association has repeatedly staked out a position against MLB's exemption, but with few exceptions it has done little to utilize the potential player lobbying muscle. This may be due to less-than-strong feelings on the union's part or to the reluctance on the players' part to become involved in a political issue that has little perceived direct connection to their economic standing.

7. The NFL's Plan B system allowed each team to designate thirty-seven out of forty-five players to be on reserve. The remaining eight—generally the eight least desirable players on the team—were available for free agency. This was an absurdly restrictive system.

8. In 1996, in *Brown* v. *Pro Football* the Supreme Court ruled that a union could not be protected by antitrust and labor law at the same time.

9. It is, however, possible that the decertified Players Association could obtain a preliminary injunction in court that would prevent the owners from imposing the new rules.

10. Press release from Senator Specter's office, August 29, 2002.

11. The New Orleans Saints, the Minnesota Timberwolves, and the Nashville Oilers are among the teams with such provisions.

12. See Paul Weiler and Gary Roberts, *Sports and the Law: Text, Cases, Problems* (West Group, 1998), chap. 7, sec. C.

13. There is an interesting discussion of this and related points in Martin Greenberg and James Gray, *The Stadium Game* (Milwaukee, Wisc.: National Sports Law Institute, 1996), chap. 8.

14. *Congressional Record*, daily ed., June 27, 1996, p. 1.

15. Pouring rights means the right to be the sole beverage merchant at the stadium.

16. Paul Weiler goes a step further, arguing forcefully for a ban on state and local subsidies for stadium construction. See Paul Weiler, *Leveling the Playing Field: How the Law Can Make Sports Better for Fans* (Harvard University Press, 2000).

17. In *Selig* v. *United States,* the Seventh Circuit Court of Appeals ruled that Selig could attribute $10.2 million to the value of player contracts in his 1969 purchase of the insolvent Seattle Pilots for $10.8 million. The origin of this case predates free agency and hence was during a period when player contracts did have a consistent asset value. For cases that originated after 1976, the IRS permits a presumption that an owner can declare the player contracts to constitute up to half the asset value of a franchise. *Selig* v. *United States*, 740 F. 2d 572 (7th Cir. 1984).

18. Under many circumstances, the owner will be obligated to recover this amortization when he or she sells the team, through recaptured capital gains. Many owners, however, find ways around this. All benefit from paying a lower tax on recaptured gains than they do on their personal income. They also benefit by deferring the payment of these taxes for several years, or decades in some cases.

19. Of course, insofar as a player suffers an uninsured career-shortening injury the team incurs a cost. Such costs can be expensed as they occur, rather than capitalized via a probability function and amortized.

20. In *Ithaca Industries* v. *Comr.,* 97 T.C. 253 (1991), aff'd., 94-1 USTC 50, 100 (4th Cir. 1994), the tax court held that an assembled work force is not a wasting asset separate and distinct from goodwill or a going concern and therefore may not be amortized. The court also characterized the turnover of employees as merely representing the ebb and flow of a continuing work force.

21. The full amount spent on player development is not the appropriate base for this purpose. A team's player development system has more functions than simply developing major league players. These include developing major league managers and coaches, promoting interest in MLB in general and the parent club in particular, maintaining a reserve of temporary replacement players for major leaguers on the disabled list, and protecting the monopoly status of MLB by hoarding player talent. (When the Continental League failed in 1960, its president, Branch Rickey, claimed that the major reason for its demise was the failure of Congress to pass a bill sponsored by Representative Kefauver that would have given rival leagues access to a specific share of minor league players.)

22. An important element in testing the antitrust legality of the ESPN deal is whether the exclusive Wednesday-night games have a combined higher rating than the combined local team telecasts would.

23. See, for one, Andrew Zimbalist, *Unpaid Professionals: Commercialism and Conflict in Big-Time College Sports* (Princeton University Press, 1999), pp. 98–103.

24. TBS was a superstation, but converted in 2000 to a national cable channel. WGN remains a superstation. Basically, the revenues that fall under the category

"domestic television and radio" in table 7-1 could be transferred to the categories "superstation" and "copyright royalty arbitration panel." If new teams have not been added to the major markets, it might be desirable to introduce additional redistributive policies.

25. Reported in *Sports Business Daily*, September 6, 2002, p. 9.

26. *Sports Business Daily,* November 26, 2002, p. 10. With the average monthly cost of NESN around $2, these increases are on the order of 25–30 percent.

27. Andrew Zimbalist, *Baseball and Billions: A Probing Look into the Big Business of Our National Pastime* (Basic Books, 1994), p. 49; *Broadcasting and Cable*, July 29, 2002.

28. Again, actual revenue growth is likely to be considerably higher than this. See the discussion in chapter one of the Yankees' YES network.

29. See Federal Communications Commission, *Annual Assessment of the Status of Competition in the Market for Delivery of Video Programming,* Seventh Annual Report (Washington, January 2001).

30. To the extent that competition from satellite has affected certain areas, cable companies' ability to pass on the increased costs of programming has been limited. Some cable companies are seeing their profit margins shrink. Similarly, in the few markets where there are cable overbuilds (more than one cable company), cable company prices have been found to be systematically lower. See ibid.

31. Of course, a few of the very largest markets have more than one team in a given media market.

32. Arguably, baseball has even more monopoly power than the NHL, the NBA, and the NFL because the seasons of the latter sports overlap so much more.

33. Drafting players out of the minors to go directly to the majors would be covered by the nonstatutory exemption and could be negotiated with the union. Thus this policy would not violate antitrust statutes should the exemption be ended. Presently, the union has a role in defining aspects of the draft (vis-à-vis the owners) because of free-agent compensation rules that involve the forfeiture of draft picks.

34. Since the scope of MLB's exemption is ambiguous, aggrieved parties are free to test the exemption.

35. The idea of compulsory arbitration has a certain appeal. The key to its implementation would lie in the definition of rules and the selection of arbitrators.

36. S.3445, 92 Cong. 2 sess., introduced March 30, 1972; quoted in Zimbalist, *Baseball and Billions*, p. 184.

37. Rivkin, "Sports Leagues."

38. For a good discussion of these issues, see Roger Noll, "Alternatives in Sports Policy," in Noll, *Government and the Sports Business.*

39. That said, an advisory council of experts with subpoena power might be a positive force. Without regulatory powers, it could at least help to clarify the economic situation of the various leagues and be a constructive voice for reform.

40. Major League Baseball Players Association, *Baseball's Antitrust Exemption: A Resource Book* (New York, 1993), p. A6.

41. Cited in Donald M. Fehr, Testimony before the Senate Judiciary Committee, February 13, 2002.

42. This approach was first suggested in a formal argument by Stephen Ross in a lengthy article, "Monopoly Sports Leagues," *Minnesota Law Review*, vol. 73, no. 3, pp. 647–761. Earlier references to the desirability of divestiture are made by Roger Noll in Testimony before the Select Committee on Professional Sports, U.S. House of Representatives, September 1976, pp. 135–37; and Roger Noll, "The Economics of Sports Leagues," in Gary Uberstine, ed., *Law of Professional and Amateur Sports* (Clark-Boardman, 1988). It is also discussed, among other places, in James Quirk and Rodney Fort, *Hard Ball: The Abuse of Power in Pro Team Sports* (Princeton University Press, 1999).

43. In the September 2, 2002, issue of *Business Week* ("Economic Trends," p. 26), Michael Mandel analyzed the advantage that a New York team has over other teams in MLB. Mandel developed the concept of a team's "economic base," or the total personal income for the region divided by the number of teams. With two teams in NYC, both the Yanks and the Mets still have an economic base ($418 billion) that is 47 percent above the third highest team, the Orioles (including the Washington, D.C., market, at $284 billion). Mandel's analysis may understate the differential because two teams in one city does not necessarily mean that the area is divided in half for each team. Econometric work that I have done suggests that when two teams are in the same city each gets the equivalent of 70 percent of the market. The explanation for this phenomenon is that there is a synergy between the teams. Having two teams in a city not only builds a rivalry but also helps build the baseball culture in an area.

44. Dave Winfield, "Labor Deal Is Nice, but Peace Deal Is Needed," *New York Times*, October 20, 2002, sec. 8, p. 9.

45. A joint study committee was established by the 1990 collective bargaining agreement. Ultimately, there was a strike in 1994–95. One might reasonably ask why a new joint study committee would have more positive results. The answer is threefold. First, the 1990 committee did not have adequate input from experts. Second, the committee did not have sufficient financial information on the teams at its disposal to discern their true economic status. Third, by the time the next joint study committee could be established, the two sides would have additional experience and insight that would be more conducive to a successful outcome. Because it failed the first time does not mean that an improved effort shouldn't be made. It is the right way to proceed.

Postscript

1. The lowest rated World Series was between the Giants and the Angels in 2002, posting an 11.9 average in seven games. The second lowest was between the Yankees and Mets in 2000, with an average of 12.4.

2. Quoted in *Sports Business Daily,* October 28, 2003. Selig also told Bill King of

the *Sports Business Journal* (October 6–12, 2003): "I'm thrilled with the way the season has gone, because it's a manifestation of everything we've done."

3. *Basic Agreement between the 30 Major League Clubs and Major League Baseball Players Association,* effective September 30, 2002, p. 106. Italics added.

4. These revenue sharing numbers come from a financial analysis the Brewers provided to prospective investors in July 2003. In December, the Brewers were telling the press that they received $15 million in transfers, not the $18.35 million estimated in their July report.

5. The coefficient of variation (standard deviation divided by mean) of team payrolls also increased, by 7.0 percent.

6. Bruce Murphy, "Storm Warnings," *Milwaukee Magazine,* December 1996. Murphy also cites a source claiming that Selig's daughter, Wendy, and her husband together received $1.1 million in annual salaries in 1996 as executives for the Brewers.

7. The quasi-public Stadium District, which manages the stadium, contends that the actual cost is $20–$30 million below the Legislative Audit Bureau's estimate. Moreover, pending litigations from some of the suppliers and contractors could result in still higher costs. Further, not included in the stadium cost estimates is $45 million for leasing certain capital equipment (such as the scoreboard, concession equipment, and the roof drive mechanism), which was arranged by the Stadium District.

8. A significant share of this sum was not paid up front. The Brewers had to finance this portion.

9. This is from the financial analysis that the Brewers provided to prospective investors in July 2003.

10. Quoted in the *Milwaukee Journal-Sentinel,* November 13, 2003. Secretary Thompson stated in a radio interview on January 21, 2004, that he considers the decision to reduce the team's 2004 payroll to around $30 million "a breach of faith with taxpayers." He went on to say: "They promised me, they promised the legislature, that they were going to field a very competitive team if we built the stadium. And we did that. We relied upon those promises and . . . they didn't come through." *Milwaukee Journal-Sentinel,* January 22, 2004.

11. *Milwaukee Journal-Sentinel,* November 16, 2003.

12. *Sports Business Daily,* December 15, 2003.

13. Quoted in Jack Curry, "Brewers Announce the Team Is for Sale," *New York Times,* January 17, 2004, p. B15.

14. The arbitration hearing in this matter was originally scheduled for October 2003 but was postponed to mid-May 2004, in part due to the Marlins' participation in the postseason.

15. Jeff Blair ("Expos Payroll Faces Axe," *Toronto Globe and Mail,* November 10, 2003) reports that "a highly-placed source" stated that the Expos' payroll could drop as much as $12–$15 million in 2004. The team has already lost two of its star players (Javier Vazquez and Vladimir Guerrero) and may lose more. The only thing preventing a more precipitous drop in the payroll is an apparent agreement in exchange

for the team's willingness to return to Puerto Rico: MLB has received a $10 million guarantee from the local promoter for the twenty-two games to be played at Hiram Bithorn Stadium in 2004.

16. Quoted in E. Schiappa, ed., *Squeeze Play: The Campaign for a New Twins Stadium* (www.comm.umn.edu/twinsreport/reference.htm).

17. Mike Berardino, "Selig Takes a Cautious Approach on California Doping Probe," *South Florida Sun-Sentinel,* October 22, 2003.

18. Quoted in Evan Weiner, Westwood One radio commentary, February 12, 2003.

19. *Sabermetricians* is the name bestowed upon baseball statistical analysts. Its root, saber, comes from the Society for American Baseball Research (SABR).

20. On some matters, Lewis is simply misinformed. Jason Grimsley, for instance, does not throw ninety-six-mile-per-hour fastballs, Chad Bradford's submarine delivery cannot add a perceived ten-miles an hour to his fastball (it would require his release point to be seven feet closer to home plate), and the players union did not create the blue-ribbon panel on baseball economics.

On other issues, Lewis is inconsistent. After arguing for chapters that Beane's system is based on an exhaustive absorption and interpretation of statistics and then stating that one of Beane's five basic rules is to "know exactly what every player in baseball is worth to you—you can put a dollar figure on it," Lewis writes that "[Beane's] approach to the market for baseball players [is] unsystematic." Either there is a system or there isn't; Lewis can't have it both ways.

21. It is notable, for instance, that the Oakland A's have been losing their top players (including two MVPs) more rapidly than they have been developing new talent. This is a problem that the Yankees and Red Sox, with their lofty payrolls, do not have.

22. The allowed debt is computed based on the team's EBITDA over the three preceding years.

23. Some of this undervaluation is being reduced. According to documents prepared by McCourt's investment bankers for prospective investors, the combined local cable and over-the-air television rights fee payments to the Dodgers will increase from $22.9 million in 2003 to $36.5 million in 2004 and grow at 5 percent annually thereafter, up to $49.2 million in 2009, the contract's last year.

24. According to one informed source, of the $430 million purchase price, McCourt is borrowing $150 million from Bank of America, $75 million from MLB's credit facility, and $165 million from seller News Corp. In order to appease the critics of the heavy debt load, News Corp. agreed to take on $40 million of equity, for which McCourt must find a buyer within eighteen months. Dan Kaplan, "Ratner to Borrow up to $150 million," *Sports Business Journal,* February 2–8, 2004, p. 9.

25. Ross Newhan, "Supreme McCourt," *Los Angeles Times,* January 30, 2004.

26. Average salaries for free agent signings during the 2003 off-season fell by 16.5 percent (as of mid-January 2003).

27. Although the debt rule states that the commissioner cannot attempt to influence clubs' player payroll decisions in order to enforce compliance, it does not prevent the clubs from taking such action on their own. Further, although the attachment to the debt rule states that it is not the *intent* of the rule to reduce payrolls, it does not preclude lower payrolls from being an *outcome* of the rule.

28. Still, Rob Manfred, MLB's labor relations chief, gave cause to wonder when he stated that MLB has given teams "advice with respect to negotiations on an individual basis" but "clubs make individual decisions on the free agent market and get no guidelines from [MLB]." Quoted in *Sports Business Daily,* February 2, 2004, p. 18.

29. Formal tampering rules would not permit this to happen, and Selig was criticized in the press for favoring the Red Sox by not implementing the rule. The tampering rule, however, is designed to protect the player's existing team from an unwanted intrusion by a new team. Selig could have required the Rangers and the Red Sox to complete a deal contingent on A-Rod's approval, but this would have been putting the cart before the horse because the restructuring was such a central part of the transaction.

30. Naturally, to the extent that coercion or threats were used in restructuring a contract, the contract could be legally voided. It still makes sense to establish a less formal, internal mechanism to avoid litigation with its attendant frictions and expense.

31. The commissioner's office may still decide, however, to arbitrate the principle of the matter, independent of A-Rod's case.

32. One might even ask whether the union policy is consistent with promoting higher salaries and longer terms in the future. Won't the union's posture give future superstars pause before signing long-term, record contracts? Might these players not fear that they would lose mobility and that they may get stuck on a losing team? And might this not induce a player to accept a shorter or smaller contract?

33. One of many e-mails I have received over the past year in response to the first edition of this book came from Mark Self in October 2003. Mark wrote: "I help with a carpool for K–8th graders and not once did I hear anybody talk about the World Series." This is one of the costs of seeking to maximize short-run television dollars by putting the World Series games on only at prime time. In the long run, baseball loses its grip on a generation of potential fans and its audience diminishes.

34. This subsidiary began operations in June 2002.

Index

Breinigsville, PA USA
22 December 2010
252039BV00002B/2/P